Sustainable Rural Livelihood Systems

About the Author

Sib Ranjan Misra (*b.* 1947 Malda, West Bengal), a Ph.D. in Economics (Jadavpur University, India) and D.E.P. (Istituto di Studi per lo Sviluppo Economico, Naples University, Italy) and a Japan Foundation Fellow (2004-05, 2008, 2009) was on the teaching staff of the University of North Bengal (1971-78), currently Professor of Economics, Department of Economics and Politics, Visva-Bharati University, Santiniketan, India. His present assignment includes research and teaching in various branches of Economics. He has completed quite a number of projects on problems of tea plantations, fisheries development, irrigation management etc. sponsored by ICSSR, UGC, ICAR etc. He has also served for quite some time as an advisor on the Fisheries Development Advisory Board, Ministry of Agriculture and Co-operation, Government of India. He has also been serving since long as a member on the Committee for Food and Nutrition Security constituted and monitored by Food and Agricultural Organisation (FAO) Rome. The author's publications have appeared in various professional, national and international, journals and also include books entitled: *Tea Industry in India* (1986), *Understanding Fisheries Sector in India* (1989), *Floriculture in West Bengal — Problems and Potentials* (1997), *Managing Canal Irrigation—Issues and Challenges* (2005).

Sustainable Rural Livelihood Systems

The Case for India's Inland Fisheries Sector

Sib Ranjan Misra

CONCEPT PUBLISHING COMPANY PVT. LTD, NEW DELHI-110059

ISBN-13: 978-81-8069-785-2

First Published 2012

Published and Printed by

Concept
Since 1974

Concept Publishing Company Pvt. Ltd.
A/15-16, Commercial Block, Mohan Garden
New Delhi-110059 (India)
T: 25351460, 25351794, *F*: 091-11-25357109
E: publishing@conceptpub.com, W: www.conceptpub.com
Editorial Office: H-13, Bali Nagar, New Delhi-110 015, India.

Cataloging in Publication Data--*Courtesy:* D.K. Agencies (P) Ltd. <docinfo@dkagencies.com>

Misra, Sib Ranjan.
Sustainable rural livelihood systems : the case for India's inland fisheries sector / Sib Ranjan Misra.
p. cm.
Includes bibliographical references (p.) and index.
ISBN 9788180697852

1. Sustainable fisheries—India—West Bengal. 2. Fisheries—Government policy India—West Bengal. 3. Rural development—India—West bengal. I. Title.

DDC 639.2095414 23

To
Mili and Saon

For their silent expression of inspiration

Give a man a fish and he eats for one day; teach him how to fish and he eats for a lifetime.

—Henry David Thoreau

Preface

India is witnessing a series of changes since early nineties. In the current phase of globalization and liberalisation, livelihood security has assumed increasing importance. This is also to be noted that sectors and industries that are integrated with the global markets may impose such vulnerabilities even on those dependent on these sectors/ industries. A large number of other occupations and livelihoods are also imposing insecurities on the people owing to different reasons. Unprecedented number of farmer suicides, big corporate houses entering into retail business and allocation of special economic zones, boom in information technology and IT enabled services, zero growth rates in employment are among many such events that need introspection. Understanding the livelihood systems of the poor is crucial to effective poverty reduction. It is true that livelihoods of the poor can never be understood in any one-track logic—be it economic, social, technical, cultural or political. The livelihood systems are made up of very diverse elements which—taken together—constitute the physical, economic, social and cultural universe wherein the families live. Thus, the livelihood system is more than just a set of physico-economic preconditions for continued existence. The livelihoods approach puts households of the poor as its central focus. It takes holistic considerations of things that the poor might be vulnerable to assets and resources that help them thrive and survive, policies and institutions that impact their livelihoods, how the poor respond to threats and opportunities and what kind of outcomes the poor aspire to.

Of course, there has been in recent years a growing recognition of the vast growth potential of production of fish, mainly from inland water bodies, thereby providing the much-needed edible protection and augmenting the income of the rural poor. India has abundant natural endowments, conventional wisdom and human skills in respect of intensified fish farming. But in spite of enormous potentials, much headway has not been made. The levels of production and productivity have not been adequate, leaving a large gap between actual and potential yield. The new technology, which seems technically attractive, has failed to produce substantial results in real world. The recipients of technology are greatly circumscribed by the factors like multiple ownership of tanks and ponds, shortage of quality fish seeds, shortage of investment capital, inadequate extension work, poaching, deliberate poisoning, inadequately organized marketing facilities and many more others. In other words, the present unsatisfactory performance may be attributed mainly to absence of rational management and judicious utilization of the resources. And, this unsatisfactory performance tells tellingly upon the livelihood system of the fisherfolk who depend squarely on this sector in rural India.

In this study, attempts have been made to examine the operational features of tanks and ponds and to identify the factors that impede the development of fisheries in West Bengal. Efforts are also made to evaluate the role of government programmes towards development of inland fisheries sector. The study is based on the data collected from selected fish farmers from different villages in the selected agro-climatic zones of West Bengal. This book is largely based on the Report of a Major Research Project on the Economics of Pisciculture which was undertaken with the financial support from the University Grants Commission. I express my deep sense of gratitude to the UGC for their support. In point of fact, it is pertinent to note that this book has drawn heavily from another exploratory research work undertaken by the author earlier.

I wish to express my thanks in abundance to Dr. Jaydev Misra who consistently took the trouble of collecting and collating the data and preparing the statistical tables appropriate for this exercise. I also received help from him for making an analysis on efficiency of the fish cultivation with the help of Data Envelopment Method (DEM). Through my frequent interactions with the Professors like Kyo Kambayashi, Tokyo Metropolitan University, Professor Ichiro

Horide, Professor Yukimasa Nagayasu, International School of Economics, Reitaku University, Dr. Kuniyo Tsubota, Director, Asian Productivity Council, Tokyo; Professor Hiroike Masanaro, Hitotsubasi University during my stay in Japan as a Japan Foundation Fellow, I have been able to enhance my understanding about the different dimensions of Indian aquaculture. I owe a special debt of gratitude to all of them for shaping my thought about it.

A word of warm appreciation is due to Sabhadipatis of Murshidabad, Malda, Bankura and South 24-Parganas, Agriculture Development Officer and members of the Panchayat Samitees of the Study area. Our obligation is due to Director of Directorate of Fisheries, West Bengal; Dr. Goutam Sarkar, Deputy Director of Fisheries (Central Zone); Dr. Samik Das, Chief Executive Officer, FFDA, Murshidabad; Sri A.K. Gorai, Fishery Extension Officer, Malda and Sri N. Barik, Assistant Director of Fisheries, Birbhum who provided me with most of the facts and figures and many of the ideas which are set out below. It is thanks to their expertise and unfailing courtesy. To the numerous fish farmer respondents of our study, I owe a debt which no expression of gratitude can fully redeem. I would like to acknowledge his contribution in making the study what it is.

The staff of the Libraries (Central Library, Visva-Bharati and Agro-Economic Research Centre, Visva-Bharati), where we spent most of the time involved in completing this work gave us their full cooperation. I am thankful to them, particularly to Prof. Kalyan Brata Bhatyacharya, Prof. Soumyen Dutta in the Department of Economics, Burdwan University and Dr. (Late). Madan Gopal Ghosh, Ex-Director, Agro-Economic Research Centre, Visva-Bharati. I have also immense pleasure in placing on record the support I used to receive from Dr. Sri Narayan Ojha, Dr. Biplab Loho Chaudhury, Sri Ram Prasad Majumdar and Sri Daya Sankar Kushwaha of Visva-Bharati in different ways. I am really grateful to them. I am thankful to the staff members of the Department of Economics and Politics in Visva-Bharati for their support during the course of this investigation and finalization of this book.

I am again really grateful to Shri Ashok Kumar Mittal of the Concept Publishing Co. Pvt. Ltd. who kept me always going and for his indefatigable interest in bringing out this book to the market. In the process, I found a very good friend in him.

Sib Ranjan Misra

Department of Economics and Politics
Visva-Bharati
Santiniketan, India
June 10, 2011

Contents

List of Exhibits

List of Figures

List of Pictures

List of Annexure

Glossary

Algae: Members of a group of mostly aquatic, photosynthetic organisms that defy precise definition. Algae provide much of earth's oxygen, serve as the food base for almost all-aquatic life and provide foods and industrial products. Algae are common as green sheens on pools and ponds. Use of algae is perhaps as old as mankind. Many species are eaten by coastal societies.

Aquatic Ecosystem: Any system of interacting aquatic life within its natural and physical environment.

Aquatic Environment: Means the natural and biological resources comprising any aquatic ecosystem.

***Aratdar*:** Commission agent of fish and moneylender.

Baor: Floodplain lake.

***Batam Cake*:** Local fish feed.

***Bati*:** Vessel used for measuring quantities of hatcheries.

Beel: Floodplain Lake.

***Bheri*:** Pond used for fish production.

Brackish Water: Water having a mineral content intermediate between fresh water and sea water (1000-10,000 mg/1 dissolved solids).

Capture Fishery: In this kind of fishery, one does not have to sow the fish seeds. Nature is doing the job for sowing. The wild untended stock of organisms is harvested with little human interventions on either habitat variables or the biotic communities.

Co-management: A valuable tool for the sustainable management in fisheries. It can also help in resolution of potential conflicts among user groups. As part of co-management, effective dialogue between local and tourism communities is needed, as it is a commitment on the part of non-resident stakeholders.

Culture Fisheries: In culture fisheries, the whole operation is based on captive stock with a high degree of effective human control over the physio-chemical water quality and other habitat variable. One has to sow the seeds, nurse it and tend it to the proper size before harvesting. Intensive aquaculture of fish and prawn in a pond is a typical example of culture fisheries.

***Dalal*:** Agents and fish availability (or quality) informants used in establishing and securing the transactions of live fish between two parties.

***Dayabhaga*:** One of Hindu laws of Inheritances. The *Dayabhaga* system provides that sons and grandsons had right in the family property even during the lifetime of the father.

Ecosystem: An integrated unit consisting of the community of living organism and the non-living, or physical, environment in a particular area such as a tropical rainforest, coral reef or grassland. The relationship among species in an ecosystem is usually complex and finally balanced, and removal of anyone species can often be disastrous.

Enhancements: These are interventions in the life/rearing cycle of the common pool resources. Enhancement technologies involve culture based fisheries/ranching, habitat modification, fertilizations, feeding and eliminations of predators. They use little feed and energy and provide high returns and inputs of labour and capitals. Resource poor sections of the population benefit greatly from the enhancements, which help in generating food, income and other benefits from underutilized, new or presently degraded aquatic resources.

***Fashijal*:** A kind of net, used by the traditional fishermen of Bengal.

Fishery: One or more stocks or species of fish or aquatic life (usually fresh water) that can be treated as a unit for conservation/ management purposes.

Food Chain: A sequence of plants and/or animals generally increasing in complexity and decreasing in numbers with each succeeding species feeding upon its predecessors.

Freshwater: Water having a low mineral content acceptable for portable purposes (< 1000 mg/1 dissolved solids).

Freshwater Ecosystem: Include Rivers, lakes, freshwater wetlands, geothermal ecosystems and underground aquifers.

Fish Farmers' Development Agencies: The FFDAs are registered societies, envisaging leasing of tanks and ponds owned by government and local bodies to the fish farmers on long-term lease, training of farmers, supply of inputs required, and provision of financial assistance in the form of subsidy for fish pond improvement and inputs. In addition, the extension services were provided to the fish farmers to spread the technology.

***Garma*:** A kind of net, used by the traditional fishermen of Bengal.

Glass Jar Hatchery: It is an example of low cost Chinese type portable hatchery, especially in respect of fresh water variety of fish species, which Government of India has helped to promote in rural and semi-urban areas.

***Goldar*:** Trader who transports large quantities of fish seed by truck (owned or hired).

Habitat: The place or type of site where a biological community naturally occurs.

***Hapa*:** Nylon net cage used for holding fish.

Hindu law of Inheritance: *Mitakshara* and *Dayabhaga* were two laws in ancient India, the dominance of which continued uninterrupted in the countryside have played an important role in the subdivision and fragmentation of tanks and ponds in India.

***Hundi*:** Small aluminium vessel used for transporting fish (also known as *patil* in Bangladesh).

Inland Fisheries: Any activities conducted to extract fish and other aquatic organism from inland waters.

***Jalkar*:** Rent of water bodies collected by the zamindars/owners.

Jhora Fishery: In the hill areas of Darjeeling, FFDAs have taken up pisciculture by impounding running water from hilly streams, which is known as 'Jhora'.

Majhi**:** Boatman.

Mangrove Swamp: Muddy swamp found on tropical coasts and estuaries, characterized by dense thickets of mangrove trees that are adapted to live in creeks of salt water and send down special breathing roots from their branches to take in oxygen from the air.

Mitaksara: One of Hindu laws of Inheritances. According to the law, father or eater-family was the steward of the property. He could dispose of the property and if he died, property succeeded to his sons who would divide them equally. The eldest son, having no special claim, could get a little consideration amounting to twentieth part of the share.

Nursery pond: This type of pond is used for nursing 2.5 to 7.5 cm fry until the desired size of fish is reached.

Reservoir: A natural or artificial, usually open, impoundment or body of water to be used for recreation, power, flood control or drinking purposes is stored.

Sewage Fed Fishery: A unique example of recycling urban waste for productive use in pisciculture. Sewage Fed Fishery in the eastern fringe of Calcutta is an eye-opener to the world and show how the urban waste can be purified through pisciculture. It not only maintains the ecosystem but also continues a major source of fish supply.

Social Fishery: This scheme was introduced in 1987-88 by the Fisheries Department aiming at stocking water bodies owned by the Government, institutions etc. by transferring management to group of persons selected by Panchayats, from among those, living below the poverty line.

Stocking: The protection of natural fish resources is a cost-effective strategy for increasing fish production in inland waters but the effect is sometimes limited by environmental conditions. In those cases, where the composition of natural fish species is not optimal for natural productivity, stocking can effectively increase fish production in inland waters. It involves the release of artificially produced fish seeds into natural water bodies and usually depends on the artificial breeding of the fish species. Two major objectives of stocking are to enhance fish resources, and to establish extensive fish culture production.

Sustainable Development (SD): SD is a requirement to the present generation to manage the resource base such that average quality of life we ensure ourselves should potentially be shared by other future generations.

Sustainable Yield Cropping: The removal of surplus individuals from a population so that the population maintains a constant size. This usually requires selective removals of animals of all ages and both sexes to ensure a balanced population structure. Taking too many individuals can result in a population decline, as in overfishing.

System Approach to Aquaculture: This multidisciplinary approach involves the following steps—stating the problem, identifying the system, classifying and describing the system boundaries and critical factors, analyzing the problem, proposing solution to the problem based on system understanding, testing the solution, and implementing the knowledge on how to solve the problem.

Threatened Species: A species or community that is vulnerable endangered or presumed extinct.

Wetland: Permanently or intermittently wet areas, shallow water and land water margins that support a natural ecosystem of plants and animals that are adapted to wet conditions.

***Zotedar*:** Landholders.

Zooplankton: Small animals or the larvae of larger animals, which drift in the surface waters of the sea and lakes.

1
Introduction

In the literature, the conventional perception is that fisheries (especially small scale fisheries in less developed countries) and rural poverty are closely interrelated. More than thirty years ago, the Food and Agricultural Organization already stated: 'The people engaged in these activities and their families continued, with few exceptions, to live at the margin of subsistence and human dignity' (FAO, 1974). This view, which is still largely accepted nowadays (*see* Smith, 1979; World Bank, 1982; Wright, 1990; Payne, 2000) is, in fact, embodied in the famous adages: 'fishermen are the poorest of the poor'(e.g., Bailey) and 'fishery is the activity of last resort for the poor' (e.g., Townsley, 1998). The underlying logic of this general perception is that fisheries due to its open access nature of the resources which acts as the safety valve attracts a large number of people, especially—but not exclusively—in rural areas where alternatives for other activities may be low. The last resort dimension of fisheries is, therefore, of great importance and relevance to the poor. Again, it is also argued that small and open access nature of the fisheries leads to the economic and biological overexploitation of the fish stock and other related resources. This eventually leads to further impoverishment of the already poor fishers.[1] This downward spiral of poverty further reinforces the second aspect of the conventional wisdom, namely the perception that the fishers are the poorest of the poor. But these two conventional wisdoms tend to oversimplify the complex social, economic and cultural interactions which take place within the community over the fisheries sector. These ideas may have led to oversimplication or misrepresentation of the reality and hence preclude understanding of the role that the sector can play in rural people's livelihood and especially in rural poor households' livelihoods. The present exercise is made to aim at improving the understanding of the exact nature of the relationship between the fisherfolk (in this case, inland fisheries) and different socio-economic parameters in the context of the changed circumstances.

1.1 Livelihood, in the Popular Sense of the Term, Describes the Means of Living and Sustenance[2]

An economic definition of livelihood could be the organization of production resources of households to maximize their standard of living. It can be described as the organization of a household's productive resources to achieve and secure a maximum standard of living. In their definition, economists like Chambers and Conway include assets and capabilities along with activities or strategies in the productive resources. To quote, "livelihood comprises the capabilities, assets and activities for means of living" (Chambers and Conway, 1992). By capabilities, they mean something akin to Sen's notion of a set of alternative "beings and doings that a person can achieve with his or her economic, social and personal characteristics" (Dreze and Sen, 1989; Sen, 1993). Assets comprise several components, some of which represent the economic categories of capital, and others—claims and access to resources. Generally, five categories of assets are identified as contributing to livelihoods. They are natural assets, physical assets, human assets, financial assets and social assets. Natural assets refer to natural resources like land and water that contribute to production and consumption activities. Physical assets are produced means of production, such as tools, machines, and irrigation systems. Human assets mainly refer to education, skills and health of household members. Financial assets are basically the stocks of cash and access to credit. Social capital could mean social networks and organizations. Interactions among people in markets, government and civil society provide access to resources or/government development of assets into commodity bundles. Institutions play a crucial role in the livelihood dynamics. Institutions are the humanly devised constraints that structure political, economic and social interactions. They consist of both informal constraints (sanctions, taboos, customs, traditions and codes of conduct) and formal rules (constitutions, laws, property rights etc.). Institutions, markets, and assets interplay in livelihood dynamics. Access to natural assets—land, financial assets, social organizations etc. is defined by rules and social norms, value of the flow of the benefits from productive assets is determined by the market forces. By impacting on the transaction costs, institutions can make markets efficient or inefficient. Institutions can affect livelihood directly. State policies on social security directly affect livelihood outcomes. Conversely, changes in livelihood might make certain institutions redundant and certain others necessary. An understanding of these and other interrelationships among assets, institutions, markets, and livelihood becomes important in unravelling the different dimensions of sustainable livelihoods. These relationships are diagrammatically represented in Figure 1.1.A:

Livelihood strategies

Institutions Arrangements

International National Regional Local

Assets

Natural
Human
Physical
Financial
Social

Market Forces
Environment

Figure 1.1A: Livelihood Strategies Structures.

Outcomes of livelihood strategies could be viewed in terms of income received or consumption achieved by households.[3] However, it could be adversely affected by the presence of livelihood risks. Livelihood risks is defined as the likelihood of occurrence of (external) shocks and stresses plus their severity. In the rural scenario, livelihood risks can be categorized among four main divisions: (a) harmful trends such as increasing soil erosion, frequent droughts, unfavourable development of commodity or input prices, (b) shocks such as earthquakes, floods, diseases, loss of jobs, violent conflicts, destruction of physical infrastructure etc; (c) harmful seasonal fluctuations such as price fluctuations in crop and livestock markets, fluctuations in food availability due to climatic change, (d) unfavourable socio-economic environments, characterized by absence of rule of law, deprivation of rights, gender related deprivation etc. As and when livelihood faces risks, households may develop strategies to overcome them. Such strategies may be of two types; risk coping strategies and risk mitigation (adaptive strategies). While the former represents ex-post short-term strategies to cope with risk mainly through smoothing consumption, the latter is ex-ante steps to mitigate risk potential in the long run through income smoothing strategies (Morduch, 1990).

Policy-makers and development specialists of today have recognized clearly the need for natural resource management including the fishery sector to be approached in the context of sustainable rural livelihood systems.[4] Of course, there has been no systematic research aiming at the enhancement of our knowledge about the relationship between the two. Rural livelihood systems embrace quite a good number of factors and forces necessary to sustain life of rural families and communities. They include physical, economic, social, political and psychological elements as well. It is, however, pertinent to structure such a notion in a manner as to situate the management of natural resources like fisheries meaningfully to ensure at the same time the livelihoods systems. A livelihood comprises the capabilities, assets and activities required for a means of living. A livelihood is sustainable when it can cope with and recover from stresses and shocks and maintain or enhance its capabilities and assets, both now and in the future, while not undermining the natural resource base. According to some economists like Scoones, five key indicators are essential for assessing sustainable livelihoods: (1) poverty reduction, (2) well-being and capabilities, (3) livelihood adaptation, (4) vulnerabilities and resilience, and (5) natural resource base sustainability (Scoones 1998). The sustainable livelihood approach, a conceptual framework, aims generally to reduce poverty. This framework is employed precisely to identify methods to advance the livelihoods of fish farmers and those others engaged in this enterprise. This approach seeks to improve rural development policy and practice by recognizing the seasonal and cyclical complexity of livelihood strategy (Carney, 2002). The sustainable livelihoods framework helps in thinking holistically about the issues that the poor might be vulnerable to the assets and resources that help them thrive and survive and the policies and institutions that impact on their livelihoods (DFID, 1999).

1.2 Contextualizing the Issue

Fisheries and Livelihood

Developing countries like India face several livelihood risks (1) In their struggle to achieve a secure livelihood, households try to cope with and even to mitigate or prevent such risks. Whether they succeed in this struggle or not is so crucial that it determines the sustainability or vulnerability of their very livelihood. A livelihood system could be sustainable if and only if it can cope with and recover from the risks and maintain (or enhance) its capabilities and assets without undermining the natural resource base (Chambers and Conway, 1988). As such, case studies of such livelihood struggles by rural people in the wake of varying risks to their livelihood, contributes significantly to the understanding and making of sustainable rural livelihoods. In case of fisheries also, there is a wide dimension of livelihood risk as informed by in-depth case studies conducted by researchers in this globe. As such, several coping strategies to enhance livelihood outcome have emerged that have strong policy implications in sustainable livelihood in rural areas.

Fishery-related livelihoods are complex, dynamic and adaptive. Some fishers engage in fishing full-time, all year round. More commonly though, people fish part-time. They may take advantage of seasonally available riverine, coastal and offshore resources, or they may fish part-time all through the year. This leaves time to engage in other activities such as farming and rearing livestock. Fishing often shows this high degree of integration with other economic activities at the local level, such as agriculture, trading and the provision of labour. Management strategies need to take into account the diverse and complex nature of fishery-related livelihoods. For example, co-management based on territorial rights of sedentary communities that exclude migrants may have a detrimental effect on people if it disrupts the mutual economic reciprocity that exists between different groups. Fish stocks fluctuate seasonally in abundance and availability producing high and low fishing seasons. When high seasons coincide with the seasonal low availability of other food sources such as agriculture, fisheries can increase food security. In addition, apart from seasonal inland fisheries where the river, reservoir or lake dries up completely, very few fisheries have periods when the catch is consistently zero, providing at least subsistence use all year round.

At a higher level, the cash income generated from selling fish can be used to invest in other assets or livelihood diversification, which can further reduce vulnerability to poverty. Some studies have found that households involved in fishing have higher incomes than non-fishing households in the same villages or districts. However, people involved in fishery-related livelihoods are vulnerable to a variety of factors. Fishing as an occupation carries its own risks, due to the fugitive nature of the resource, the hostile environment of the seas, and perishability of the product. Additionally, ready access to cash can result in fishers being exposed to other problems such as alcohol consumption or other luxury consumption. Fishing communities often lack access to basic service provision such as education, health care and formal credit services. This situation is exacerbated for those fishers, who as temporary in profession, are often marginalized from democratic decision-making structures.

Fisheries are vulnerable to overexploitation of the resource, which can result in the loss of benefits that can be derived from them. Therefore, management must control exploitation so that the fish stock is sustainable. Fish stocks may suffer negatively from external impacts, shocks and trends such as environmental degradation or changes in climate, which are beyond the control of most fishers. This demands a cross-sectoral approach to management and planning Fishery-related livelihoods are both complex and dynamic. The importance of fisheries to livelihoods is being increasingly recognized and their various roles understood. Hence, increasing understanding of the different roles of fisheries in the livelihoods of the poor in different contexts and the issues that threaten their contribution must be looked into close supervision. Also, policy planners should identify management arrangements and actions that support livelihood strategies and contribute to reduce the vulnerability to risks of poor people, dependent on fisheries. In these processes, therefore, promoting the inclusion of fisheries in poverty reduction strategies through recognition of their importance to the livelihoods of the poor should be the call of this hour.

1.3. Livelihood in Indian Fisheries

India is a major maritime state and an important aquaculture country in the world and Indian fisheries is a sunrise sector. With third position in fisheries and second in aquaculture, the country has high potentials in the sector for rural development, domestic nutritional security, employment generation, gender mainstreaming as well as export earnings, that only few other activities can provide. 'Look to the Seas' is the recent thinking for harnessing the fish-related wealth, as also a number of related products from the waters. This is not only an option, but also a necessity for us to sustain over 16 per cent of the global population, with 2.4 per cent of land and 4.2 per cent of water of the whole world. India, with water ranging from the seas to cold hill streams and over 10 per cent of the fish biodiversity on earth, has high scope for producing fish, along with a high possibility of utilising a variety of wastewaters, also rendering them better in the process of fish cultivation. Non-water-consumptive nature of aquaculture, coupled with its compatibility with other farming systems and neutrality to scale of investments, enable integrated fish farming on a large scale. With a heritage in marine and riverine fisheries, recent innovations, entrepreneurial enthusiasm and a creditable performance in the global market, the sector is poised to make greater contributions in the coming years.

Fisheries, now recognized as a sunrise sector in India, has recorded faster growth than any of the other agriculture and allied sectors in the post-independent India. The last two decades of twentieth century has been the real boost in fish production in the country. The share of fisheries in agricultural domestic product (Ag-GDP) increased from 1.7 per cent in the year 1979-80 to 5.94 per cent in 2007-08 and is now regarded as an important sector for country's nutritional security and food production. The livestock and fisheries sector contributed over 4.07 per cent to the total GDP during 2008-09 and about 29.7 per cent to the value of output from total agricultural and allied activities. The sector contributes to the livelihood of over 14 million people, a large section of which fall in the economically underprivileged category of country's population. Growing at an average annual growth rate of 7.12 per cent during 1980-81 to 2008-09, the fish production in the country was 7.15 million tonnes in 2008-09, bringing fish availability for fish eating populace of the country to 9.96 kg per capita. The Eleventh Five Year Plan envisages an overall growth of 6-7 per cent per annum for the sector. Fish production increased from 7.14 million tonnes in 2007-08 to 7.85 million tonnes in 2009-10. This rise in fish production has been possible due to quantum jump in inland fish production, especially pond aquaculture, which is now growing at an average annual growth rate of 13.87 per cent.

Fish as health food and its role in ensuring nutritional security of the country has been appreciated, with non-traditional fisheries states taking to fisheries and aquaculture and large scale movement of fish becoming a reality all-over the country. Paradigm shifts from marine fisheries to inland fisheries in terms of production became clear during the last decade, and further increasing contributions from culture practices overcapture fisheries in both marine and inland sectors. Diversification has been significant at all stages from production to consumption, whether it is from food fish to ornamental fish, carps to catfish and scampi, exportable items from shrimp to a variety of products and further the overseas markets to a number of countries.

Fisheries is one of the main sources of livelihood for the rural poor, particularly the fisher community. The country is endowed with enormous inland and marine waters, which provide immense livelihood and employment opportunities. In case of inland waters, fisheries in open waters (Rivers, Reservoirs, Floodplains and Estuaries) are, although, of subsistence type, yet, have high potentials for production enhancement. The fish catches from these waters contribute significantly to their food and nutritional security. Inland aquaculture has witnessed the highest growth rate and emerged as the most important and contributing activity to fisheries sector. The livelihood options exist for both the poor and large fish farmers through horizontal and vertical integration of the enterprise. Similarly, marine fisheries is a major source of livelihood for lakhs of people along the coast. While the inshore fishery has almost attained its potential, immense scope exists in deep sea fisheries, along with mariculture and post-harvest value addition. The total output of fisheries sector was Rs. 31,672 crores during 2003-04 with net domestic product valued at Rs. 27,026 crores (CSO, 2005). With this level of output, over 90 lakh people may be employed at subsistence level of annual income of Rs. 30,000. Fisherman. The share of marine and inland sector is 54 and 46 per cent respectively.

Indian fisheries constitute an important sector of our national economy for various reasons. The importance of this sector can be better appreciated in the light of the fact that this sector provides wholesome protective food containing animal protein in the dietary of the country's undernourished population. In the country like India, where half of the population still does not get two square meals per day, it is important to pay attention to any alternative source which, besides being within the reach of the people, will constitute a nutritive diet.

Inland fisheries sector remains a sector of much promise. Unlike agriculture, because of expansion of culture based fisheries enterprises, the contribution of inland fisheries sector to grow domestic product has been increasing at a significant rate. This sector is complex enterprises which operates under the intensified network of natural resources, other enterprises with fisheries and other socio-political variables. This is evident from Exhibit 1.1 that during the period 1995-96 to 2001-2003 the percentage of possible changes in output values with respect to time has mined by 30 per cent with inland fisheries, constituting more than 55 per cent of the growth. The rate of growth of value of output of the fisheries sector has been targeted 7 per cent per annum during the fourth and element during five year plan (GOI, 1999). Fish consumption is also expected to increase from 5.05 kg/capita in 1996-97 to 9.30 kg/capita in 2011-12. (GOI, 1999).[5]

Exhibit 1.1: Change in Value of Output in Fisheries and Agriculture

Sector	*1995-96*	*1996-97*	*1997-98*	*1998-99*	*1999-00*	*2000-01*	*2001-02*
1	2	3	4	5	6	7	8
Agriculture	103.60	113.65	110.19	118.68	119.43	116.43	122.40
Fisheries	112.25	117.77	120.75	128.20	139.70	140.78	145.78

Source: National Account Statistics, Central Statistical Organization.
Note : This is of course worked out on the basis of expected population growth rate and the elasticities of demand with respect to per capita consumption expenditure.

According to National Income Statistics, Indian fisheries contribute about 1.4 per cent of the total Gross Domestic Product (GDP) and 4.73 per cent of the GDP from agriculture. The vast resources which are capable of yielding 10 million tonnes of fish per year as against only an average annual production of 5.65 million tonnes per year will go a long way in increasing the national income.

Foreign exchange earnings from export of fish and fishery products have been steadily rising during the recent years.[6] In absolute term, the export earnings have steadily increased from Rs. 234.84 crores in 1980-1981 to Rs. 5,114 crores in 1999-2000 which accounted for 1.76 per cent of the total export of the country. It is also estimated that with adequate facilities, the export earnings can be more than doubled within three or four years.

Photo 1.1: Fishermen in Action

It is generally difficult to assess correctly the population engaged in Indian fishing industry because of the general inadequacy of statistical data on fisherman population, the system of casual labour prevalent in the industry, the difficulty in distinguishing fishermen wholly or partly dependent and fishermen directly or indirectly dependent on this industry.[7] However, an important advantage of employment opportunities in this sector is that it is mostly the rural section of the population which is benefited most. It is also observed from the Census of India data that about 73 per cent of the Indian fishermen and related workers are engaged in the rural sector. Heavy pressure of the population on arable land, coupled with conditions of the backward technology and organization has resulted in severe unemployment and low output per engaged person. Pisciculture may provide some additional employment. Most importantly, it is the source of livelihood for a large section of economically backward population of the country.

Public revenue from fisheries would be welcome in the context of present financial position of a large number of Indian states. Leaving aside the justification or otherwise of making fisheries as a source of public revenue, it is important to evaluate the revenue potentialities of fisheries. The revenue from fish culture has reached a level of about 20 per cent in the case of Gram Panchayat of some states like Orissa and Uttar Pradesh.

The fishing industry, when developed on a commercial scale, gives rise to a larger number of ancillary industries. Important among them are shipbuilding, marine engines, nylon manufacturing, marketing, freezing, canning, fishmeal and fish oil, cold storage, ice manufacturing and various others. It is difficult to formulate an idea about Indian fishing ancillary industries through the published data. But it can be stated that a state like Kerala alone has 24 cold storages, 21 freezing factories, 40 boat building yards etc. It should be noted that USSR has invested more than half of her food industry investments since 1952 into the fishing industry. The potential forward and backward linkages through these activities contribute to diversification and strengthening of the regional and national economy.

There is no doubt that the development of fishing and allied industries in India has a special significance for different reasons.

This sector is eminently suited to assist a large mass of backward and economically weaker section of rural community. This implies simply that this is a sector which provides a reasonable degree of provisions for livelihoods to the rural population. It provides a huge protein subsidiary food at reasonable prices to satisfy certain rigid consumer preferences and it has a large export potential.[8]

The fisheries of India broadly consist of two types—(a) marine fisheries and (b) inland fisheries that include fresh water, estuarine and backwater fisheries. Of the total fish production of 5.66 million tonnes during 2000-01, about 2.84 million tonnes came from the marine sources and the rest from the inland water. Inland fisheries resources consist of two types of water—brackish and fresh. The fisheries of this type of water can be further classified into two types—culture and capture fisheries. Capture fisheries consist of rivers and their tributaries and estuaries, lakes etc., wherein fisheries are harvested without having to sow the seeds, nature is doing the job of sowing. In case of culture fisheries, one has to sow the seeds, nurse it and tend it to a proper size before harvesting. Culture fisheries comprise ponds, tanks, swarms, marshes etc. These different segments—capture, culture and culture-cum-capture fisheries have different settings and require entirely different types of inputs, infrastructure and development strategy.

India has a vast potential for development of inland fisheries. Indian fishery resources are vast and varied comprising rivers, canals (1,91,000 km), reservoirs (3.15 million hectares), ponds and tanks (2.25 million hectares), floodplain, lakes and derelict waters (1.3 million hectares) and brackish water areas (1.42 million hectares). Marine fisheries resources in the Indian EEZ have been estimated at about 3.934 million tonnes, constituting 51 per cent demersal, 43 per cent pelagic and 6 per cent oceanic.[9]

The performance of the fisheries sector is quite consistent. It is quite evident from Exhibit 1.2 that fish production was 0.75 million tonnes in 1949-50. It increased to 2.34 million tonnes during 1979-80 and then to 3.68 and 5.26 million tonnes in 1989-90 and 1998-99 respectively. In terms of growth, production rose by 4.78 per cent during the period from 1979-80 to 1989-90 and then by 4.70 per cent during the period from 1989-90 to 1998-99.

Again, the structure of fish production in the country has undergone significant changes over the years. During the 1970s and 1980s, the share of inland fisheries was just above one-third of the total fish production. Later, it gradually increased to reach nearly 40 per cent in 1990-91 and more than 50 per cent in 2000-01 (Exhibit 1.2). Fish consumption is likely to increase from 5.05 kg. per capita in 1996-97 to 9.30 kg. per capita in 2011-12 (Government of India, 1999). By 2020 AD, the domestic demand for fish is expected to be anywhere between 125 lakh tonnes and 200 lakh tonnes. The inland fisheries production will have to increase seven-fold even if minimum expected demand is to be satisfied from the inland sector.[10] In this situation, it is essential to fill the supply-potential gap rather than supply-demand gap.

With a catchment area of over 3.12 million km, 14 large, 48 medium and innumerable small rivers carrying a surface run-off of 167.23 million hectare through their drift exhibit a kaleidoscopic variety of environments, such as the cold-streams of the uplands, fast and slow moving stretches in the plains, floodplain lakes, deep pools, placid backwaters and estuaries (Exhibit 1.3). Development and rational exploitation of ourcapture fisheries resources are

Exhibit 1.2: Production and Growth Rates of Some Major Agricultural Commodities

Commodity	*Production (million tonnes)*				*Growth Rates (per cent per annum)*					
					1979 to 1989-90			*1989-90 to 1998-99*		
	1949-50	*1979-80*	*1989-90*	*1998-99*	*Area*	*Production*	*Yield*	*Area*	*Production*	*Yield*
1	2	3	4	5	6	7	8	9	10	11
Rice	23.54	42.33	73.57	85.99	0.45	4.29	3.82	0.49	1.70	1.21
Wheat	6.39	31.83	49.85	70.78	0.57	4.24	3.65	1.64	3.64	1.96
Foodgrains	54.92	109.70	171.04	203.04	-0.11	3.54	3.33	-0.18	1.80	1.42
Fish	0.75	2.34	3.68	5.26	--	4.78	--	--	4.70	--

Source : Tenth Five-Year Plan, 2002-07, Vols. II, III, Planning Commission, Government of India, New Delhi.

challenging tasks, unlike culture fisheries, where ecosystem manipulation and production monitoring are easy. Large open waters, spread among varied agro-climatic conditions exhibit diverse geo-dynamics and hence no uniform guideline can be formulated for their managements.

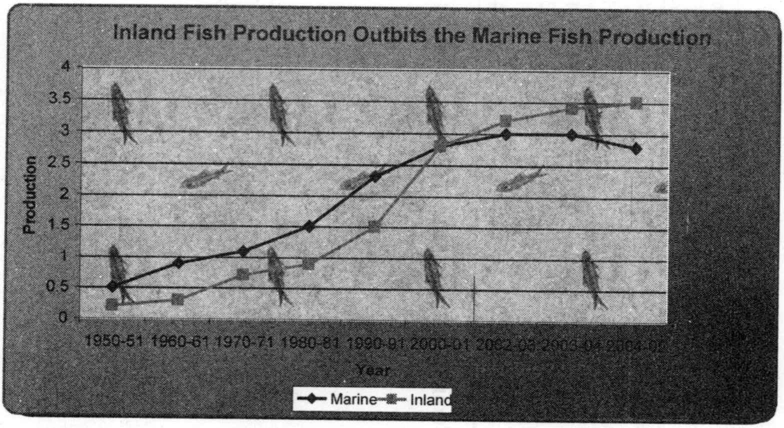

Figure 1.1: Fish Production in India.

1.4 West Bengal Fisheries and Livelihood

West Bengal is well endowed for inland water fisheries. It is situated in the monsoon belt. It has an annual precipitation of 1000 mm. It has extensive inland water resources in the form of hill streams, rivers, canals, wetlands, ponds and tanks etc. According to the West Bengal State Statistics (Directorate of Fisheries), the following (Exhibit 1.4) are the water resources available in the State:[11]

West Bengal produces the largest quantity of fresh water fish. About 65 per cent of total production of fish comes from fresh water, mainly, tanks and ponds. The estimated demand for the State is eight lakh tonnes. The shortfall is made up to an extent by import of fish from other states.

The Government of West Bengal has recently taken steps for intensifying fish culture and a considerable investment has already been committed. Fish Farmer Development Agencies (F.F.D.A.) which has been established in the State have extended facilities like fish seed supply at cheaper rates and subsidy. Extension services have

Exhibit 1.3: Inland Water Resources of India

No.	Resources	Quantity
1.	Rivers (km)	29,000
2.	Irrigated Canals (km)	1,20,000
3.	Flood Plains Lakes (ha)	2,02,213
4.	Upland Lakes (ha)	72,000
5.	Reservoirs (ha)	3,15,798
6.	Estuaries, Mangroves, Brackish Water Lagoon	60,00,000
7.	Estuaries Wetlands (ha)	50,000
8.	Brackish Water Aquaculture	9,02,000
9.	Fresh Water Aquaculture	7,53,000

Source : Handbook of Fisheries Statistics, Government of India.

Exhibit: 1.4: Water Resources in West Bengal

Tank/Pond	2,76, 201.90 ha
Beel/Baor	41,781.65 ha
Rivers	1,72,586.36 ha
Reservoirs	16, 738.8 ha
Sewage Fed	4,083 ha
Canal/Creek	30, 000 ha

Source : ME & MS Wing, Government of West Bengal.

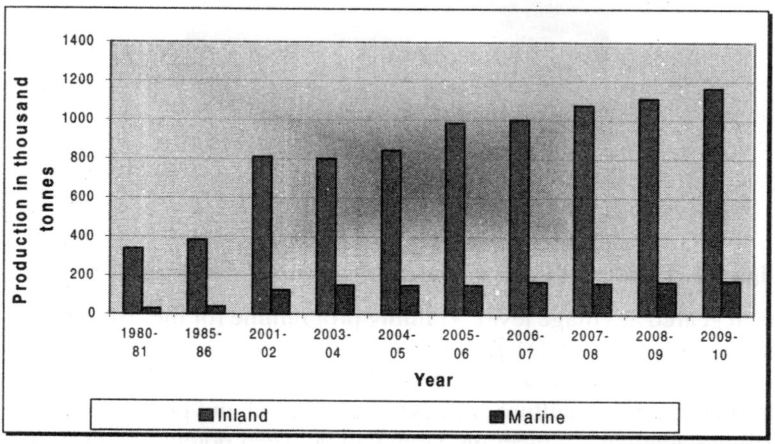

Figure 1.2: Fish Production in West Bengal

Source : ME & MS Wing, Government of West Bengal.

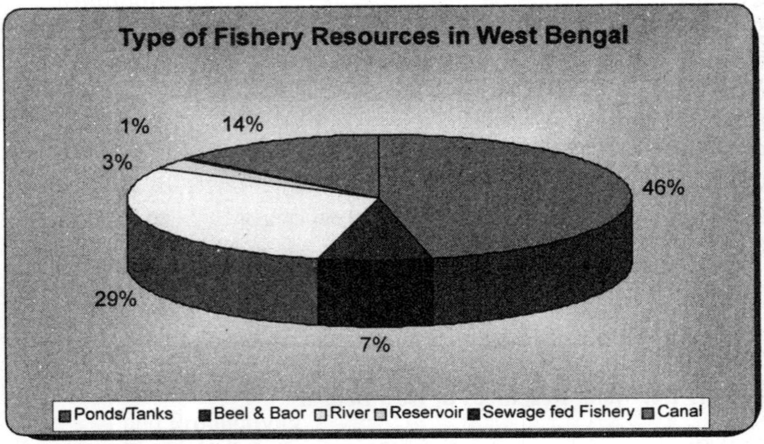

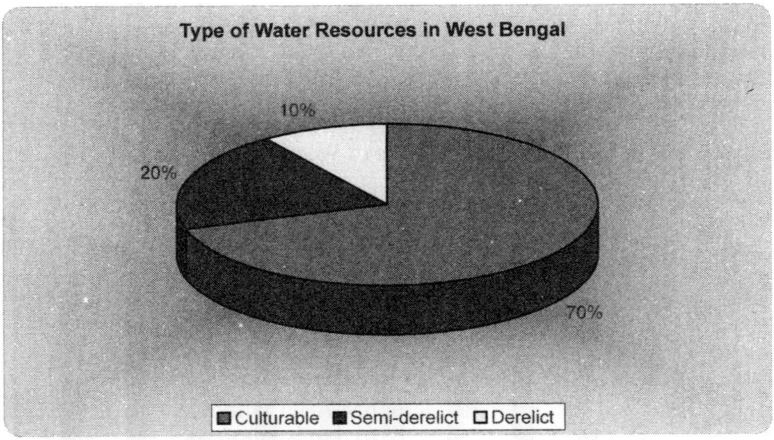

Figure 1.3: Different Types of Water Resources in West Bengal

been geared at village level. Training programme for the fish farmers has been introduced. Despite all these efforts and enormous potentials for intensified fish farming, these water bodies have not been utilized optimally for fish culture. The production level and productivity are still not adequate to meet the large gap between potential and actual yields. Improved technology has not yet disseminated to the level of common fish farmers in the villages. The recipients of technology are generally circumscribed by different factors. When the technology has been developed and resources available, one should expect reasonably that production should increase several folds in the next few years. There is an urgent need to make institutional efforts in the field of research, extension and training to exploit the fish production potentiality. This, in fact, has been in utter negligence in our country. There is hardly any comprehensive research in the field of fish culture in general and economics of inland fish production in particular.

1.5 Objectives of the Study

It is quite clear that inland fisheries sector (aquaculture and fisheries) consisting mainly of ponds and tanks, constitutes currently one of the most important sectors of India's national economy. In the case of West Bengal, the main production systems relate to extensive and semi-intensive pond-tank poly-culture of Indian major carps. All these account for quite a remarkable proportion of the total freshwater aquaculture production. Fish production is crucial for livelihoods within the agro-based economy of the country.

The study aims to understand how production under inland fisheries has led to poverty reduction. The aim of the study is to illustrate how the principles underlying the Sustainable Livelihoods Approach (SLA) (DFID, 1999) can be applied to support the development of fish farming in rural West Bengal. It is expected that the use of the livelihoods framework as a diagnostic tool can help bring a fuller understanding of farmer's adaptive strategies into the policy arena, and the SLA principles can then be applied in using this knowledge for development.

1.6 Study Outline

The Scheme of the study proceeds, in Chapter One, by setting out in more detail contextualizing the issue and identifying the importance of the inland fishery sector in our national economy. Efforts are also made to explain, in short, the Indian fisheries resources (both inland and marine) and their contributions to sustainable livelihood system. Explanations about the objectives of the study are also made in this chapter. The Second Chapter deals with a short review on the conceptual framework of the Sustainable Livelihood Systems. Attempt is made in Chapter Three to make a critical review of the literature on livelihood study relating to fisheries sector. Attempts also are made in Chapter Four to explain the methodology of the study. In Chapter Five, structure and operational features of inland fisheries resources, i.e., the tanks and ponds are explained. Also, technical efficiency of the fish farmers has been examined in Chapter Six. Chapter Seven offers a systematic overview of the adoption behaviour of the different packages of practices. In this context, some of the major constraints faced by the fish cultivators are also explained. Chapter Eight provides an explanation of the role and inadequacies of the institutional interventions like Government programmes, precisely like the Fish Farmers Development Agencies (FFDAs) in the development of inland fish cultivation. In the final chapter, Nine, the main conclusions of the study are summarized and the policy implications thrown up by the study are also elucidated.

Notes

1. Small scale fisheries play extremely important 'economic and welfare' functions at the local level (including safety net and labour buffer mechanisms). But these are still very rarely adequately documented and evaluated and the role that this sector has been playing as an engine for rural development by strengthening local communities' empowerment and fostering gender equity (through women economic empowerment).
2. Livelihood, according to the *Oxford English Dictionary*, not only refers to a manner of life, but also to the various means of maintenance. From these two terms, one gets an impression of the broad field of significance extending around the notion of livelihood. Livelihood seems to be melody and money at the same time. As a matter of fact, this refers to a way, a habit, or a custom and even to a melody or a tune, including food, income, property or inheritance.
3. It is important to realize that livelihood security has to be understood from the farmer's perspective. Food security is a subjective concept defined as an individual farmer's own perception as to whether s/he has been able to support the family's food and fodder requirements adequately round the year using all resources under the control. Food security is only one (although extremely important) element of livelihood security (See Appendix on 'Food Security' which explains how food security has assumed critical importance and hence, fishery sector is to play a role to rejuvenate livelihood security). But since farmers never make their decisions in a one-track logic, it seems possible that the one track security—based on food alone would have

to be enlarged to the more holistic notion of security of livelihood or speaking more simply-life security. Livelihood security encompasses food security, social security and psychic security. Each one of them has some basic minimum threshold level to achieve and maintain and also must be pursued in a balanced way.

4. Development assumes a human dimension when, through vigorous human activity, it seeks to establish for men and women the world-over the conditions essential to the maintenance and blossoming of life. (Chaudhury, 2010)
5. National Income Statistics, Central Statistical Organization, Government of India, 2004.
6. Export Prospects of Fish and Fish Products: National Council of Applied Economic Research, New Delhi.
7. Fishing News International, July 2004, pp. 21-22.
8. Kerala Fisheries—Facts and Figures: 1999-2000, Directorate of Fisheries, Government of Kerala, Tiruvanantapuram. Fishing News International, Vol. 5, No. 10, pp. 10.
9. It is sometimes argued that the increase in the share of inland fisheries in India was, on the one hand, due to deceleration in the growth of marine fish production and on the other, because of a policy shift in favour of inland fisheries, especially aquaculture. Again, the strong traditional knowledge base supported by scientific inputs in various aspects of management of inland fish cultivation is one of the factors responsible for growth in inland fish production (Jana and Sena, 2004).
10. 35 per cent of population in India has been estimated to be fish eaters, it being 46 per cent in the coastal and 27 per cent in the non-coastal states. With increase in population and per capita income, the demand for fish in India is likely to increase in the coming years. Own price elasticity of demand for fish is high and has not shown any sign of decline. There are some studies which mentioned that the responsiveness of demand for fish to changes in price and income (expenditure) varies for fish across income classes, regions and urbanization (Ayyappan, 2004).
11. The preponderance of small tanks and ponds and the existence of large number of derelict and semi-derelict ponds in West Bengal are quite evident from Annexure 4.

2

Sustainable Livelihood: Approach and Framework

2.1. Livelihood Framework in Fisheries

It is generally recognized that lack of knowledge and capital, higher risks, high opportunity costs for land and water, and access to markets usually limit small aquaculture entrepreneurs. As a result, new technologies and innovative culture systems for sustaining livelihood have been developed that specifically target the poorest of poor. Sometimes, the contribution of pond aquaculture on the livelihood depends on number of factors, even some of which are not directly related to fisheries and aquaculture. A number of studies explore the integration of aquaculture with agriculture, capture or inshore fisheries, fruits or vegetable, livestock, duckery or piggery. For example, Integrated Aquaculture Agriculture (IAA) scheme developed by FAO for understanding importance of intersectoral linkages became a popular model for the researchers. Natasja Sheriff *et al.* (2008) evaluate the role of high-value fish culture in the livelihoods of coastal households in southern Thailand. The study shows that fishing and aquaculture play contrasting roles in the livelihoods of coastal fishers and should be considered as complementary rather than alternative occupations. Dang K. Nhan *et al.* (2007) show that promotion of integrated aquaculture with agriculture, including crops and livestock requires consideration of both bio-physical and socio-economic contexts. The major factors influencing the adoption of IAA-farming by households at three sites in the Mekong delta were identified in their study. Special attention was given to the multiple roles ponds play in IAA-farming systems. Information was collected through semi-structured interviews and discussions with focus groups and key individuals. Data were analyzed using multivariate factor analysis, analysis of variance or participatory ranking methods. Three major IAA-systems were identified: (1) low-input fish farming integrated with intensive fruit production (system 1), (2) medium-input fish farming integrated with less intensive fruit production (system 2), and (3) high-input fish farming integrated with less intensive fruit production (system 3). System 1 was commonly practised in a rural fruit-dominated area with fertile soils, while systems 2 and 3 were more evident in peri-urban rice-dominated areas with less fertile soils. In the study area, only 6 per cent of poor farmers adopted IAA-farming, while this was 42 per cent for intermediate and 60 per cent for rich households. Richer farmers tended to intensify fish farming and seek a more commercial orientation. The major factors why farmers did not start aquaculture were the inappropriateness of technology, insufficient landholding or poor access to extension services, limited farm management, and through a fear of conflicts associated with pesticide use on crops. The main motivations for practising IAA-farming included increased income and food for home consumption from the available farm resources while reducing environmental impacts. Further improvements to IAA-systems can be realized by strengthening nutrient recycling between different IAA-system components while enhancing farming output and safeguarding the environment. M. Prein (2002) reviews the status of integrated agriculture-aquaculture (IAA) in Asia with an emphasis on rural small-scale systems. Existing IAA-systems within mixed farming systems are characterised and the economic and ecological role of aquaculture described. The analysis shows that in comparison to other enterprises, the pond offers relatively greater potential for integration on farms and for flows of nutrients to and from the new enterprise. Based on examples from Bangladesh, China, India and Thailand, Prein concludes that considerable potential exists for further aquaculture integration in Asia, with notable improvements in the livelihoods of rural small-scale farmers.

2.2 In Search of Alternative Development Theory

While tracking along the path of recorded theories of rural development, we came across different innovative ideas, where it might be taken for granted that enhancement of well-being of the poor depends directly on growth and modernization of their working environment. Modernization as a way of development can be traced back the first half of the 20th century in the history of western-industrialized countries. Modernization became in reality an economic development theory. It was taken generally that for Third World countries to develop; they had to follow the same stages as European Countries went through some decades ago. The theory emphasized that poor countries of the world were poor because they were dependant on agriculture, used traditional means of production, lacked technological innovations and generally had an illiterate society. Development is by the modernization theorists characterized as a movement from a state of backwardness with subsistence economy, to a modern, industrial society with higher income and productivity rates. This school of thought however ignores the concrete and complex processes of change and struggle in real social formations. Modernization appeared as an environmentally and socially destructive ideology, which retains a power to shape trajectories of economic development within which sustainability is problematic (Lee, 2000).

Against the backdrop, concept of alternative development theories comes into the picture. This paradigm rejects economic growth as an end in itself, and instead emphasizes welfare and human development with increased choices (Martinussen, 1999). It emerged in the 1970s as a critique to mainstream economic model of modernization that failed to address the problem of massive poverty and environmental sustainability. It was inspired by the works of John Friedman who saw the previous attempts to development as 'failure' and alternative development as 'hope'. As a new approach, alternative development hoped to improve the living conditions of the poor especially in rural areas and at the same time be compatible with emerging environmental concerns.

The main idea about alternative development was not to replace mainstream development path of modernization through the state but rather to transform them so that the disempowered poor are included in political and economic processes and have their rights as citizens and human beings acknowledged. It, therefore, starts with a bottom-up approach with the major concern on people and not only on production and profits and ends with top down coping strategies. Alternative development focuses on the fulfilment of practical and strategic interests through collective mobilization—the empowerment approach. This has increasingly been used to mean increasing people's capacities so that they become self-sustaining, independent and able to make decisions that affect their lives. The theory points out that its only through people-centred and bottom-up approaches to development through which people are empowered; socially, economically as well as psychologically. Through this 'basic needs approach' of alternative development theory, fish farming in small water bodies is very important as an alternative source of food (proteins), source of income for farmers thus able to meet other basic needs like clothing, housing and education. That is, policies to develop small scale rural aquaculture should be so developed that are sustainable in long run.

2.3 The Concept of Sustainable Development

Broadly speaking, sustainability is a key indicator of success or failure in development projects. The term 'sustainable development' was first used in early 1980s in the World Conservation Strategy but became popular after the publication 'Our Common Future' by the World Commission on Environment and Development (WCED) in 1987. The concept has been defined as "development that meets the needs of the present without compromising the ability of future generations to meet their own needs". By this time, international debates had been characterized more and more by considerations about the impact of growth and socio-economic change upon the physical environment. From this definition, the emphasis on 'needs' is closely related to problems of poverty especially in the Third World. It is emphasized that fulfilling of human needs and aspirations is the most important goal for all development efforts throughout the world. Globally, the concept of sustainability has been the major focus in the formulation of development objectives as well as in connection with the design of strategies, which increasingly take into account environmental concerns. In simple terms, sustainability may be taken to mean that, a specific activity can continue or a resource can be available for at least the medium, and it is not associated with or dependant upon rapidly depleting inputs (Helmore and Singh, 2001).

Sustainability can mean different things to different people, though most would agree that it involves three elements of futurity, equity and the environment. It is important to note that the term has acquired different connotations within particular fields; for instance, in an institutional pond aquaculture project, particularly in economically deprived areas, the term sustainable development is used to define whether fish farming are still profitable and are likely to continue once external support has been withdrawn. It relates with project effectiveness, financial viability, technical capacity and social acceptability. Sustainability is important because it implies that progress in poverty reduction is lasting, rather than fleeting because there is accumulation of broad capital base that provides the basis for improved livelihoods, especially for poor people. With regard to this study, the term sustainability is used to determine whether the long term objectives of augmenting the livelihood options of poor fish farmers are achievable through the pond aquaculture.

Thus, since, sustainability of poverty reduction is now a major goal of almost all the developing countries, the role of fisheries decision making units is changing as a result. Previously, managers were concerned mainly with safeguarding or increasing fish production. Now they are also involved in activities that aim to improve the standard of living of rural fisherfolk. These include helping local communities increase their involvement in formulating policies and programmes concerning the management and development of pond aquaculture resources. This explained role requires fisheries managers, at all levels from local communities to government, to broaden their perspectives of fisheries, the work involved and the place of fishing and fishing related activities in the wider communities. To do this, requires examining the circumstances of rural people, their access to various assets and resources, their vulnerabilities and the major outside influences on their live, culture and society. This new way of looking at fisheries management is popularly known as Sustainable Livelihood Approach (SLA).[1]

2.4 Sustainable Livelihood Approach—Theory and Concept

'Sustainable livelihoods' is a cross-thematic approach that was identified in early 1990s to eradicate poverty; on the basis of the energies and talents of the poor people (Helmore *et al.*, 2001) thus encouraging activities that are pro-poor. Poor people are taken to be actors, that is, capable to identify and address their livelihood priorities while outsiders listen and respond. The latter need to support and enhance existing livelihood strategies and copying mechanisms of the poor. The approach is built on ideas such as adaptive strategies, participation and empowerment, governance and policy. For instance, it is very important to understand livelihood strategies and vulnerability of the poor as a starting point in livelihood analysis. Activities need to be conducted in partnership with both the public and the private sectors thus making SL approach holistic in nature, encouraging local people to draw up integrated, multi-sectoral development strategies in order to restore and maintain the health of all aspects of the local social ecosystem. Much as the approach recognizes multiple actors, it also puts into account the multiple livelihood strategies that people adopt to secure livelihoods. Sustainable livelihoods approach is neither a bottom-up nor a top-down but stresses that all levels should work together (holistic) as mentioned above. It aims to promote development that is sustainable not just ecologically, but also institutionally, socially and economically and to produce positive livelihood outcomes (Ashley and Carney, 1999).

In the popular sense of the term, livelihood describes the means of living or sustenance. An economic definition of livelihood could be the organization of productive resources of households to maximize their standard of living. In their definition, Chambers and Conway include assets and capabilities along with activities or strategies in the productive resources. To quote: 'Livelihood comprises the capabilities, assets, and activities for a means of living' (Chambers and Conway, 1992: 7). By capabilities, they mean something akin to Sen's notion of a set of alternative beings and doings that a person can achieve with his/her economic, social, and personal characteristics (Dreze and Sen, 1989; Sen, 1993, 1997).

The livelihoods approach has its origins partly in a literature concerned with understanding the differential capability of rural families to cope with crises such as droughts, floods, and diseases. This literature focuses attention on the assets of rural people, and how different patterns of asset holding (land, stock, food stores, savings etc.) can make big differences to the ability of families to withstand shocks. This set of concerns also links to the concept of vulnerability; defined as a high degree of exposure to risk, shocks and stress and proneness to food insecurity. Vulnerability has the dual aspect of external threats to livelihood security due to risk factors such a climate, markets or sudden disaster; and internal coping capability determined by assets, food stores, support from kin or community, or government safety net policies.

The approach also borrows ideas from an ecological literature concerned with the sustainability of ecosystems or agro-ecological systems. Here, sustainability is defined as "the ability of a system to maintain productivity in spite of a major disturbance, such as is caused by intensive stress or a large perturbation". The concepts of resilience and sensitivity as livelihood attributes also originate in this context. Resilience refers to the ability of an ecological or livelihood system to "bounce back" from stress or shocks; while sensitivity refers to the magnitude of a system's response to an external disturbance. It follows from these ideas that the most robust livelihood system is one displaying high resilience and low sensitivity; while the most vulnerable displays low resilience and high sensitivity. These ideas are relevant to fishery-based livelihoods, as will become apparent in due course. The concept of 'a livelihood' seeks to bring together the critical factors that affect the vulnerability or strength of individual or family survival strategies. These are thought to comprise, chiefly, the assets possessed by people, the activities in which they engage in order to generate an adequate standard of living and to satisfy other goals such as risk reduction, and the factors that facilitate or inhibit different people from gaining access to assets and activities. These considerations result in the following definition of a livelihood.

Both material and social resources and activities are required for living. A livelihood is sustainable when it can cope with and recover from stresses and shocks and maintain or enhance. A livelihood is generally defined as comprising the capabilities, assets, including its capabilities and assets both in the present and in the future, while not undermining the natural resource base.

Thus, the livelihoods approach seeks to improve rural development policy and practice by recognizing the seasonal and cyclical complexity of livelihood strategies, helping to remove access constraints to assets and activities that complement existing patterns, and identifying ways of making livelihoods as a whole more able to cope with adverse trends or sudden shocks. A fundamental precept of the approach is that it seeks "to identify what the poor have rather than what they do not have" and "[to] strengthen people's own inventive solutions, rather than substitute for, block or undermine them". The livelihoods approach centres on the links between individual or household assets, the activities in which households

Photo 2.1: Homestead Pond—Congenial for Good Monitoring.

Photo 2.2: Female Involvement in Livelihood through Fish Culture.

can engage with a given asset profile, and the mediating processes (institutions, regulations etc.) that govern access to assets and to alternative activities.

Several research approaches have developed out of the concept of Sustainable Livelihoods. They include the Asset Vulnerability Framework (SIDA, 2002; Moser, 1998) and the Social Risk Management Framework (Heemskerk *et al.*, 2004; Holzmann and Jorgensen, 2000). While strengthening the capital assets of communities is the primary focus in the former framework, protecting basic livelihood as well as assisting the poor to develop appropriate risk-management instruments is the emphasis in the latter. The latter framework, according to Holzmann and Jorgensen (2000), will help the poor to engage in riskier but also higher-return activities and hence gradually move them out of chronic poverty. Both frameworks are useful for analyzing livelihoods. However, they take a very limited view of poverty.

The definition of poverty, or well-being, is commonly based on estimates of income or consumption expenditures (Campenhout, 2007; Headey and Wooden, 2004; Khan, 2001). These analysts, however, do not acknowledge the complex nature of poverty (Kingdon and Knight, 2006). While poverty is associated with a lack of income and productive assets (such as cultivable land), poverty is also associated with higher morbidity and mortality, limited or no access to basic sanitation, minimal health services, unhygienic living conditions, illiteracy and lack of formal education, lack of political power or exclusion and overall marginalization (DFID, 2002; Narayan *et al.*, 2000). These features of poverty make the poor vulnerable. Individuals and households in poverty are, therefore, exposed to food insecurity and diseases, and are often forced into occupational and livelihood displacement. These vulnerabilities are very complex. Understanding them requires a comprehensive approach that is capable of integrating diverse factors in a meaningful manner.

The theoretical foundation for SLA is in the realm of poverty and environment (Baumann, 2002). In Baumann's report on *Improving Access to Natural Resources for the Rural Poor*, reference is made to "approaches", meaning a set of principles supported with a set of tools rather than a single method (Baumann, 2002, pp. 6-7). Baumann stresses that the single most important factor in understanding livelihood strategies is determining the ability of the poor to access assets. This research, uses SLA principles and tools, and is designed to address access to assets, livelihood strategies and outcomes in the context of resource dependent households of pond fishing communities.

2.5 Sustainable Livelihood Framework (SLF)

People draw on a set of 'capital assets' as a basis for their livelihoods. Carney (1998) identifies five sets of assets: human, natural, financial, physical and social. The capital available to individual households reflect their ability to gain access to systems (the resource base, the financial system, society) through which these capitals are produced. Assets comprise several components, some of which represent the economic categories of capital, and others—claims and access to resources. Generally, five categories of assets are identified as contributing to livelihoods. They are natural assets, physical assets, human assets, financial assets, and social assets (Scooner, 1998; Bebbington *et al.*, 1997; Bebbington, 1999; Carney, 1998; Serageldin and Steer, 1994).

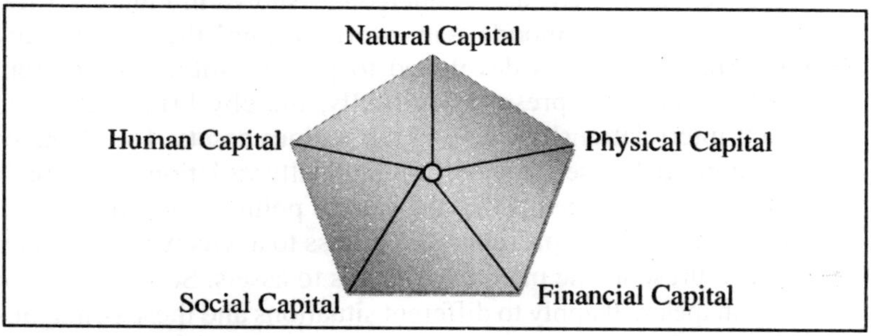

Figure 2.1: Asset Pentagon used in Sustainable Livelihood Framework

Source : DFID, 2005.

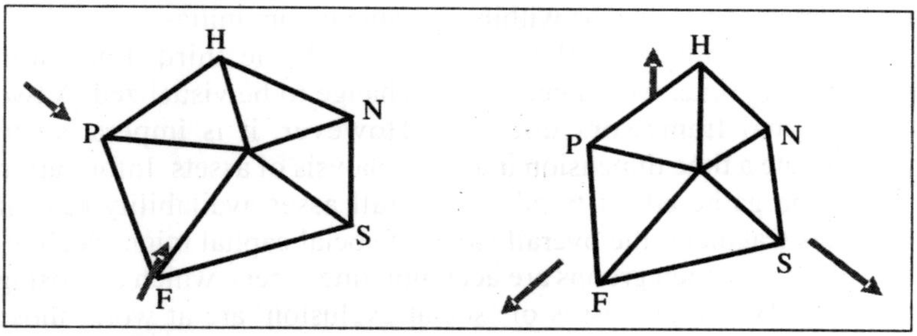

Figure 2.2: Different Shaped Pentagons—Change in Access to Assets

Source : Adapted from Sustainable Livelihood Guideline sheet, DFID.

Natural assets refer to natural resources like land and water that contribute to production and consumption activities. Physical assets are produced means of production such as tools, machines, and irrigation systems. Human assets chiefly refer to education, skills and health of household members. Financial assets are basically the stocks of cash and access to credit. Social asset could mean social networks and organizations. Interactions among people in markets, government and civil society provide access to resources or/and development of assets into commodity bundles (Sen, 1981; Evans, 1996; Bebbington, 1999). As such, we can identify the 'access profile' of households that defines their ability to gain access to capital assets. It seeks to gain an accurate and realistic understanding of people's strengths (assets or capital endowments) and how they endeavour to convert these into positive livelihood outcomes.

For analyzing the access of people to various capitals, we use the 'asset pentagon'. The asset pentagon as shown in Figure 2.1 lies at the core of the livelihoods framework 'within' the vulnerability context. The pentagon is developed to provide information about people's assets to be presented visually, thereby bringing to life important interrelationships among the various assets. The shape of the pentagon can be used to show schematically variations in people's access to assets. The idea is that the central point of the pentagon, at which the lines meet, represents zero access to assets while the outer perimeter represents the maximum access to assets. So pentagons of different shapes will apply to different situations and these pentagons change over time. So the asset pentagon should be considered a dynamic presentation of the assets of a social group. On this basis pentagons of different shapes can be drawn for different communities or different social groups within the same communities.

A three dimensional framework, with the third dimension representing time, would enable this change to be visualized. A two dimensional framework does not. However, it is imperative to incorporate a time dimension into any analysis of assets. Information should be gathered on trends in overall asset availability (e.g. if societies fragment, the overall stock of social capital might decline) as well as on which groups are accumulating assets, which are losing and why. Where processes of 'social exclusion' are at work, those who are already poorly endowed, with assets may well be becoming gradually, but notably, more marginalized. Change in the asset status would be clearer with the following figures.

The left hand pentagon shows reasonable but declining access to physical capital and limited access to natural capital. Social capital is also falling. Perhaps the people whose livelihood assets are represented do not have the skills or finance to invest in infrastructure maintenance. The decline of social capital also constraints their ability to form shared work groups. The right hand pentagon shows the situation after support that has extended access to financial capital (e.g. through group based micro finance schemes that also help build social capital) as well as providing skills and training (human capital). Together these enable the people to maintain and extend their physical capital. Access to natural capital remains unchanged.

Along with Asset mix, institutions play a crucial role in livelihood dynamics. A classic definition of institution is given by North (1991:97):

Institutions are the humanly devised constraints that structure political, economic and social interaction. They consist of both informal constraints (sanctions, taboos, customs, tradition, and codes of conduct) and formal rules (constitutions, laws, property rights).

Institutions, market and assets interplay in livelihood dynamics. Access to natural assets like land, financial assets, social organizations etc. is defined by rules and social norms (institutions); value of the flow of benefits from productive assets is determined by the market forces. By impacting on transaction cost, institutions can make markets efficient or inefficient.

Institutions also affect livelihoods directly. State policies on social security directly affect livelihood outcomes. Conversely, changes in livelihoods might make certain institutions redundant and certain others necessary. An understanding of these and other inter-relationships among assets, institutions, markets and livelihoods becomes important in unravelling the different dimensions of sustainable livelihoods. These relationships are diagrammatically represented in the Figure 2.3.

Now, outcome of livelihood strategies could be viewed in terms of income received or consumption achieved by households (Ellis, 2000). However, it could be adversely affected by the presence of livelihood risks. Livelihood risk is defined as the likelihood of occurrence of (external) shocks and stresses plus their severity (OECD development association committee network on poverty reduction).

In the rural scenario, livelihood risks can be categorised among four main divisions (Figure 2.4):

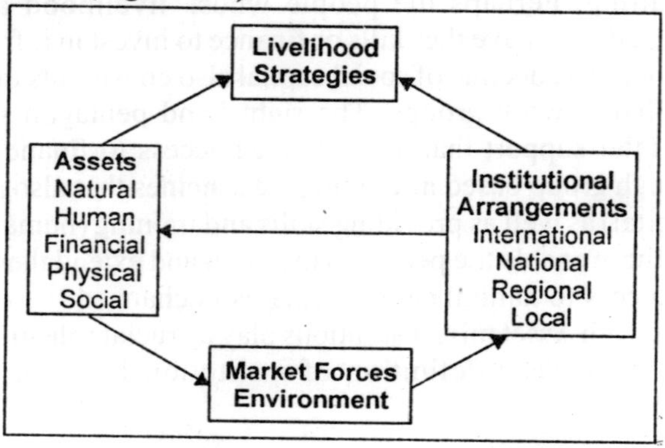

Figure 2.3: Interplay between Different Components of SLF.

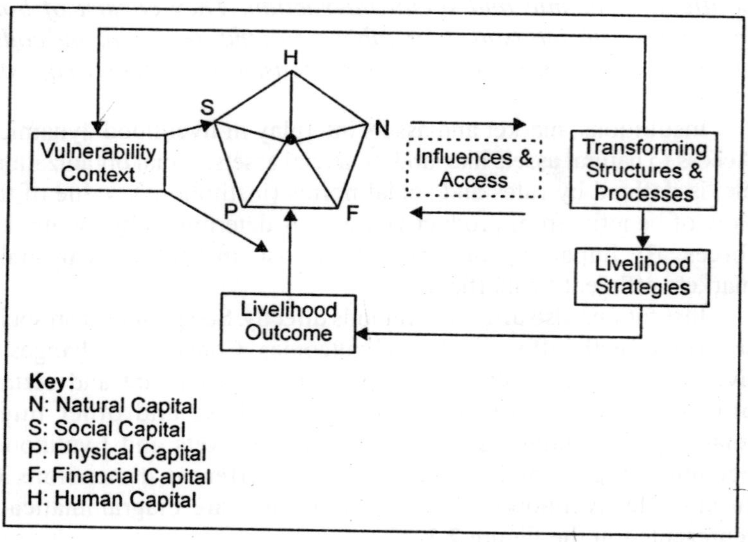

Figure 2.4: Overall Sustainable Livelihood Framework under Analysis.

Source : Carney, 1998.

(i) harmful trends such as increasing soil erosion, frequent droughts, unfavourable development of commodity or input prices; (ii) shocks such as earthquakes, floods, disease, loss of jobs, violent conflicts, destruction of physical infrastructure etc., (iii) harmful seasonal fluctuations such as price fluctuations in crop and livestock markets, fluctuations in food availability due to climatic changes, and (iv) unfavourable socio-political environments, characterised by absence of rule of law, deprivation of rights, gender-related discrimination etc.

As and when livelihood faces risks households may develop strategies to overcome them. Such strategies may be of two types: risk coping strategies and risk mitigation (adaptive) strategies. While the former represent ex-post short-term strategies to cope with risk mainly through smoothing consumption, the latter is ex-ante steps to mitigate risk potential in the long-run through income smoothing strategies (Aderman and Parxson, 1994; Morduch, 1990; Dercon, 2000).

In a nutshell, therefore, framework for Sustainable Livelihood Approach (SLA) can be summarized as the search for a particular livelihood strategies that combines the assets they can access, taking account of their vulnerability context, supported or obstructed by the policies, institutions or processes and throughway leads to livelihood outcome. The relationship between different parts of SLA framework are represented in the Figure 2.5.

The empirical unfolding of this framework may be illuminated well in an appropriate micro location, since the analysis of livelihood has to be studied at close quarters holistically. It may be noted that livelihood is conditioned by extra local factors. Therefore, understanding the micro-macro linkages is important to obtain a comprehensive grip on the factors and processes conditioning livelihood strategies.

2.6 Fisheries and SLF

A livelihood comprises the assets (natural, physical, human, financial and social capital), the activities, and the access to these (mediated by institutions and social relations) that together determine the living gained by the individual or household. The livelihoods approach is typically set out in the form of a framework that brings together the principal components that are thought to comply with the livelihoods definition, as well as demonstrating the interactions between them.[2] There are many different diagrammatic representations of this framework. The reference social scope of this framework is typically considered to be the extended household, including members who are away from home but send remittances back to the resident homestead. The starting point of the framework is the assets owned, controlled, claimed, or in some other means accessed by the households. The livelihoods framework recognizes five main asset categories, comprising physical capital (sometimes also called produced capital or economic capital); natural capital (land, trees, fish stocks etc.); human capital (people, education and health); financial capital (savings, credit); and social capital (kinship networks, associations). Access to both assets and activities is enabled or hindered by the policy and institutional context of livelihoods, including social relations, institutions and organizations.

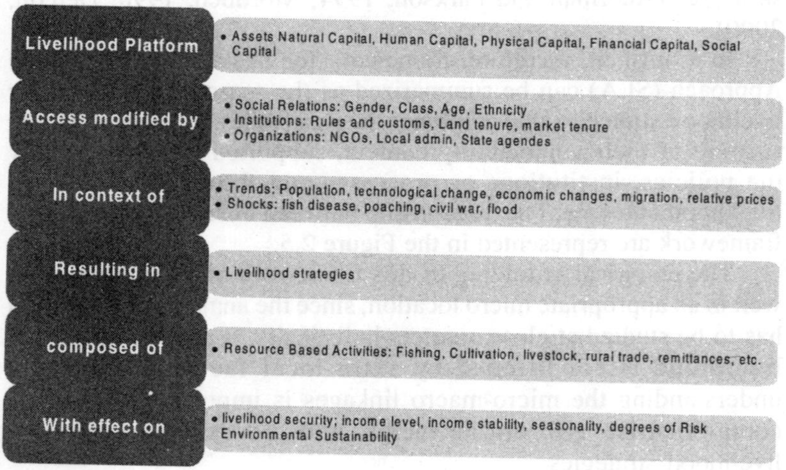

Figure 2.5: Micro Policy Analysis of Rural Livelihood in Pond Aquaculture.

Source: Adapted from Ellis, 2000, p. 30.

It is also affected by external factors, sometimes referred to as the vulnerability context, comprising trends and shocks that are outside the control of the household. Assets permits livelihood strategies to be constructed, and these are composed of a portfolio of activities, some of which may be natural resource based and others not so. Finally, this framework points to outcomes of livelihood strategies, distinguished here between livelihood security effects and environmental sustainability effects. The livelihoods of artisanal fisherfolk are readily described by this type of framework. In this instance, key assets are fishing gears (boats and nets), although many artisanal fishers may also possess land and combine fishing with farming. The policy and institutional context of artisanal fishing includes, but is not limited to, the role of state regulations and 'community' based rules that affect access to resources. Social relations can also determine who has access to fishing opportunities (e.g. the ethnicity of fishing families may differ from other families in coastal communities, and roles within fishing activities are often strongly gender-differentiated). Fishing families are no less prone than other rural dwellers to adverse events and trends, with natural fluctuations in fish stocks being especially critical for them. Finally, fishing families often engage in diverse activities in order to achieve livelihood security.

The livelihoods approach is utilised in different ways, according to the goal of the study or programme. In development practice, it is being used as a 'process' tool to enable participants in development programmes to identify key constraints and opportunities for development intervention. The livelihoods framework also forms the basis for recent policy-relevant empirical research that seeks to capture the cross-sectoral nature of rural people's income-generating and subsistence activities. In this chapter, we are using the livelihoods approach as a conceptual tool to re-examine past strategies in fisheries management and development from a perspective different to the more usual sectoral analyses. The remaining sections of this chapter attempt a re-examination of the literature on small-scale fisheries in the light of our preliminary experiences with the application of the livelihoods approach.[3]

2.7 Analysis of Asset Pentagon

For assessing the asset status of households in some study area and for plotting the pentagon, a quantification method was developed. In this method, appropriate proxy variables are generally identified in order to represent each asset and developed the quantification method for the particular variable.[4] After quantifying the proxy variable, we plotted a pentagon for all the households taken together and analysed it visually; later we plotted pentagons separately by occupation, by community and according to Monthly Per Capita Consumption (MPCC). The category of households with significant difference in the form of lying away from 'all households', was taken into consideration and named as the 'poor' (poor defined as households which have MPCC below Rs. 500). Households lying in the inner most pentagon inside the pentagon plot for the poor, were households belonging to the marginal communities.

In order to examine the phenomenon further, we tested the association among various variables by a correlation analysis. The actual data for consumption expenditure, the land owned and the investments made were fed into the analysis, whereas for variables of education, housing and participation on social organisations, the ranks were used. The results show that there is significant correlation between all types of assets; that it is the highest between land and investment, and land and education. It is obvious that those with larger landholdings have better access to finance and education. Naturally, their consumption expenditure, which is considered one of the main livelihood outcomes, is also on the higher side. That is to say, land—the natural capital—is the determining capital.

From the analysis carried out above about various assets possessed by different social groups and their level of consumption we may draw two major conclusions:

1. From the pentagon plot analysis, it is found that there are households inside the pentagon plot which can be defined as poor. They lie in the innermost pentagon. They are the poorest of the poor and are considered 'marginalized households'.
2. There exists a significant correlation among all types of assets which the households possess and access. This correlation is the highest between land and investment, as well as between land and education. It is obvious that those with higher landholdings have better access to finance and education. Naturally, their consumption expenditure, which is considered one of the main livelihood outcomes, also is on the higher side. In other words, land, the natural capital, is the determining capital.

Notes

1. The livelihoods approach has its origin partly in a literature concerned

understanding the differential capability of rural families to cope with crises such as drought, floods or diseases. This literature focuses attention on the assets of rural people, and how different patterns of asset holding (land, stock, food stores, savings etc.) can make big differences to the ability of families to withstand shocks. This set of concerns also links to the concept of vulnerability, defined as a high degree of exposure to risk, shocks and stress, and proneness to food insecurity.

2. The livelihood approach centres on the link between individual or household assets, the activities in which the households can engage with a given asset profile and the mediating processes (institutions, regulations etc.) that govern access to assets and to alternative activities. The first major fisheries development and management project explicitly adopted is the sustainable fisheries Livelihood Programme in West Africa (1999-2004) funded by DFID and implemented by FAO. It involved 25 countries, within which 7 million people are directly dependent on freshwater and marine resources.
3. The advantages of SLA are that it is helpful in structuring fieldwork and data collection by proving a holistic approach and help grasp all components of livelihoods in the target areas of study. The combined use of both participatory methods (qualitative) and sample survey (quantitative) is complementary in providing an understanding of the reasons behind livelihood strategies adoption. It is a reconciliation of traditional economic methods and participatory qualitative methods.
4. The use of small scale sample survey provide a detailed and quantifiable insight into the problem. However, the operationalisation of the SLA leaves something more to be desired. The difficulties mostly relate to time management and timing of multiple data collection. The bias induced by snapshot perceptions of a situation applies to the system also. The questionnaire survey also captures information specific to a particular point of time. The researchers' perceptions of the situation would be affected by prevailing conditions. The participatory appraisal or the sample survey do not address forward or feedback arrows linking the SLA components.

3

Fisheries and Livelihood: Review of Literature

3.1 Livelihood Approach in Practice

The subject of livelihood enhancement and diversification among different fishing communities has been debated since the early 1980s, especially when doubt started cropping up about the capacity of open water fisheries to contribute sustainable to the livelihood of the poor.[1] These doubts sprang from the fact that most fisheries had begun to show the sign of distress due to overfishing, urban and industrial pollution, reduced flow of freshwater and many more others. As a result, both fish catches and productivity had fallen, incomes had declined and the misery of fishers have aggravated by rampart indebtedness. Problems had become much more acute as technology driven, production focused government policies overlooked the knowledge and expertise of fishers and proved to be a major handicap in making viable interventions into the very distress.

In search of an alternative, promotion for livelihood strategy has become popular policy to uplift the socio-economic status of small scale fishers and to reduce fishing pressure on overexploited fisheries. The first is to raise the economic standard of living of small scale fishers, and the second is to reduce fishing effort. Alternative livelihood as a solution to overfishing has been proposed for more than two decades. Smith (1979) recommended alternative income sources such as seaweed farming as one type of incentive to reduce fishing pressure as long as they are attractive enough to reduce full-time fishing. However, he also reported that

Philippine surveys at that time indicated that only 50 per cent of fishers are willing to change their occupation, with households more dependent on fishing more receptive to occupational change. Willingness to change was also higher in more geographically isolated locations, among poorer, younger, less educated and less successful fishermen, groups less likely to accept the risks of a new activity. Therefore, he recommended an emphasis on supplemental rather than alternative employment, encouraging a shift from full-time to part-time fishing. In another example, from Central America, brackish water farming was proposed as an alternative economic opportunity to reduce pressure on fisheries resources in the Gulf of Nicoya even though few such solutions had been tested (Phillips, 1985). A report on bivalve farming in the Philippines recommended mari-culture as a means of uplifting the socio-economic status of small-scale coastal fishermen to counterbalance increased fishing and population pressures as well as declining catches (Delmendo, 1989).

In the early 1990s, people centred, subsistence oriented Sustainable Livelihood Approach (SLA) has appeared as a meaningful policy option to address the context of livelihood enhancement and diversification of fishing communities. Significant is that, most of the studies in the nineties have adopted SLA only in the context of coastal fishing communities.[2] If a long history of livelihood diversification of this traditional fisheries economy is one reason behind such tendency, another one must be the fact that destruction of critical coastal habitat and nurseries due to overfishing had a direct negative impact on the livelihood of these communities. However, the results of those studies have brought to the fore a number of strategies and responses to fluctuating resource availability employed by poor fish farmers in coastal fishing. Review of those case studies and regional reviews deserve particular mentions.

In *Cambodia*, Vannaara (2003) used a livelihood approach to assess the aquatic resources targeted by the Au Svay community fishery in Stung Treng province, Northern Cambodia. One of his objectives was to, 'provide additional information and experience related to sustainable abstraction of natural resources to government institutions and NGOs that could then be implemented in other community fisheries'. Marschke (2006) explored livelihood strategies that build resilience in Cambodian fisheries. In *Lao PDR*, Shoemaker *et al.* (2001) used the approach to understand the complex interrelationships between resources and livelihoods in the Xai Bang Fai River basin. They found, 'from place to place and from season to season, different ethnic groups take advantage of the natural wealth of the basin in different ways'. Mollot *et al.* (2003) employed the approach to study how the livelihoods of rural communities living in seasonally flooded habitats in southern Lao PDR were closely linked to the preservation of biodiversity in these ecosystems. By getting the communities to share their local knowledge, they were able to obtain a greater understanding of the balance between the benefits and threats resulting from seasonal floods. Through this analysis, Mollot *et al.* aim to prevent 'the implementation of incomplete poverty alleviation strategies', that is, development activities that do not take fully into account the benefits of the flood.

In *Thailand*, the Thai Baan research followed a livelihood approach in demonstrating the great diversity of activities taken up by rural people, including fishers. Furthermore, the long-enduring Village Fish Pond Programme (VFP) developed a strategic management approach to emphasise aquatic resource development for alleviating rural poverty in north-east Thailand, which makes use of a number of principles of the livelihood approach. In doing so, it emphasised the unique socio-economic and biological characteristics of each village and water resource under consideration, as well as the importance of multiple variables encompassing social, agro-biological, institutional, and organisational components (Virapat, 2002).

In *Vietnam*, the livelihood approach was used 'to characterize the poor, identify their dependence upon aquatic resources, describe the nature and status of these resources, and emphasize the vulnerabilities of the poor in relation to loss or mismanagement' (Sultana, *et al.*, 2003). Furthermore, 'livelihoods' figure prominently in a series of activities that inform the implementation of the Ministry of Fisheries (MoFI) Strategy on Sustainable Aquaculture for Poverty Alleviation (SAPA) under the Vietnamese Government's Hunger Eradication and Poverty Reduction (HEPR) Programme (STREA M., 2002). These examples are taken from the studies that used livelihood analyses to achieve a more complete understanding of the role of aquatic resources, particularly fish, in the livelihoods of rural people in the Lower Mekong Basin. However, livelihood approaches involve more than just livelihood analysis; they also require that the understanding of livelihoods that these analyses produce, is taken up in policies and procedures for fisheries management. To do this requires a more structured categorisation of livelihoods, their characteristics and functions.

Recently, Smith *et al.* (2005) used livelihood approaches to generate a framework in which to analyse and categorise fishing-related livelihoods. Their analysis is based on the view that, 'in contrast to the stereotype that all fishers are poor and that fishing is the activity of last resort, actual fishing communities are likely to be varied in terms of wealth, social status, fishing methods and livelihood roles performed by fishing' (pg. 375). They recognise four principal types of 'livelihood strategies' which include fishing:

(i) As a primary livelihood of last resort—a fisher or fishing household that fishes as a subsistence activity;
(ii) Part of a diversified semi-subsistence livelihood—a fisher or fishing household that fishes and gathers other natural resources (such as other aquatic animals or non-timber forest products) as a subsistence activity;
(iii) A specialist occupation—a fisher or fishing household that makings a living or an income from fishing primarily for trade; and
(iv) Part of a diversified accumulation strategy—a fisher or fishing household that gains income from fishing (or letting fishing grounds) as one of a diverse set of activities that may involve other water resources, or work outside the sector such as farming. The fisheries associated with these 'livelihood strategies' have different characteristics and functions.

This analysis, as they have argued, has important consequences for policymaking as it identifies a need for more diverse and flexible management measures, tailored to local priorities and conditions, which also ensure that poor people can access the benefits of inland fisheries whilst achieving conservation objectives. This calls for greater differentiation of fisheries management policies than often currently exists, and recognition that the best combination of policies may be very location specific.

Cunningham (1993) in his article "Fishermen's Incomes, Fisheries Management" reveals that the level of income in fishing cannot be divorced from income levels in other parts of the economy. According to Cunningham, this is due to the fact that fisherfolk might be in a position to enter in the event of a collapse in income from

Photo 3.1: Harvesting of Fish.

fish. That is, the number of individuals and families engaged in fishing as a main occupation depends on the opportunity income available to them. On the other hand, if fishing income rises above that for comparable trades in the rest of the economy, there will be an influx of new entrants that will drive income down. On the other hand, if incomes elsewhere in the economy rise, then individuals may leave fishing, or become part-time fishers, allowing those left behind to experience rising incomes. Therefore, much of the effort expended by fisheries departments to raise fisherfolks' incomes in the context of generally low incomes has reflected misplaced optimism about what can be done for a single sector taken in isolation from the rest of the economy. Clearly, Cunningham's paper directs us towards the need to recognize the interdependence of fisheries with other allied services in agriculture or petty trading, thereby the need to prescribe a well integrated cross-sectoral development policies.

Inspired by the observations developed by Cunningham, several case studies have been made to analyze the livelihood outcome of coastal communities in South East Asia and Sub-Saharan Africa. Baily *et al.* (1996)'s paper "Resource Dependency and Development Options in Coastal Southeast Asia" and paper named "Sub-Saharan

Africa betwixt and between: Rural Livelihood Practices and Policies" by Bryceson (1999) are two important contribution in this regard. Both the studies have observed that fisheries policies in developing countries in early nineties were based on faulty presumption. In viewing fishing as a full time occupation taking place within a single, well developed economic sector. Actually, in the past, mobility of individuals between fishing and other activities has tended to be seen as a substitution between full time occupations. Panayotu and Panayotu (1996) had found that higher inward mobility of labour towards fishery sector leads to overexploitation of an open access resources. On the other hand, outward mobility due to diminishing returns of labour leads to lower fish productivity. Authors, taking examples from Thai fisheries have suggested that introduction of specialized capital, tied up in fishing assets can reduce the labour mobility between sectors. But, higher capital investment may reduce relative profitability and this question has remained unanswered in the study.

The search of alternative development policies in fisheries has gained momentum in late nineties, especially after the pioneering work by Robert Chambers. In IDS working paper "Poverty and livelihoods: whose reality counts?", Robert Chambers (1995) explores how universal, reductionist and standardized views of poverty differ from those of the poor themselves. Poverty line thinking concerned with income-poverty and employment thinking concerned with jobs, project Northern concerns on the South, where the realities of the poor are local, diverse, often complex and dynamic. Examples illustrate how poor people's criteria differ from those assumed for them by professionals. The paper also discusses neglected dimensions of deprivation including vulnerability, seasonality, powerlessness and humiliation. In the new understandings of poverty, wealth as an objective is replaced by well-being and "employment" in jobs by livelihood. The final sections argue for altruism and reversals to enable poor people to analyze and articulate their own needs, and they conclude with the implications for policy and practice of putting first the priorities of the poor.

Frank Ellis *et al.* (2003) in their article "Livelihoods and Rural Poverty Reduction in Malawi" in World Development seeks to provide a critical viewpoint on these macro-level processes based in micro-level investigations of rural livelihoods. Ellis shows that the truly desperate livelihood circumstances of most rural Malawians are emphasized by qualitative and quantitative information on assets, activities and outcomes. Taking data from eight villages in Dedza and Zomba districts of Malawi, Frank Ellis, Milton Kutengule, Alfred Nyasulu have established the fact that poor rural Malawians confront multiple severe constraints that can only be addressed by some combination of raising agricultural productivity, diversifying farm output to reduce risk and shift towards higher value outputs, and diversifying livelihoods towards non-farm enterprises. The paper has paid particular attention to the public sector institutional environment required to facilitate and encourage the latter option, and finds that the Poverty Reduction Strategy Paper (PRSP) of Malawi Government offers little guidance in this regard. The fiscal decentralization strategy of the government, according to them, contradicts the funding needs of local government.

Smith *et al.* (2001), taking evidences from two rural districts in Uganda, have shown that despite the continuing centrality of agriculture to the rural economy of Uganda, households engage in diverse livelihood strategies. This paper has brought to the fore the role of various factors that influence livelihood trends and strategies. Qualitative and quantitative analysis of the study reveals differences according to wealth, gender, and between traditional and non-traditional occupations. Comparisons drawn between the two districts—Kumi in the eastern region, and Rakai in the central region—identify social and historical, as well as contemporary levels of investment as the determinants of varying levels of livelihood diversification. The intension of Smith, Gordon, Meadows and Zwick is to establish that along with economic and financial effort, culture and tradition of a community plays an important role in finding the coping strategy from vulnerability.

C. Béné *et al.* (2003) in their article entitled "Inland Fisheries, Poverty, and Rural Livelihoods in the Lake Chad Basin" published in Journal of Asian and African Studies, described the livelihoods of the rural populations of the Lake Chad Basin area (Sub-Saharan Africa), and in particular to assess the role of inland fishing activity in these livelihoods. For this purpose, a combination of activity and wealth ranking exercises was carried out in 64 villages of the Basin, completed by a series of comparative analyses of the ethnic composition, accessibility to fishing grounds and fishing gear ownership across the different socio-economic strata of the populations. The analysis shows that for the entire area, households, irrespective of their wealth levels, still rely to a very large extent on subsistence-based economy where the three major activities (fishing, farming, and herding) are closely integrated. With respect to fishing activity the survey demonstrates the central role of this activity (in terms of income, labour, and food supply) for all wealth groups. But the analysis also reveals that there is no one-to-one relationship between the contribution of fishing activity and the wealth (or poverty) level of the households. In particular the analysis suggests that well-known adages such as "the fishermen are the poorest of the poor" or "the fishery is the activity of last resort" do not reflect the complexity of the real situation.

The paper entitled "Participatory research supporting community-based fishery management" written by Melanie Wiber, Fikret Berkes, Anthony Charles and John Kearney (2004), published in Marine policy paper was based on a project to engage researchers and fishers together in adapting social science approaches to the purposes and the constraints of community-based fisher organizations. The work was carried out in the Scotia-Fundy Region of Atlantic Canada (the Bay of Fundy and Scotian Shelf). Its rationale reflects arguments that (1) effective community-based management requires that managers are able to pose and address social science questions, (2) participatory research, involving true cooperation in all stages, can support this process, and (3) there is a need to overcome practical and methodological barriers faced in developing participatory research protocols, to serve the needs of community-based management while not demanding excessive transaction costs. In this paper, we report on work with fisher organizations, both aboriginal and non-aboriginal, in which social science priorities were set by each organization, and small-scale research projects designed and carried out to meet these needs. This work identified interests among fishers in research on three different levels of meaning: (1) practical livelihood concerns, including what, when and where to fish, and with what intensity of effort, (2) social, economic and political issues (e.g., on institutional structures, politics of access and allocation, overlap and conflict between regulatory regimes), and (3) values and ethics that implicitly or explicitly guide policy development and implementation. Several research themes proved crucial, including those of power sharing, defining boundaries of a community-based group, access and equity, designing effective management plans, enforcement, and scaling up for effective regional and ecosystem-wide management. The research results demonstrate the effectiveness of extending participatory methods to challenge traditional scientific notions of the research process.

Some of the social and cultural aspects of marine fishing communities as a vulnerability coping strategy are also emphasized by John Kurion (2000). Kurion shows how social and cultural dimensions emerge in the course of the pursuit for food and livelihood in coastal areas in Kerala. This working paper of Centre for Development Studies, Thiruvanantapuram attempts to show how these dimensions evolved in the context of very specific resource and ecological determinants. Social and cultural dimensions have been often considered a "drag" on the transformation of societies into modern entities. However, the numerous failures encountered when development is given an exclusively techno-economic orientation, provide the basis for a new search to give meaning to previously neglected socio-cultural norms. This search is all the more relevant in this era of globalisation that set into momentum the tendency to homogenize social and cultural specificity. The sustainability of any society will depend in large measure on the degree of diversity and self-reliance that it is able to maintain with regard to reproducing its social and cultural concomitants. At the core of this are issues pertaining to the food and livelihood security of its people. The paper examines the visible manifestations of deeper social and cultural attributes in the marine fishery sector, which have been fashioned over a very long history. The list includes the nature of the sharing patterns in the fishery; traditional knowledge and technology; the old and new institutional arrangements in fishing communities; fish and the question of food security; and the role of women.

Patrick Dugan, Madan M. Dey and V.V. Sugunan (2006) have felt that against the growing pressure upon freshwater resources, increased water productivity in agriculture is essential. Efforts to do so, however, need to consider the wider role of water in sustaining food production. Their paper considers the importance of water management in sustaining fish production in tropical river basins, and the potential for enhancing food production and income to farmers by integrating fish production into some farming systems. Specific examples from selected river systems and irrigated farming systems in Africa and Asia are provided in this study. The results highlight the benefits of integrating the water requirements for fish into water allocation decisions. In some cases, these benefits can be realized without any reduction in the water available for other purposes, while in others, a trade-off needs to be considered. The nature of this trade-off needs to be better understood by analyzing the livelihood diversification strategy which will create an environment for better decision making in water management.

In order to explain the trends in the development and farm attributes of Integrated Agriculture-Aquaculture systems in the Mekong Delta of Vietnam, Phong *et al.* (2007), in their paper in Asian Journal of Agriculture and Development, a participatory community appraisal and two surveys are carried out in three districts with contrasting fish culture input systems. The first survey, undertaken in December 2002, covers 90 households; the second, held in December 2004, covers 80 households.

Photo 3.2: Local Trade of Fish

The factors driving changes in the farming systems are the introduction of modern rice varieties, the policy of economic liberalization, market demand, and natural disasters. The principal components of agriculture-aquaculture systems in the Mekong Delta which the study examines are the land use intensity, market access, farm diversity, farm inputs, and household income. The study finds that some farm characteristics are hard to change, some are easy to monitor. The hard-to-change farm characteristics are the land use intensities of rice, orchard and cash crops. In contrast, the easy-to-change farm characteristics are the number of farm components, the land use intensity of fish ponds, on-farm family labour, off-farm and non-farm income, and farm inputs. The main drivers of the changes over the two years are market demand and a poultry disease outbreak (Avian Influenza). Well-off farmers with good farming practices and enough capital tend to intensify their farming practices, while the poorer farmers tend towards diversification in order to safeguard their livelihood and avoid risks.

Nathanael Hishamunda (2009) in their paper "Commercial aquaculture in Southeast Asia: Some policy lessons" published in Food Policy Journal observed that globally aquaculture has been increasing rapidly and already accounts for nearly half of all food fish consumed. For developing countries, which produce ninety per cent of the world's output, aquaculture is a source of protein, employment, income and of foreign exchange. Southeast Asia is an area which has experienced this "blue revolution". Total aquaculture output in the region increased from less than two million tonnes in 1990 to more than eight million tonnes in 2006. Moreover, the region's pace of expansion has accelerated. Annual average growth rates in output from 2000 to 2006 were more than double those from 1990 to 2000. Already more than a quarter of food fish in Southeast Asia comes from aquaculture. Aquaculture matters because fish products are important in the diet of much of Southeast Asia. The population generally has a high per capita consumption of fish, and fish are a major source of animal protein in a region where levels of animal protein are below the world average. Output from the capture fisheries has increased but growth rates are slowing. To maintain present levels of per capita consumption of fish in the region, whose average population is projected to grow by 16 per cent by 2015, requires continued expansion of aquaculture.

Najma Mohamed and Belinda Dodson (1998) in their research project "Sustainable rural livelihoods—Evaluating the potential of small-scale aquaculture in the Western Cape" have shown that rural unemployment is exacerbated by the decrease in demand for farm labour on commercial farms; therefore, alternative livelihood opportunities for rural dwellers require investigation. The production of fish in dams offers such an opportunity. An existing aquaculture project in De Dooms in the

Western Cape was evaluated in terms of its ability to provide an alternative source of income and a cheap animal protein source. The results indicate that, potential to create sustainable livelihoods in Western Cape depends on socio-political issues as well as bio-technical and economic considerations. Through decentralized legislative measures, those socio-political issues should be accorded equal consideration to biotechnical and economic measures.

3.2 Some Case Studies

Several studies have sought to understand the relationship between (coastal) fishing communities, their livelihoods, sustainable development and the environment (*see* for example, Chuenpagdee and Bundy, 2005; Bouahom *et al.*, 2004). Most of these studies analyze these relationships at macro levels, since secondary data are often available at national, state and, in some cases, district levels. These studies are important in many ways, indicating general trends and spelling out policy implications. However, they fail to highlight the specific choices people make for their survival, the livelihood strategies that have evolved, and the decisions governments make in mediating these relationships at the micro level. Therefore, this research makes an important contribution by filling that gap.

The coastal areas in which the marine fishing communities make their day-to-day livelihoods contain marine and terrestrial ecosystems with a high level of primary productivity. Fishing communities have traditionally lived mainly off the fauna, and especially fish, of this zone. Many studies have documented how these communities have organized themselves to maintain the harmony of the coastal ecosystem, while at the same time drawing sustenance from it, up until the beginning of fisheries modernization (Mensah *et al.*, 2006; Kurien, 2003; Sebastian, 2002; Leival *et al.*, 2001; McGoodwin, 2001). The modernization of the fisheries has resulted in overfishing and fish-resource depletion (Pauly *et al.*, 2002; Kurien and Paul, 2001; Porter, 2001). It has also led to increasing conflict between the industrial and mechanized sector and artisanal small-scale fishers (Kura *et al.*, 2004). These conflicts combined with lack of empathy from government to the artisanal sector put the small-scale fishers at a disadvantage compared to the industrial sector.

There are several other factors such as fish trade and food security that threaten their livelihoods (Kurien, 2004; Kent, 2002). The threats arise from decline of traditional institutions, which used to bind the fishers with a sense of ownership of the community resources. This sense of ownership had given rise to common set of rules and regulations, and also, sharing of resources. However, with the introduction of modern technologies and fisheries policies, the deeply instituted traditional process of care and concern was replaced with gain and profit (Kurien, 2004). Threats also arise from the declining fish resources. Households in artisanal fishing communities are impacted adversely when fish stocks are depleted particularly when there are fewer options available to them in terms of local employment. The location of land and houses close to the shore, where fishers have easy access to the sea, is a major physical asset and is a right they enjoy, although property rights in the coastal zone are relatively ill defined (Damodaran, 2006; Ramachandran *et al.*, 2005; Kurien, 2003). However, this could also be a limiting factor as often artisanal fishers develop fishing methods and fishing gears tailored to catch particular species within their home/fishing ground (Kura *et al.*, 2004). The crisis in many of the worlds fisheries due to open access and unregulated common-property regimes, are major concerns in fisheries management (Eggertson, 2002; Mutunga, 2002; Adhikari, 2001). Historically, communitarian social structures, environmentally friendly technologies and limited market extension kept populations and ecosystems in a relative balance. The present situation is quite different. New developments and technological advancements have helped increase production, but the disparity between the rich and poor has widened. Increasing profits have also attracted new claimants to the resource, and this has led to competition and conflicts. Having been drawn into the mainstream of modernization, several communities have played an active role in achieving high production, and contributed to state and national income. However, these communities are now threatened because of the fluctuations in, and access to, the resource. This is elaborated in the following section. The case studies chosen here are also representative of issues relating to resource dependency and livelihoods within the context of the poverty-environment nexus.

With the degradation of the resource, members of these communities diversify their occupational strategies and move into other sectors. This is evident in studies relating to migration and remittances (Adger *et al.*, 2002; Kannan and Hari, 2002). Adger *et al.* (2002) investigates the relationship between demographic change, social resilience and sustainable development, and the effects of migration and remittances on resource-dependent communities in population source areas of coastal Vietnam. A sizable population constituting ten per cent of the workforce in Kerala, India, works in Middle Eastern countries and sends remittances that constitute a significant share of state income (Kannan and Hari, 2002). These studies acquire importance as coastal fishing communities in this study form a large number of labour migrants to the Middle East (Zacharia, 2001a).

In a study for the FAO, Tietze *et al.* (2000), conducted macro-level studies and field surveys at the community level, to understand fertility indicators; occupational mobility; income and education; perception of environment, resources and economic situations; and changes in livelihood of fishing communities in Bangladesh, India, Malaysia, the Philippines, Senegal and Tanzania. For comparison, they included control populations of non-fishing communities within the same ecosystem. The study revealed that among coastal fishing communities, there is slightly higher fertility and mortality than among other rural residents. Moreover, the younger generation has markedly different attitudes from those of their elders regarding fertility and family; fisheries no longer seem to be a 'last resort employment' (Tietze *et al.*, 2000). The majority of the fisherfolk in the selected countries, Tietze *et al.* (2000) noted that resources and the environment have seriously declined because of an increase in the number of fishers and fishing fleets (and due to domestic and industrial water pollution). However, they also observed an overall decline in the number of fishers in the countries studied.

Investigating gender, welfare and labour in India, Nieuwenhuys (1989), reports that over 200 million children contribute to family livelihoods. She argues that the Kerala case study provides a blueprint for the ways in which the women and children among artisanal fishers are excluded, while the sector itself is confronted with increasing competition from modern fishery sector. She suggests that although women and children are perceived to be marginal, they are in reality playing an indispensable role in on-shore activities, very much connected with the well-being of poor consumers in coastal areas. This, in turn, has allowed fishers to stay in the fishery even when modernization could lead to their exclusion. At the same time, as conditions worsen, alternative gender and age roles came into existence in response to new work opportunities, growing demands in terms of schooling and the need to cope for oneself following the out-migration of men (Nieuwenhuys, 1989).

In most of the recent studies on coastal fishing communities, particularly artisanal fishing communities, lives and livelihoods rely on the methodology developed by Kurien (2005, 2004, 2003, 2001, 2000). The basic idea in Kurien's work that is relevant to this research is to give a sense of history of the life and livelihoods of coastal fishing communities. The artisanal fishing communities are not depicted or regarded as passive victims and recipients of government policies or external aid. Rather, they are people with immense knowledge who are assertive of their rights. In his paper on 'Factoring Social and Cultural Dimensions into Food and Livelihood Security Issues of Marine Fisheries', Kurien (2000) examines the visible manifestations of artisanal fishing communities' deeper social and cultural attributes in the marine fishery sector. This, according to him, is fashioned over a very long history.

The visible manifestations of social and cultural attributes include the nature of the sharing patterns in the fishery, traditional knowledge and technology, old and new institutional arrangements in fishing communities, the question of food security, and the role of women (Kurien, 2000). Reduced vulnerability through social security is investigated by analysing various supply and demand factors that influence the provision of social security measures in Kurien and Paul (2001). This study also provides useful information on individual earning dynamics such as the variability of individual income, which is a share of the sum of income from an enterprise.

According to Kurien and Paul what matters to the fisherman is that: A fisherman would depend in large measure on his contribution to the labour of the specific fishing trip and to his overall share, if at all, in the capital of the enterprise. This, and the fact the harvest from the sea is a fluctuating fortune and the price of first sale is by no means predictable, results in highly fluctuating daily incomes (Kurien and Paul, 2001, p. 9).

Kurien's (2005) paper is written in the style of a personal statement. It moves from social security and livelihoods to provide insights into the manner in which Kerala's fishery has become unsustainable since the 1980s. A description of the important aspects that led to this unsustainable fishery can be found in his earlier work with Thankappan, in which they restricted their assessment to five major areas:

(a) the open access nature of the fishery, (b) the use of inappropriate technology, (c) the demand-pull factors that create galloping prices, (d) financial subsidies offered by the state which encourage investment and (e) the pressure of population on the coastal commons (Kurien and Thankappan, 1989, p. 11).

The studies reviewed here have attempted to express the relationships between coasts, coastal fishing communities and the resources they depend on for their livelihoods. They leave several questions unanswered, namely how the households in community respond to changes in the status of bio-physical, social, cultural, political and institutional assets on which they base their livelihoods and whether the status of these assets are impacted by environmental degradation or changes in their access/rights. The sustainable livelihoods framework is useful in this regard, to fill in these gaps and explore different types of information on assets and strategies of the coastal artisanal fishing communities that can help policy-makers, researchers and resource managers explain the circumstances of fishers and their households and to develop management strategies to ensure their well-being and conserve marine resources.

The study entitled "Aquaculture and the poor—Is the culture of high-value fish a viable livelihood option for the poor?" conducted by Natasja Sheriff, David C. Little, Kwanta Tantikamton (2008) published in Marine Policy evaluates the role of high-value fish culture in the livelihoods of coastal households in southern Thailand. The study shows that grouper culture, promoted as an alternative to destructive fishing practices, can make a substantial contribution to household incomes. However, fishing and aquaculture play contrasting roles in the livelihoods of coastal fishers and should be considered as complementary rather than alternative occupations. The study found that poorer households can benefit significantly from raising grouper in cages if certain conditions are met, including access to credit and the substitution of financial for natural capital.

Promotion of integrated aquaculture with agriculture, including crops and livestock (IAA-farming), requires consideration of both bio-physical and socio-economic contexts. In the article "Integrated freshwater aquaculture, crop and livestock production in the Mekong delta, Vietnam: Determinants and the role of the pond" in the journal Agricultural System, Nhan *et al.* (2007) identified the major factors influencing the adoption of IAA-farming by households at three sites in the Mekong delta. Special attention was given to the multiple roles ponds play in IAA-farming systems. Information was collected through semi-structured interviews and discussions with focus groups and key individuals. Data were analyzed using multivariate factor analysis, analysis of variance or participatory ranking methods. Three major IAA-systems were identified: (1) low-input fish farming integrated with intensive fruit production (system 1), (2) medium-input fish farming integrated with less intensive fruit production (system 2), and (3) high-input fish farming integrated with less intensive fruit production (system 3). System 1 was commonly practised in a rural fruit-dominated area with fertile soils, while systems 2 and 3 were more evident in peri-urban rice-dominated areas with less fertile soils. In the study area, only 6 per cent of poor farmers adopted IAA-farming, while this was 42 per cent for intermediate and 60 per cent for rich households. Richer farmers tended to intensify fish farming and seek a more commercial orientation. The major factors why farmers did not start aquaculture were the inappropriateness of technology, insufficient landholding or poor access to extension services, limited farm management, and through a fear of conflicts associated with pesticide use on crops. The main motivations for practising IAA-farming included increased income and food for home consumption from the available farm resources while reducing environmental impacts. Further improvements to IAA-systems can be realized by strengthening nutrient recycling between different IAA-system components while enhancing farming output and safeguarding the environment.

Globalization of the agro-food system has led developing nations to orient their production to meet global markets. Consequently, local agricultural systems are increasingly linked to global commodity networks, and generate complex intersections and sometimes tensions. Cultured shrimp in Bangladesh is such a global commodity that connects the local producers with the global consumers starting from pond to plate via a network of diverse actors in a complex manner. Field research in Bangladesh conducted by Md. Saidul Islam (2008) shows that shrimp aquaculture in Bangladesh is moving towards a twin-driven commodity chain in which lead firms govern supply network, while the Shrimp Seal of Quality Organization (SSOQ), a recently emerged third-party certifier, as well as other environmental NGOs define regulatory aspects of the industry. In his paper entitled "From pond to plate: Towards a twin-driven commodity chain in Bangladesh shrimp aquaculture" published in Marine Policy, Islam argued that while governance in twin-driven commodity chain offers opportunities for a sustainable aquaculture, it also poses many questions which have significant policy implications for different stakeholders involved in the chain.

Pomeroy (2006), in his paper entitled "Coping with disaster: Rehabilitating coastal livelihoods and communities" published in Marine Policy journal examines lessons from past approaches to natural disasters, as well as early lessons from the post-2004 Asian tsunami rehabilitation, to draw out general principles for rehabilitating livelihoods in poor coastal communities. We contend that avoiding the mistakes of the past requires: (1) a framework for understanding the diversity of coastal people's livelihood strategies and the sources of their vulnerability, (2) a process for designing interventions that build on this understanding in order to strengthen and revitalize coastal communities, including a means of assessing and selecting the most promising livelihood options, and (3) a focus on the longer-term challenge of building future resilience and sustainability in the communities by addressing the root causes of vulnerability.

Small-scale fisheries in developing countries are often perceived as being a low-productivity and backward informal sector. As a result they are rarely considered in poverty reduction programmes and rural development planning. In this paper, we investigate the dual role of fish as a food and cash crop through data collected in river fisheries in Democratic Republic of Congo (DRC). Christophe Béné *et al.* (2009) in his article "Fish as the bank in the water—Evidence from chronic-poor communities in Congo" published in Food Policy journal have shown that fishing in this very remote rural region of DRC is operated both by men and women, as part of a household multiple activity livelihood strategy. The data shows that poor households rely heavily on fishing for their supply of protein-rich food, in particular through women's subsistence catches. Fishing also appears to be the main source of cash-income for the majority of households, including local farmers. Based on these findings and a review of the literature, the paper argues that small-scale fisheries can play a fundamental role in local economies, especially in remote rural areas where they strengthen significantly the livelihoods of people through their role in both food security and cash-income generation.

3.3 Literature on Indian Fisheries

Economic information on the various aspects of inland fish cultivation have seldom appeared in literature, though much research works have been done in the biological and marine sciences. It is not properly coordinated with the economic ideas. One of the major reasons for the unsatisfactory performance may be low availability of appropriate reliable data and standardized terminologies necessary for comparability and aggregation of data over time and across regions.

B.S. Saxena (1968) observed that lack of detailed data on resources, their utilization, production levels and marketing practices have affected adversely the development of the inland fish cultivation. He suggested that the steps should be taken to improve credit arrangements to the farmers.

Dinesewar Prasad (1968) in his paper "Economic Aspects of Fisheries Development" made an attempt to investigate that the economic problems of fisheries development normally arise from various factors, e.g. a high degree of risk and uncertainty involved in fish production. Over and indiscriminate fishing of juvenile fishes is another problem. As the fishermen sometimes may not be the owners of the ponds and tanks, the fishermen harvest and sell their product to minimize their risk. Generally, the fishermen do not have any long-term interest in stocking of large and matured fish. They have a tendency to maximize yield at the earliest shortest possible time. Among numerous other problems, Prasad pointed out mainly the factors like existence of middlemen, lack of governmental incentives, sale of undersized fishes, general poverty and low purchasing power of the people and absence of organized centres for fish marketing. Measures suggested by him are proper exploitation of huge water resources through effective planning like appropriate stocking, proper manuring of tanks and training of the fishermen for improved method of fish rearing, catching and storage were also suggested.

S.K. Chakrabarty (1968) observed that inland fisheries, particularly pond culture, would provide the best opportunity for rapid increase in fish production—because fresh water in tropical regions has a higher rate of production per unit area than the brackish water. According to his estimate, production in the study area (a village in Birbhum district of West Bengal) was fairly very small. The main reasons behind low productivity of fish production identified by him are deplorable condition of the tanks and ponds as also their low level of maintenance as the large number of tanks and ponds were weed infested and semi-derelict. Due to continuous deposition of silt in the bottom layer of the water area—the average water level has been gradually going down. He suggested that there is a need for immediate desiltation of the tanks and eradication of excess vegetation and water hyacinth to maintain the mere existence of as many as two-thirds of the tanks. Sometimes, it was found impossible to carry on fish cultivation as water dries up completely in the summer.

Measures suggested by him for improvement of production are the formation of Fisheries Co-operative Societies. Institutions like Directorate of Fisheries and Local Administration (Panchayat) can play an effective role in formation of such societies. He emphasized that demonstration of successful fish farms in the matter of the adoption of improved techniques will provide the incentive to other fish farmers to go in for the adoption of scientific packages and hence, higher yields. Among other measures, he also suggested measures like provision of adequate financial help in the forms of grants and loans, effective legislation for better and efficient management of water bodies. In case of multi-owned ponds, by legislation, an efficient management should be established in order to obtain and maintain a minimum level of production. Another important measure suggested was that for higher production, tanks should be leased out to a single person on the guarantee that he will produce the minimum level of production and for a reasonable period of time.

Another important aspect of pisciculture is about multiple ownership of most of the private ponds and tanks. Most of the private tanks and ponds are not owned by the single owner. People, particularly in West Bengal have incentives to hold the percentage of ownership of inherited ponds with their other family members and division of the ownership continues from one generation to next generation. Thus, as generation proceeds, share of ownership by single owner decreases, which gives rise to a very complex plurality of ownership. Such problem often impedes new investment for the improvement of ponds and tanks and also the intensive application of new technologies. M.M. Bhalerao & Kalicharan (1968) recognized the problems of existence of plurality of ownership and interference of middlemen as senior deterrents.

S.P. Sinha and M.N. Jha (1968) in their paper "Development in Fisheries" raised some relevant socio-economic problems. Their investigation in the context of co-operatives reveals the following—

1. The influential and rich persons in the place like Darbhanga, Bihar do not want fishermen co-operative societies to grow at all. They do not want that the society should earn a substantial profit and give their members a stable profit. They assumed it would be a challenge to their socio-economic status.
2. As most of the farmers are landless labourers, no financial help or subsidies or help of any kind were available to them. Rather, a stringent measures for recovery of the loans, result in disincentiveness of functioning of co-operatives on the one side and on the other side, encourage private trades to operate freely in their study area.

For the development of co-operative system, their suggestions were—

1. Fisheries operating in a scattered way should be brought within co-operative system. Private trading, contract and auction system should be abolished.
2. Fisherman Co-operative Societies should be aided with substantial financial help. Loans and grants are to be supplied to the members of the society at the right time and right occasion.
3. Modern training and equipments should be supplied to them at a reasonable rate.

Difficulties in Co-operative Societies have been explained by G.S. Galgotia in his article "Operation of Co-operative Societies—Problems and Prospects" (1968). His findings in many ways are similar to those of Jha and Sinha. But in addition to socio-economic analysis, he takes over the problems of marketing and storage. His findings can be summarized in the following way—

1. The societies do not have sufficient accommodation facilities in the market for storage and hence they have to sell fresh fish within three or four hours and the members are compelled by circumstances to sell their produce to other dealers at much lower rates than the prevailing market prices.
2. The societies have to face cut-throat competition from the private traders. At the time of heavy supply, the traders' joint efforts artificially push down the prices. Hence, it becomes

difficult for the members of the societies to meet up their cost and earn some minimum profits.

Galgotia has the same view with the previous investigators that government's discriminatory and unhelpful attitude are the main problems faced by the co-operatives. His suggestions were not much different than those of others. He alleged against government's insincere attitude in supplying finance and credit. Similarly, the institutional credit for the processing units and transportation are not available up to the desired extent.

In the book "Inland Fisheries Resources in India" (1983) by Srivastava and Vasistha, published by the Concept Publishing Company, New Delhi and "Fisheries Development in India" by Srivastava and Dharma Reddy, published by the Concept Publishing Company, New Delhi, analysis on nature and problems of fisheries, both inland and marine, have been done. In the articles, like "Economic Aspects of Fisheries Development of Bihar" by D. Prasad in Indian Journal of Agricultural Economics (IJAE, 1968), Vol. XVIII; "Fisheries Co-operative in India" by Bhalara and Kali Charan in Indian Journal of Agricultural Economics (IJAE), Vol. XVIII; "Benefit-Cost Ratio in Fish Culture" by Dhondy and Singh in IJAE Vol. XVIII, attempts were made to identify some of the basic constraints.

In the monographs like "Potentials and Problems of Composite Fish Farming in West Bengal" by S.M. Murshed, CIFRI Bulletin No. 5; "Scope for Scientific and Commercial Fish Farming in West Bengal" by A.V. Natarajan, CIFRI Bulletin No. 9 and "Export Prospect of Fish and Fish Products" (1986) by NCAER, New Delhi, some of the issues relating to the problems of marketing of fish production have been dealt with.

V. Gautam (1983) pointed out that the inland fisheries are equally vast and diverse and potentially one of the richest in the world. The progress and development of the inland fisheries have so far been impressive. There is greater potential in still water resources than in flowing water. His study highlights the points that fish production in ponds and tanks is much higher than the larger water reservoirs and lakes resources. He estimated that by 2000, the domestic demand for fish is going to be 200 lakh tonnes. Even if expected demand is to be satisfied from the inland sector, inland fisheries production will have to increase seven times in the next two decades. He advocated a need to practise aquaculture in combination with agriculture. However, he did not take care of, among others, the financial condition of the poor fishermen, inadequate supply of better inputs and at reasonable rate.

G.S. Gupta (1983), in his article "Freshwater Fisheries—Present Status, Prospects and Policy Measures" showed that there is an inverse relation between pond size and yield rate. That is, as pond size increases, the productivity decreases. The conclusion was derived from the data, which is based on the new concept of Effective Storage Level (ESL). On the basis of its biological implication, it has brought two other concepts—(1) Full Storage Level (FSL) and (2) Dead Storage Level (DSL). Still, it can be said that the conclusion is not always valid, as it did not consider input-output ratio. It may happen that if inputs are increased along with the pond size, rate of fish production increases by the same amount or more than the input growth, depending on whether there is increasing or constant returns to scale in inland fish production.

Opposite view regarding farm size-productivity relation in Pisci-cultures was also explained by some other researchers. At least two of them deserve particular mention. Vatshala (1983) opines against the assumption of negative correlation of pond size and productivity debate. According to Vatshala, in a big pond, if cultivators take intensive care, by incorporating various improved technologies and with proper training, then it is not difficult to get a positive return from big size ponds.

Ram Charan (1983) in his study makes a point that there is not much difference between composite fish culture, yield and traditional yield. He assumes that it may be important and essential for maintaining the eco-system, but as regards its economy, it certainly does not make any difference whether we have poly-culture, mono-culture or composite culture.

A.J. Singh and V.K. Gupta (1983) dealt with the problem in relation to demand, supply and production, marketing and distribution of fish seed. In their in-depth study in West Bengal, the biggest seed producing and exporting state in India, they have developed a clear picture about the infrastructural developments taking place in seed production. The authors then examined the notional idea that the gap between existing supply and demand in the nineties would be highest in West Bengal in detail.

The study conducted by Indian Institute of Management (I.I.M.A.) (1983) has made some recommendations for the development of pisci-culture. These recommendations like database and statistics, research on specific problems of commercial fish culture issues like classification of districts into good, medium and poor on the basis of some criteria of potential and stage of development and adequate supply of quality fish seed, more intensive stocking and partial stocking and partial harvesting at intervals, long leasing system and fixation of lease amount, improvement of fish farmers co-operative for supply of inputs, harvesting and marketing, improvement of Fish Farmers Development Agencies (F.F.D.A.) which have significant bearing upon fish cultivation have been clearly explained.

T.A. Mammen (1983) points out that the farmers are not always interested to learn about the technical know-how; that is, what he suggests is that farmers should accept technical knowledge whenever it is available and in innovating new techniques, the fish farmers should be open-minded.

In an article entitled "Institutional Structure for the Governance for Freshwater Aquaculture" in Indian Journal of Agricultural Economics (IJAE), Marothia (1984) examines the factors that affect the perfect utilization of multipurpose common water bodies. He employed the contingent valuation method. On the basis of the data collected from common pool water body in Chhattisgarh, he arrived at the conclusion that success in management of common pool water bodies for fish culture does not depend exclusively on the technical-physical nature of the resource or the decision making arrangements or the behaviour of the members, but on the interrelationship of all the key parameters.

A.V. Natarajan in the monograph "Present Status and Policy Issues in Inland Fisheries" (1985) from a study at 24 Parganas observed that a number of tanks and ponds are used for seasonal irrigation purposes. An antagonistic relation for water availability for irrigation and for the purpose of pisciculture seriously affects fish cultivation.

An in-depth study by Agro-Economic Research Centre (1986), Visva-Bharati, Santiniketan in its "Use of Tanks for Minor Irrigation and Pisciculture in West Bengal" made an attempt to explain the actual position of the uses of tanks for irrigation and fisheries purposes. The main findings of the study are that the scope of using tanks for irrigation is rather limited; while potentialities of pisci-culture are quite large. Some institutional and legal reforms are urgently called for to overcome the existing constraints. Improvement of the technical characteristics of tanks like depth, siltage, weeds etc. are of crucial importance for long-term improvement of tanks. The importance of existing social forestry in the embankment of tanks has also been highlighted in the study. The result was derived by examining the effects of some 'cause' (independent) variables on a number of dependent variables.

Sibranjan Misra (1987), in his book "Fisheries in India", by Concept Publishing House reveals that poaching acts as a major constraint leading to poor performance of fish production particularly in West Bengal tanks and ponds. Misra, on the basis of data collected from tanks and ponds owners in three districts of West Bengal, arrived at the conclusion during 1983-84 that poaching or deliberate poisoning due to rivalry, enmity or jealousy are widespread. Among other problems, lack of proper transport facility, suitable marketing management, non-availability of opportunity for soil and water testing etc. were considered by the poor fishermen as the major inhibiting factors. In consideration to non-adoption of new techniques, he observed that lack of information regarding various improved practices is one of the important factors. The financial difficulties due to bureaucratic delay, etc. make the practice of composite fish-farming technologies much more difficult. Other problems emphasized by Misra were erratic and inadequate supply of quality fish seeds or fingerlings in time and at reasonable rate, multiple ownership and adulteration of inputs etc. According to Misra, this unsatisfactory performance can be attributed mainly to absence of rational management, judicious utilization and appropriate exploitation of the resources.

Measures suggested by Misra are the utilization of canal irrigation (from which water can be released to the fish ponds in winter season) or rainfed farming on watershed basis, desilting of about to dry-up ponds, long-term lease arrangement, Government legislation to evict multiple ownership, development of appropriate technologies (keeping in view the regional, environmental and ecological differences), organized marketing channels, mixed farming etc. Pumping of more money into the economy, by itself, may not necessarily generate the desired result. According to Misra, more village-based co-operatives should be set up and existing ones should have to be reformed and galvanized.

K.S. Chattopadhyay (1987) in his "Problems and Prospects of Pisciculture" discussed various institutional, technical and financial factors, which are found detrimental to smooth functioning, and augmentation of growth of fish production in a district like Birbhum district in West Bengal. He was optimistic that if such vast water bodies are properly exploited, both the level of production and productivity of fish in this district could be increased several folds. But he severely criticized the role of the government while rendering extension programmes at the grassroots level. Functioning of F.F.D.A. in his study area was also subjected to criticism.

In an article entitled "Input Resource Management in Fisheries" published in Indian Journal of Agricultural Economics (IJAE), Katiha (1988) *et al.* attempts to explain the suboptimal utilization of inputs. There exists scope for increasing fish production if inputs are used optimally. The marginal value productivities of inputs like gear weights, fishing efforts are sufficiently large. They employed the standard Cobb-Douglas type of production functions to estimate the elasticities of inputs.

U.K. Srivastava (1990), along with other economists from Indian Institute of Management, Ahmedabad in the Report "Fish Farmers' Development Agency Programme for Fresh Water Aquaculture" made a thorough study about how the large numbers underutilized fallow culture fishing resources could be brought under optimum fish production in the area of its operation. They have exhaustively analyzed the primary data they had collected. They arrived at the conclusion that a large number of institutional and technological factors are there to affect adversely the production of fish. The suggestions they made were to rationalize the leasing arrangements, to provide subsidy and effective training programme, to arrange smooth supply of fish seeds at reasonable prices and also to develop the marketing facilities.

Kazi M.B. Rahim and Katar Singh (1992) extensively studied the functioning of Central Fishermen's Co-operative Societies (CFCS) in West Bengal. Their findings highlight some mixed results about functioning of Co-operative Societies in West Bengal which may be quoted as follows—

> "The CFCS do not run profitably every year. It has to face negative net return from its business activities. The Primary Fishermen's Co-operative Societies (PFCS) do not avail of any extra benefit other than the right of catching fish in the brackish water. The non-members too are not debarred from

> catching the fish in the same water resources. Lack of administrative help is the main cause for these unlawful activities. The poor image about co-operatives in the mind of the members due to their experience is distinctly conveyed."

In an article entitled "The Bengram Majhipara Common Pool Fish Ponds" by K. Singh and S. Bhattyacharya (1994) in "Managing Common Pool Resources: Principles and Case Studies", they observed in their study in the case of West Bengal that ponds and tanks under common property regime had a low fish productivity. They clearly suggest that the government should promote this kind of water units on a co-operative basis and provide funds for the restoration of degraded common village properties, in addition to provision of technical guidance to fish farmers. In this context, Marothia, in his article "Village Ponds and Aquaculture Development: Is Conflicts Inevitable" stated that the multiple use of Common Village Ponds (CVPs) created conflicts and disorders among the fishers and village community. The study also revealed dissatisfaction over the caste-based preferential allotment of CVPs for aquaculture.

It is worth mentioning here that, in the light of the observations made by S.R. Misra (1995), in his project entitled "Identification of constraints in the Development of Inland Fish Cultivation with Special Reference to West Bengal", the suggestions to overcome such problems seem more realistic. According to Misra, when canal irrigation is the source of water, water should be released to fishponds at a very nominal rate. Again, since water is sometimes exhausted due to irrigation purposes, measures may be directed towards rainfed farming on watershed basis. The run-off water collected into farm ponds should be used for irrigation.

Jha (1997) in an article "Salient Ecological Features of the Chaurs and Mauns in Bihar and their Fisheries" in "Fisheries Enhancement of Small Reservoir and Floodplain Lakes in India" edited by Sugunan and Sinha, argued that the short-term leasing policy of the water bodies by the fisheries department might affect productivity. He observed that in case of short duration of lease, lessees are not interested in investment in fisheries development. The fishers tend to catch out the entire stock of fish, resulting in further depletion of the fish stock. This amounts to convert these most fragile eco-systems into fishery deserts.

In an article entitled "Enhancement and Culture-based Fisheries", V.V. Sugunan (2001) mentioned that considering the possible environmental impact and the socio-economic scenario of the country, it is not feasible to develop intensive aquaculture in the inland sub-sector, beyond certain limit. He also justified his analysis against the background of sustainable development of inland fishery resources. In another article entitled "Present Status of Inland Fishery Resources in India and the Need for Their Enhancement" by A.K. Ghosh (CIFRI, Barrackpore, Bulletin (2001), it is stated that enhancement of fish production from open waters has become a difficult proposition unless pursued on scientific lines. There is a need for holistic management policy, precisely for those inland waters which fall under common property resources.

Radheysham (2001) in an article "Community-based Aquaculture in India" in Aquabite studied the relevance of the community-based aquaculture founded on the principles of common interest groups working together regardless of sex and age. This has been an effective tool for implementing scientific aquaculture programme in India. He used Strength, Weaknesses, Opportunities and Threats (SWOT) method.

P.K. Katiha (2001) in one of his articles "Socio-economic Aspects of Culture-based Fisheries" (CIFRI, Barrackpore, Bulletin, 2001) observed that the interventions in the forms of the management and institutionalization of the water bodies might be constrained by the wide variety of social considerations. Since the fishery development and management involve and affect primarily the fishers, it is necessary to consider the social aspects involving employment mobility, subsistence orientation of production and income distribution with regard to culture-based fisheries.

M. Sinha and P.K. Katiha (2002) in their article published in "Institutionalizing Common Property Resources", edited by D.K. Marothia, Concept Publishing Company, New Delhi, mentioned that, in addition to the activity of FFDA, aquaculture should be promoted with the necessary credit and technical support to fish farming agencies. Necessary changes in the lending norms of banks are a must for an easy flow of credit to the aquaculturists. They also pointed out that the preferential allotment of this water to production-oriented co-operatives with sufficient representation of fisheries would be an effective strategy for the development of the enterprises.

R.K.P. Singh (2003) in his book entitled "Economics of Aquaculture", published by Daya Publishing House, New Delhi, made an attempt to study the various socio-economic aspects of inland fish farming enterprises in Bihar. The specific objectives were to examine the culture practices, costs, returns, labour, and employment, marketing practices and constraints in the fish production, on the basis of primary data. He identified some of the institutional and technological constraints like low level of input use, non-existence of fish nurseries, lack of institutional credit etc.

S. Ayyappan and M. Krishna (2004) in their article entitled "Fisheries Sector in India: Dimension of Development", published in Indian Journal of Agricultural Economics (IJAE) made an attempt to review the production potentialities and export possibilities of Indian fish production. They suggested different measures to meet the domestic requirements with an emphasis on earning reasonable amount of foreign exchange by way of extensive export measures.

Ratna Reddy *et al.* (2004) in their article "Ecological and Economic Aspects of Shrimp Farming in Andhra Pradesh", published in Indian Journal of Agricultural Economics, made an attempt to understand the economic incentives and ecological compulsions associated with shrimp farming. It was brought out that while the fish cultivation like shrimp farming has attracted a huge number of farmers in many states like Andhra Pradesh, its environmental consequences seem to be catching up fast. There is a need for judicious and sustainable management practices. It so happens in some states that the profits are vanishing as fast as they occur. In the process, the poor farmers are getting affected severely. The sector should be made responsible for the livelihood of the poor small and marginal farmers.

S.S. Shyam (2004) in the article "Export Performance of Indian Fisheries in the Context of Globalization", Indian Journal of Agricultural Economics tried to articulate the export performance and potentials of inland fish products under the liberalized trade regime and explore the possible impacts of WTO agreements on the Indian Fisheries sector. He also identified the different factors like the commodity concentration, geographical concentration and the share of world import as the causal factors for the export instability.

In an article entitled "A Study of Modelling of Household Demand for Fisheries in India", in Indian Journal of Agricultural Economics (2004), P. Kumar and M.M. Dey tried to analyze the long-term changes that took place in fish consumption in India. An attempt has also been made to study the demand modelling on multistage budgeting framework and examined the demand elasticities (price and income) for fish. The responsiveness of demand for fish to changes in price and income (expenditure) varies for fish across income classes, regions and urbanization. Own price-elasticities of 'demand for fish is high' and has not shown any sign of decline during the last fifteen years.

Pradip K. Katiha *et al.* in their article entitled "Governance, Institutions and Policies for Fisheries of Floodplain Wetlands" in Indian Journal of Agricultural Economics (2004) presented the set of challenges for governance, institutions and policies towards development of fisheries. The study was based upon personal surveys and discussions with different stakeholders like fishers, Government agencies lessees, fishery co-operatives etc.

S.K. Chandan also in his article entitled "Institutional Management in Reservoir Fisheries", in Indian Journal of Agricultural Economics ((2004) discussed, with the help of data collected from one hundred fishermen randomly selected from a reservoir fisheries in the Western Himalaya the socio-economic conditions of the fishermen, cost of fish capturing and marketing of fish through various channels in addition to the production and marketing management aspects.

3.4 Literature of Efficiency Analysis

On the issues of evaluating input use efficiency through the DEA, the findings of certain research works have been stated below.

Many studies have analyzed the relationship between technical efficiency and size, although the first wave of research dealing with this issue looked at the relationship between productivity (measured as output per acre) and size (measured by acres of land). In an influential paper, Sen (1962) found an inverse relationship between farm size and yields per acre in Indian agriculture, giving rise to a large set of follow-up papers attempting to confirm his results or studying related issues such as the impact of technical progress on the productivity of small and large farms (Deolikar, 1981).

While average productivity can be a relevant concept, partial productivity measures are problematic when making performance comparisons across farms. Total Factor Productivity (TFP) measures, which are ratios of output and input aggregates, are most appropriate for this endeavour. In a single output process, the output-oriented index of technical efficiency can be interpreted as TFP measure. In fact, the numerator in the index of technical efficiency is the observed output and the denominator is the potential output obtained using the production frontier, which can reasonably be interpreted as an input aggregator.

An easy way to try to account for the effect of technical efficiency on size (output) is to estimate production functions including a dummy variable for size and test whether its coefficient is significantly different from zero. For example, Bagi (1982) estimated a Cobb-Douglas production functions for three groups of Indian farms, including a size dummy (based on land) both additively and interactively with the rest of the inputs. He found that, given a level of inputs, small farms produced more output than large farms.

Another group of papers is based on production frontiers. As a first step, a technical efficiency index is calculated. In the second step, the estimated technical efficiency index is regressed on a set of variables, including size (Helfand *et al.*, 2004; Galanopoulas *et al.*, 2005; Sharma *et al.*, 1999; Townsend *et al.*, 1998). The second step (Timmer, 1971) is pervasive in this literature. Sharma *et al.* (1999) and Galanopoulas *et al.* (2005) use a Tobit model to accommodate the fact that they have an accumulation of observations with efficiency score equal to one. In general, the second stage is problematic since the statistical properties of the DEA efficiency scores are not well known. Townsted *et al.* (1999) report a negative relationship while Sharma *et al.* (1999) finds the opposite.

Ray (2004) has also shown size productivity relationship in Indian Banking sector using DEA method. In his paper, Ray used data covering the period 1997 through 2003 to measure size levels of efficiency of individual Indian banks. Following Maindiratta (1990), Ray consider a bank to be too large if breaking it up into a number of smaller units would result in a larger output bundle than what could be produced from the same input by a single bank. When this is the case, the bank is not size efficient. Our analysis shows that many of the banks are, in deed, too large in various years. While results from anyone year can be affected by random variation in outputs and inputs, banks like State Bank of India (SBI) and others that are persistently found to be size inefficient. He also found that often a bank is operating in the region of diminishing returns to scale but is not a candidate for break-up.

The results to analyze the relation between farm size and productivity also used the parametric techniques of Stochastic Production Frontier Approach. Two most important literatures in this direction are Page (1984) and Yuengert (1993). Page calculates the technical efficiencies for four Indian manufacturing Industries. The paper includes a size dummy variable (based on number of employees) but he fails to find out conclusive relationships for most of the industries.

Alvarez *et al.* (2004) analyze the relationship between technical efficiency and the size in the framework of a simple production model. With the help of simple economic theory, they suggest the importance of a conditional analysis of the relationship between farm size and technical efficiency. The theoretical model suggests a positive relation between farm size and efficiency. In its empirical application they find a positive and significant relationship between technical efficiency and farm size when controlling for the effects of output prices, input prices as suggested by theory.

Overall, the empirical analysis in previous studies makes little reference to the underlying economic model. At the same time, the studies are strongly confined in the areas of agricultural development (except Sharma *et al.*, 1999). In this section, farm size efficiency relationship has been developed, first with the help of descriptive statistics and then a non-parametric meta-frontier analysis defined by Hayami and Ruttan (1971, pp. 82) has been carried out to see whether technology indeed varies among different size class of fish farms.

Battese and Rao (2002) and Battese, Rao and O'Donnell (2004) provide frameworks for comparisons when efficiency is measured using parametric stochastic frontier models. With the main objective of providing comparable technical efficiency scores for firms across groups, the technical efficiencies of firms has been estimated. In addition, they present a more transparent analysis of the technology gap of different groups and their efficiency levels by using a decomposition result.

Rao, O'Donnell and Battese (2003) provide clear frameworks and an empirical application for meta-frontier functions for the study of interregional productivity difference. The paper has three components. The first deals with the analytical framework necessary for the definition of a meta-frontier function. The second component studies the properties of a meta-frontier function estimated using non-parametric Data Envelopment Analysis (DEA). The third component focuses on the estimation of a meta-frontier function within the parametric framework of Stochastic Frontier Analysis (SFA). The empirical application of the models uses FAO cross-country agricultural sector data on 97 countries, comprise of about 99 per cent of global agricultural production and 99 per cent of total population of the world also.

Das, Ray and Nag (2005) use the concept of meta-frontier as a national or grand frontier to study branch level labour-use efficiency of a major public sector bank in India. For each branch, they obtained two different measures of efficiency—one based on data from only the region where it is located and the other on the data from all the four regions. In second stage, comparison of the two different measures of efficiency brings out the effect of regional factors that would restrain branch from attaining the level of efficiency that would be possible if it could use branches from any region (rather than from its own region) as role models.

All in all, a review of the existing literature on this issue reveals that no systematic and comprehensive study has so far been made with regard to the problem that the technology developed which seems technically attractive has failed to produce substantial results in real world. The reasons behind this are varying in nature.

3.5 By way of Summary

This chapter has reviewed the approaches and framework of the concept of Sustainable Livelihoods that is the basis of this study. It gave an overview of the approach as well as other approaches that attempt to address poverty issues. It then focused on the Sustainable Livelihoods Framework, exploring different components in the schematic diagram that was developed by DFID and UNDP. It also explained the modifications made in the framework that would help this study map key priorities, identify links between localized phenomena to wider national and international processes.

The chapter also reviewed the literature on Resource Dependency, which is fundamentally important in this research, but is generally poorly understood in the developing countries context, and is distinct from dependency in developed countries. Finally, a few case studies have been reviewed to highlight the particularities of specific choices that people make for their survival strategies that have evolved, and the decisions governments make in mediating these relationships at a micro level.

Notes

1. Thierry Lemaresquier of UNDP's Social Development and Poverty Elimination Division (SDPE) had stated: "Projects that are based on empowerment and improvement of livelihoods of the poor stand a much better chance of surviving once the initial funding and effort has run out of gas" (Helmore and Singh, 2001, 5)
2. The first major fisheries development and management project to explicitly adopt this framework is the Sustainable Fisheries Livelihoods Programme in West Africa (1999-2004), funded by DFID and implemented by FAO. It involves 25 countries, within which 7 million people are directly dependent on freshwater and marine resources.

4

Methodology

4.1 The State of West Bengal is divided into the following six agro-climatic zones depending on soil characteristics and climatic conditions (Fig 4.1).

1. *Coastal and saline region*: Comprising Southern part of North and South 24-Parganas, Howrah and Midnapore districts. The soils are of tidal origin.
2. *Old alluvial region*: Comprising Mursidabad and Hoogly districts, part of Birbhum and Bankura districts, central part of the Burdwan and Midnapore. The soil in this region ranges from light to heavy texture according to the land situation. In general, soils are moderately well drained, low in organic matter and phosphate but high in potassium. Soil reaction ranges from acidic to neutral.
3. *New alluvial region*: Comprising Nadia district and parts of Malda, Mursidabad, West Dinajpur, Burdwan and Hoogly. In this region, soils are deep, moderately well drained and light texture, usually neutral to alkaline in reaction (pH level of 7.0 to 8.0). They are acidic to neutral (pH 6.0 to 7.0) in uplands. The soils have moderately high base saturation and medium to medium-low NPK status. Their calcium content is moderate to high.
4. *Red and laterite soil zone*: Comprising Purulia district, parts of Birbhum, Burdwan, Bankura and part of Midnapur district with small pockets of Malda and West Dinajpur districts. The land is undulating with tiny rivulets and soils are highly

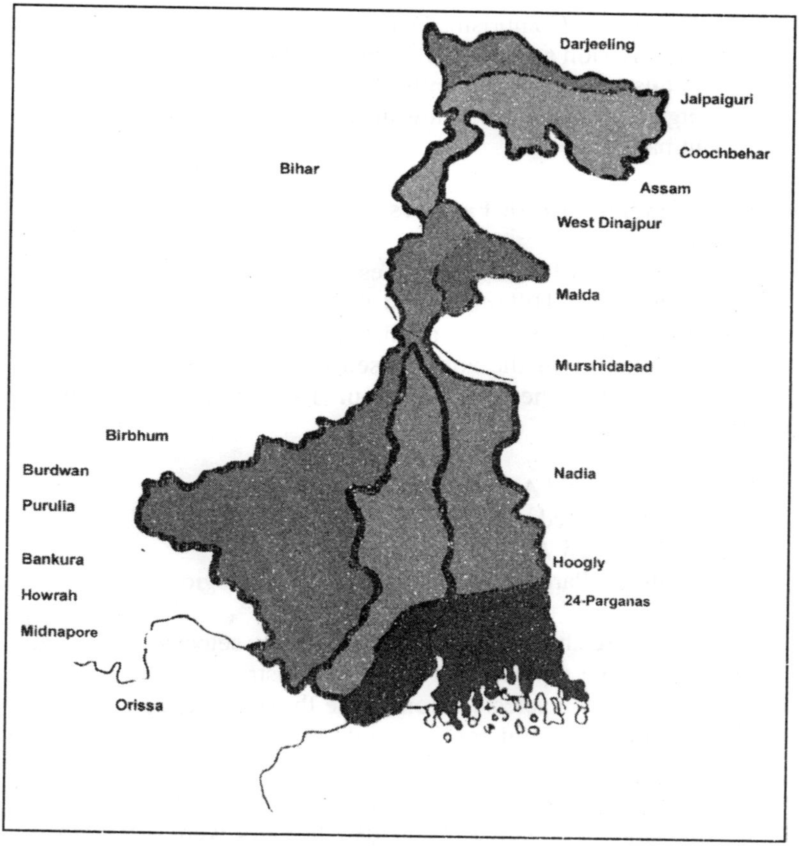

Figure 4.1: Agro-climatic Zones of West Bengal.

eroded. They are mildly acidic (pH level of 6.2 to 6.8), poor in organic matter content, low in base status and have low nitrogen, calcium and available phosphate contents.

5. *Terai region*: Comprising the plains of Jalpaiguri and Cooch Behar districts, Siliguri sub-division of Darjeeling district and Islampore sub-division of West Dinajpur district. Soils are deep and light textured, highly permeable and porous. Soils contain moderate level of organic matter without appreciable mineralization, highly acidic (pH level of 4.7 to 5.8) and low in bases, phosphorous, potash and micronutrients.

6. *Hill region*: Comprising Darjeeling district excluding Siliguri sub-division and northern fringe of Jalpaiguri district. Soils in this region are generally shallow, coarse textured, high in organic matter content, low in bases and phosphate and acidic in nature.

4.2 Identification of Fish Farmers

Altogether four out of six zones in West Bengal were selected for the study. Two zones viz. Hill region and Terai region had been excluded purposively. From each zone, one district considered comparatively more representative of the zone, based on agro-climatic situation, was selected. Thus, the following four districts represented their respective zones—

1. Bankura (Old Alluvial Region)
2. Birbhum (Red and Laterite Region)
3. Malda (New Alluvial Region)
4. South 24-Parganas (Coastal and Saline Region)

A total of three blocks had been purposively selected with equal probability without replacement from each district. Again a total of six villages had been selected from these three blocks according to equal probability without replacement. Village-wise list of pond-owners had been prepared from the mouza. The list of fish farmers with the number and area of ponds operated by them were prepared for all the villages selected. Then fish farmers were arranged in descending order on the basis of their water area (the aggregate of the water areas of different ponds held by an individual fish farmer). Then a sample of fifteen fish farmers in each identified village (or cluster of villages) were selected randomly, with the help of the random sample. Thus, a sample of 90 fish farmers had been selected from each sample district. Finally, a total of 360 (three hundred sixty) fish farmers were selected from four sample districts for the study. The unit of observation will be the fisherman's household. Sampling design is shown in Figure 4.2.

In this connection, it should be mentioned that in case of non-availability of 15 fish farmers in an identified nucleus village, two to four adjacent villages were identified to make a cluster of villages to have sufficient number of fish farmers for drawing its sample

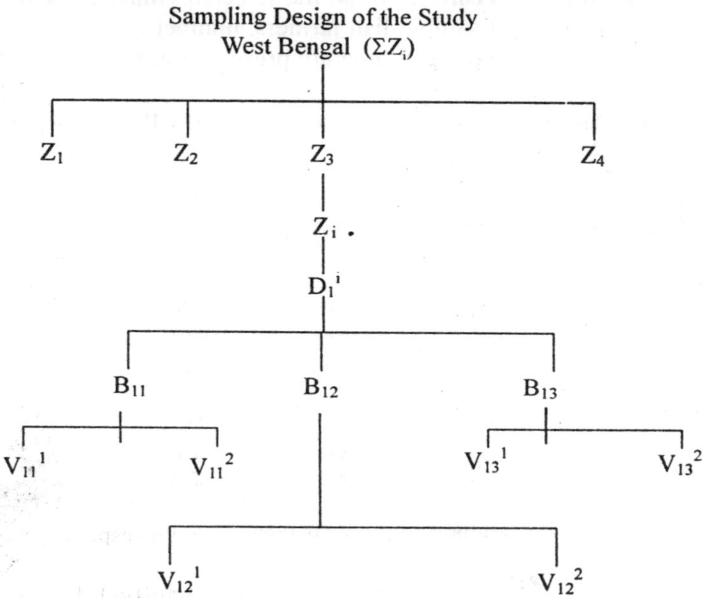

Where, Z_i : ith zone
D_1^i : district in representative zone
Bij : ith Block in jth district, i = 1,2,3; j = 1,2,3,4
Vn : nth village in ith Block of jth district, n = 1,2,3,4,5.
Fû : ûth fish farmer in respective village, û = 1, 2, ...15.

Thus,
No. of Fish Farmers in a district = 6 × 15 = 90
Total Sample Size = 90 × 4 = **360**

Figure 4.2: Sampling Design.

respondents. Names of block-wise identified villages (nucleus and associate villages) along with number of fish farmers, fish ponds and water area are presented in Exhibit 4.1.

Selected fish farmers were categorized into three groups on the basis of the size of ponds they held; that is,

Small pond owners: less than 0.39 acre
Medium pond owners: 0.4 acre to 4.99 acre; and
Big pond owners: 5.00 acre and above.

This exercise was carried for all the selected villages. Pond size group-wise number of sample fish farmers, number of ponds, water area and average size of water area are presented in the Exhibit 4.1.

Exhibit 4.1: Size-wise Sample Fish Farmers along with their Ponds, Water Area and Average Size

Category of Ponds	*No. of Sample Farmers*	*No. of Sample Ponds*	*Water Area (acre)*	*Average Size of Water Area*
Small	261 (72.5)	298 (66.51)	83.52 (26.64)	0.32
Medium	88 (24.5)	127 (28.34)	158.4 (50.53)	1.8
Large	11 (3.0)	23 (5.15)	71.5 (22.81)	6.5
Total	**360 (100.0)**	**448 (100.0)**	**313.42 (100.0)**	**0.87**

Note: Figures in the parentheses indicate percentage to the respective totals.

The names of the selected blocks in each identified district are also presented in the Exhibit 4.2.

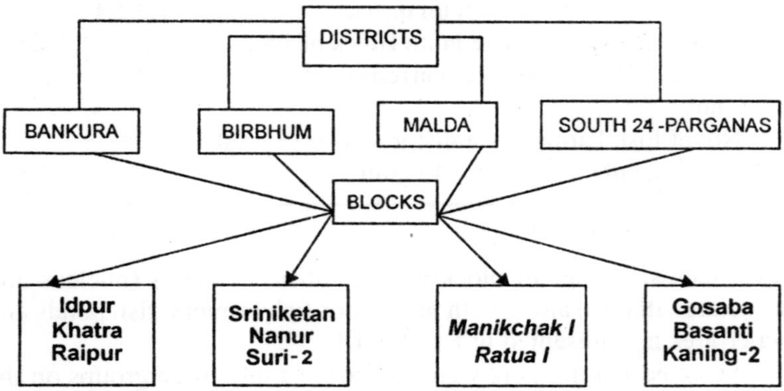

Figure 4.3: Names of the Selected Blocks.

4.3 Selection of Nucleus Villages

The names of the villages of identified blocks along with their number of fish ponds and water area were obtained from the respective Block

Exhibit 4.2: Block-wise Sample Villages along with Number of Fish Farmers, Ponds and Water Area

Sl. No.	*Block*	*Sample Villages*	*No. of Fish Farmers*	*No. of Ponds*	*Water Area*
1.	Idpur	Lotihir, Basudevpur	30	38	26.6
2.	Khatra	Nakaijhuri, Ontha	30	36	24.8
3.	Raipur	Samsundarpur, Kalasole	30	37	25.7
4.	Sriniketan	Mahidapur, Ruppur	30	32	28.1
5.	Nanur	Lavpur, Langalhata	30	34	23.7
6.	Suri-2	Purandarpur, Aushgna	30	36	22.8
7.	*Manikchak I*	Kahala, Surjapur	30	37	28.4
8.	*Ratua I*	Kahala, Surjapur, Debupur	30	38	25.1
9.	*Gazole*	Kudbari, Birpara	30	39	24.3
10.	Gosaba	Vijaygarh, Rangaberia	30	40	32.9
11.	Basanti	Varatpur, Narayanpur	30	39	25.5
12.	Kaning-2	Rangaberia, Betberia	30	42	25.4

Development Offices. Those villages are listed in Exhibit 4.2.

The data pertaining to the yield during the period, type and extent of water resources, physical characteristics, ownerships, adoption behaviour, costs incurred, marketing and other micro-details were culled by administering pre-designed structural questionnaires to all the fish farmers selected. Preliminary pilot survey was conducted in the villages in Sriniketan Block in Birbhum district to obtain first hand information about the problems. Visits were also made to different District Fisheries Offices (Meen Bhavan) in order to elicit technological and institutional problems of inland fish cultivation of the respective districts through interaction with the officers.

The unique feature of the study is that the survey was confined to the areas of the four selected districts. In point of fact, it is pertinent to note that in the choice of the districts, certain considerations weighed most. In the first place, the impounded water units, mainly ponds and tanks, constitute a significant proportion of the total inland water resources; that is, heavy concentration of tanks and ponds in these districts. Secondly, in spite of the broad dissimilarities of soils, climate and other agro-climatic features among the selected districts, there were certain similarities in respect of different infrastructural facilities like availability of credit facilities, marketing etc. Finally, in all these districts, the Fish Farmers Development Agency (FFDA) programme had been in operation.

It is the family home which forms the core of the economic, social and cultural universe that constitutes the livelihood system.

Since livelihoods are family centred and all important decisions are taken at the family level, studying the livelihoods at family level provides a better understanding of the livelihood system. Two, it is possible to attain livelihood security without drastically changing the existing farming systems, but by simply fine tuning the existing traditional farming systems so as to increase their resource use efficiency.

4.4 Method of Enquiry

In this study, we have had a relatively open-ended and exploratory research design, which allows us to look at everything that appears to be relevant. But as with all similar studies, the study suffers from certain general limitations. Firstly, the duration of the reference period is short. So, what one gets is a cross-sectional picture about an issue at a point of time. Secondly, the lack of specialized enumerations, the unwillingness or inability on the part of the fish farmers to provide detailed information, the widely scattered location of the production units and areas are some of the major problems. Incidentally, the maintenance of accounts by the fish farmers was not in evidence in the study area. Respondents were interviewed by the project fellow. However, the random checking was also done by the principal investigator.

A combination of the following participatory, qualitative and quantitative methods was used for primary data collection.

Questionnaire with fish farmers were preceded by preparation and testing of the questionnaire, use of statistical procedures to determine the sample size and sampling method, and the use of enumerators to fill in questionnaires. The pre-survey activities included reconnaissance for the pilot survey, revision of survey instruments and preparation of the sampling frame.[1] A total of 360 farmers, 90 in each district, were interviewed at their houses/and/or farm sites. The interview lasted for about two hours.[2] It focused to elicit information on issues like fish production systems, productivity, farming constraints, farming costs and returns, livelihood assets of the respondents, vulnerability concerns and livelihood outcomes.[3]

Participatory Rural Appraisal (PRA)

PRA is a group of members to collect information in a participatory fashion from rural communities. The advantage of PRA over other methods is that it allows wider community participation. Therefore, the information is likely to be more accurate. For this study, the PRA tool—Focus Group Discussion (FGD)—was conducted with fish farmers and associated groups such as fish fry traders, fish traders, labourers, FGD was used to get an interview of particular issues such as existing fish farming systems, fish marketing and the socio-economic conditions of farmers. A total of 28 FGD sessions were conducted where each group consisted of 8 to 10 individuals.

Cross-check Interviews with Key Informants

A key informant is someone with special knowledge on a particular topic. Key informants are expected to be able to answer questions about the knowledge and behaviour of others and about the operation of the broader systems. Cross-check interviews were conducted with fisheries officers, researchers and relevant NGO workers. Where information was found to be contradictory, further assessment was carried out. A total of 20 key informants were interviewed.

4.5 Period of Study

All the primary data obtained from fish farmers referred to the period 2008-09.

4.6 Analytical Framework

Tabular analysis was done to arrive at relevant conclusions. In order to study the association between output and various inputs used, Cobb-Douglas production function was used. A very widely used method known as Data Envelopment Analysis (DEA) has also been employed to examine the efficiency of the different production units.

The following model of Cobb-Douglas production function was used.

$$Y = Ax_1^{b_i} x_2^{b_2} x_3^{b_3} x_4^{b_4} x_5^{b_5} e^u$$

Where,

Y : Value of gross fish production
A : Intercept (constant)

x_1 : Fertilizer and manure (Rs/kg)
x_2 : Mahua oil Cake (Rs/kg)
x_3 : Fish feed (Rs/kg)
x_4 : Fingerling (Rs/kg)
x_5 : Labour (Rs/kg)
e^u : Error term
b_i : Regression coefficients of respective variables

To examine the productivity of different inputs used in fish production, marginal value productivities of inputs were estimated by the following formula:

$$MVP_{xi} = \frac{b_i Y}{X_i}$$

where

Y = Geometric mean of the gross fish production.
X_i = ith input
x_i = geometric mean of the ith input; and
b_i = Elasticity of production of the ith input

Test of association like chi-square test, correlation etc. were used. Bar diagram, pie charts and other descriptive statistics were also used.

Efficiency of the fish farms may be assessed with the help of non-parametric Data Envelopment Analysis (DEA). Though logit model is generally being used to assess the determinants of the adoption practices, DEA remains another principal theoretical framework of the study. Based on the objectives of the study, two different DEA models have been used—one measures technical efficiency and analyses input use efficiency of the fish farms; while another, usually called as meta-frontier DEA model, helps to differentiate technical efficiency of a farm on the basis of socio-economic or farm-specific subgroups. The DEA methodology can be explained with the following model.

We consider the situation with 360 fish farms or Decision Making Unit (DMUs), each producing output Y from a bundle of 4 inputs. The jth DMU ($j = 1, 2, \ldots, 360$) uses X_k^j units of kth input in the production of Y^j units. A separate Linear Programming (LP) problem is solved for each of the j DMUs ($j = 1, 2, \ldots, 360$) in the sample.

The input based technical and scale efficiency for the jth DMU can be obtained by solving the following LP problem—

$$\underset{\lambda^j,\theta^j}{Minimize}\ \theta^j$$

Subject to—

$$\sum_{j=1}^{360} \lambda^j Y^j \geq Y_0^j \text{ (output constraints)}$$

$$\sum_{j=1}^{360} \lambda^j X_k^j \leq \theta^j X_k^0 \text{ (inputs constraints, } k = 1, 2, 3, 4, 5)$$

$$\sum_{j=1}^{360} \lambda^j = 1$$

$$\lambda^j \geq 0, j = 1,2,...,360$$

Where, θ^j = is the dual of the variable indicating proportional increase in output possible by firm j;

λ^j = weight or intensity variable (or, shadow price) used to derive all possible linear combinations of the sample observations.

Y_0^j = Actual output produced by firm j.

X_k^0 = Actual input used by firm j

Where θ is the proportional reduction in inputs possible and λj is the weight or intensity variable used to derive all possible combinations of the sample observations. Here, θ determines the efficiency score of jth DMU. The value of $\theta = 1$ shows a technically efficient DMU; θ less than one shows a technically inefficient DMU. In order to obtain efficiency score of each farm, equation (9) has to be solved N times, once for each farm.

The DEA problem mentioned above has an important intuitive interpretation. Essentially, the problem takes the jth firm and then seeks to radically contract the input vector, X_k^j, as much as possible, while still remaining within the feasible input requirement set. The inner boundary of this set is a piece-wise linear isoquant, determined by the observed data points, (i.e. all the firms in the sample). The radial contraction of the input vector, X_k, produces a projected point, $(X_k^j\lambda^j, Y^j\lambda^j)$, on the surface of this technology. This projected point is a linear combination of this observed data points. The constraints in the above LP problem ensure that this projected point cannot lie outside the feasible set.

One interesting point to note here is that a technically efficient DMU may still be over- or under-producing if it is found that altering the size of the farm towards optimal size increases (or decreases) the efficiency of that farm. It does mean that the DMU is not scale efficient. To analyze the performance of a farm, it is important to take care of this information since the magnitude of scale efficiency will tell us how much productivity gain would be feasible if that DMU can be moved to its optimal size. Scale efficiency of a particular DMU can be determined by running the CRS and the VRS models (the VRS model includes one more constraints that weighted value of the intensity variable, λj, must be equals to one) on the same data. A difference between these two scores indicates the scale efficiency of the DMU. Hence, scale efficiency (SE) is TE^{CRS}/TE^{VRS}.

Once θ and λj can be determined it is easy to find out the optimal value of the input from the above LP equation. A comparison of the actual quantity of input used with the corresponding optimal quantity of that input reveals whether a particular DMU is using too much or too little of that input. Hence, for any particular input I, input use efficiency can be calculated by the ratio—

$$\alpha^i = \frac{L_0^i}{L_*^i}$$

A value of α^i greater (less) than unity implies over (under) use of that input.

In the present study, technical and scale efficiency score has been determined by solving those LP problems with the use of DEAP 2.1 (Coelli, 1996). The software also gives us the optimal use of each inputs, which will help to find out the input use efficiency.

4.7 Graphical Interpretation

The DEA methodology can also be shown through the following diagram.

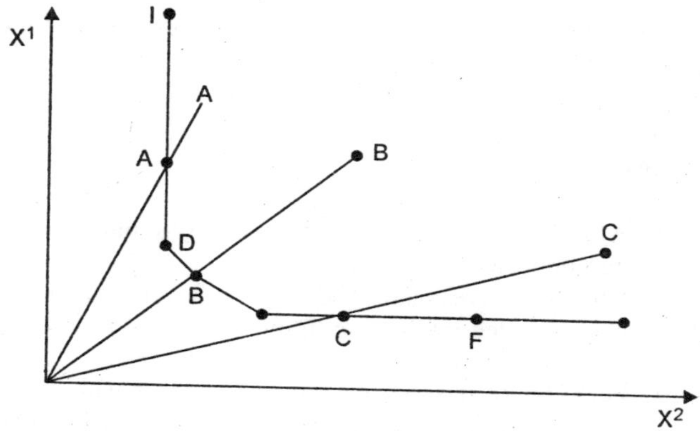

Figure 4.4: Radial Movements and Input Slacks in DEA Model.

In this diagram, six firms, A, B, C, D, E and F are producing output with two input X^1 and X^2. Among them, A, C, D and F are best practice firms, which determine the DEA frontier. In those four points, inputs are optimally used. But, firm B and E are using more input than required. They can produce even the same output even by reducing inputs radically to the point B′ and E′, where and reduces to and respectively. Hence, technical efficiency at each of the points A, C, D and F is one but at points B and E, technical efficiency must be less than one, because

$$TE_B = \frac{AP^B}{AP^*}$$

where, numerator is the weighted average productivity at point B and denominator is that at point B′, i.e. at the corresponding point on the frontier.

4.8 Limitations of the Study

But as with all similar studies, the study suffers from certain general limitations. Firstly, the duration of the reference period is short. So, what one gets is a cross-sectional picture at a point of time. Secondly, lack of specialized enumerations, the unwillingness or inability of the fish-farmers to provide detailed information, the widely scattered location of production units and areas are some of the main problems. Incidentally, the maintenance of the accounts by operators is not in evidence in the study area. Hence the study suffers from these drawbacks.

Notes

1. After making a detailed pilot survey, some modifications in the questionnaire were made.
2. Often, the investigator had to pay several visits to an individual to elicit detailed information from its selected respondents on various items of interest through probe questions.
3. For example, it is true that estimates of catch with a reasonable degree of precision can be obtained at a very high cost. For inland waters, the areas are generally scattered and unorganized with irregular catch operations.

5

Structural and Operational Features of Sample Tanks and Ponds

In this chapter, attempt has been made to examine some of the important aspects of structural and operational features of the ponds and tanks like size of the water units, types of possession, size productivity relationship etc.

Ponds and tanks vary in size and therefore, a study of the size distribution of the sample water units would be relevant for economic analysis. The ponds and tanks are grouped into three different size classes. Exhibit 5.1 gives the distribution of the number of water units and the area (percentage-wise) for these three size classes (as defined earlier in chapter four).

It is evident from Exhibit 5.1 that average size of the water units (under survey) is approximately 0.87 acres. It is also observed that more than 88.5 per cent of the water units with more than 40 per cent of the total water area are of size less than the average size. Water units of size 5.00 acres and above constitute only 3 per cent of the total water units but dominate a sizeable proportion (22.8%) of total area. And water units of size between 0.40 to 4.99 acres constitute 50.6 per cent of the water area with an average size of 1.8 acres. In figure 5.1, the Lorenz curve clearly depicts the heavy concentration of water units into small size.

Size group-wise ownership and extent of proprietorship of ponds and tanks were estimated and shown in the Exhibits 5.2 and 5.3. It was found that in the study area, the water units (ponds and tanks) were either owned or leased in through different sources. The water units were operated either as solo proprietorship or by the multiple of operators as partners. From Exhibit 5.2, it is evident that 294

Exhibit 5.1: Size Class-wise Distribution of the Number and the Area of Currently Operated Water Units in 2008

Size Class of Water Units (Acres)	*No. of Ponds*	*Percentage of the Number of Units*	*Percentage of the Area of Water Units*	*Area per Unit (Acres)*
Up to 0.39 (Small)	298	66.52	15.4	0.32
0.40-4.99 (Medium)	127	28.34	56.9	1.80
5.00 and above (Large)	23	5.14	27.7	6.50
Total	**448**	**100.00**	**100.0**	**0.87**

Source: Field Survey, 2008.

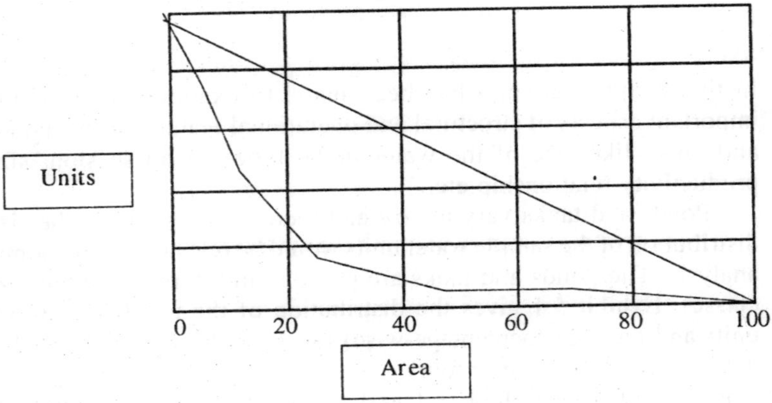

Figure 5.1: Lorenz Curve for Size and Area of Water Units.

Exhibit 5.2: Size Group-wise Distribution of Ownership of Water Units

Category of Ponds	*No. of Ponds*	*Ownership Status*	
		Owned	*Leased*
Small	298 (100.00)	209 (70.13)	89 (29.87)
Medium	127 (100.00)	78 (61.42)	49 (38.49)
Large	23 (100.00)	7 (30.44)	16 (69.56)
Overall	448 (100.00)	294 (100.00)	154 (34.38)

Source: Field Survey, 2008.
Note: Percentages in parentheses indicate the respective percentages.

(65.62%) of the total sample water units were cultivated by the owner-operators; whereas 154 units (34.38%) of the total sample units were leased in. A significant proportion of the owned and cultivated by the owners were found in the cases of small and medium size of water units i.e. 70.13 per cent and 61.42 per cent of the total sample of the respective size groups. Only a small fraction of the large sized water units are operated by the owners i.e. 30.44 per cent; whereas, 16 units or 69.59 per cent of the total units under large size group were found leased out.

During the course of investigation, it was observed that the preponderance of the owner-operators and relatively less importance attached to leasing out system might be accounted for by two reasons. One, with the advent of new technology of composite intensive fish culture, self-cultivation is being considered by the owners a paying proposition; and two, because of a series of tenancy legislations in recent years giving more rights to the tenants, the owners have become more apprehensive of losing the occupancy rights in their leased out water units.

It can be mentioned that water units in the study area were found to be usually operated by different agencies like individuals, either singly or jointly, co-operatives, government or local bodies. Joint private operations and solo private operations were found to be the major agencies.

From Exhibit 5.3, it is evident that quite a significant proportion of the water bodies were found to be operated by more than two partners, particularly in the cases of large and medium sized water units (23.63% and 30.43%). Comparatively, a large number of water units (29.24%) were operated by solo pond owners. It is important to note that quite a good proportion of water units are cultivated by a large number of operators. Unlike other States in India, it had been found in our study area, in West Bengal, the preponderance of multiple ownerships of water units, irrespective of size-classes.

As we have already mentioned in Exhibit 5.2 that in our study area, 34.38 per cent of all the ponds surveyed were leased-in. Three distinct sources were mainly identified with which lease agreements were made—they were private owners, public bodies and others like Panchayat, Zilla Parishad, trust or institutions like schools etc. The duration of lease was of various time period ranging from one year to ten years.

Exhibit 5.3: Size Group-wise Distribution of Proprietorship of Water Units

Category of Ponds	*No. of Ponds*	*Extent of Proprietorship*		
		Sole	*Only 2 Partners*	*More than 2 Partners*
Small	298 (100.00)	93 (31.21)	178 (59.73)	27 (9.06)
Medium	127 (100.00)	32 (25.19)	65 (51.18)	30 (23.63)
Large	23 (100.00)	6 (26.09)	10 (43.48)	7 (30.43)
Overall	448 (100.00)	131 (29.24)	253 (56.47)	64 (14.29)

Source : Field Survey, 2008.

It is evident from the Exhibit 5.4 that 118 out of 154 water units leased-in (i.e. 76.62%) were found to be obtained from private sources; whereas, 22 out of 154 (i.e. 14.29%) of the total water units were found to be leased-in from government or public bodies. Interestingly enough, in West Bengal, most of the water units of all size-categories were leased-in from the private sources. 76.40, 79.59 and 68.75 per cent of the water units belonging to small, medium and large size-groups respectively were leased-in from the private sources.

Exhibit 5.4: Size Group-wise Leased-in Ponds along with their Leasing Sources

Category of Ponds	*Leased- in Ponds*	*Leasing Sources*		
		Private	*Public*	*Others*
Small	89 (100.00)	68 (76.40)	12 (13.48)	9 (10.11)
Medium	49 (100.00)	39 (79.59)	6 (12.25)	4 (8.16)
Large	16 (100.00)	11 (68.75)	4 (25.00)	1 (6.25)
Overall	154 (100.00)	118 (76.62)	22 (14.29)	14 (9.09)

Source : Field Survey, 2009.

It may further be observed from Exhibit 5.5 that majority of the water units (i.e. 115 out of 154 ponds or 76.68%) were leased-in for a short duration i.e. for one year; whereas 32 and 7 water units out of 154 water units surveyed i.e. 20.78 per cent and 4.54 per cent respectively were found leased-in for a period of two years or more than two years respectively. Pond size-wise analysis of the duration of the lease period reveals that majority of the water units of small and medium size-groups (79.78% and 77.55% of the total water units of the corresponding size-groups respectively) were leased-in for a short period of one year only. However, the duration of lease period for more than four years was found conspicuous by its absence in the case of medium sized water units. Only one-fourth of the large ponds (25%) were leased-in for more than four years. 37.50 per cent of the large water units were leased in for only one year and also for a period of two to four years.

Exhibit 5.5: Size Group-wise Leased-in Ponds along with their Lease Duration

Category of Ponds	*Leased-in Ponds*	*Lease Duration*		
		One Year	*2-4 Years*	*More than 4 Years*
Small	89 (100.00)	71 (79.78)	15 (16.85)	3 (3.37)
Medium	49 (100.00)	38 (77.55)	11 (22.45)	-- (0.00)
Large	16 (100.00)	6 (37.50)	6 (37.50)	4 (25.00)
Overall	154 (100.00)	115 (74.68)	32 (20.78)	7 (4.54)

Source : Field Survey, 2008.

The figures in Exhibit 5.6 bring out the fact that most of the water units (52%) were acquired through inheritance and only 10.5 per cent of the total water units were purchased. The share of the construction of new water units in the total number of water units was 3.12, whereas 34.38 per cent of the total units were acquired through leasing arrangements. It should be stated that it is the inheritance factor which is mainly responsible for fragmentation of ownership (that is, multiple ownership).

The range of uses of water units is very large and includes uses like irrigation, duck rearing, cattle watering, pisciculture field drainage and also for crop production for crop for both cattle and human being. Exhibit 5.7 demonstrates that almost all water units are

Exhibit 5.6: Percentage Distribution of Water Units by Means of Acquisition

Means of Acquisition	*Percentage of the Number of Water Units (of 448 Water Units)*
Inheritance	52.0
Purchase	10.5
Construction of new water units	13.12
Lease	34.38
Overall	100.00

Source: Field Survey, 2008.

Exhibit 5.7: Use of Water Units

Household Purposes	*Fish Production*	*Field Irrigation*	*Duck Rearing, Cattle Watering etc.*	*Percentage Reporting Combination*
1	2	3	4	5
6	14	5		25
6	*	*	13	19
4		6		10
4	10	6		20
	8		4	12
	3	5		8
6				6
22	35	20	17	100

Note : Percentages are reporting this use.
Source : Field Survey, 2008.

used for multipurpose with a wide variety of combination of uses. 'Household uses' in our case include bathing, dishwashing, cloth-washing, supply of water for cooking etc. 22 per cent of the water units are used for household purpose, 20 per cent of the ponds and tanks are also used for irrigation purposes. There are inlet and outlet channels indicating that the units may be used for drainage and irrigation also.

It can also be pointed out that the water units sometimes provide both water and space for growing vegetables. Dried out parts of the ponds are sometimes used for winter (Boro) paddy cultivation—either for nursery seedbeds or for transplanting the paddy itself.

In point of fact, it may be stated that there is no systematic relationship between size and yield of ponds. The correlation coefficient is found statistically insignificant. During the course of interview, it was observed that some ponds owned and operated by an enterprising fish farmers located in an ideal situation may yield higher fish production, irrespective of the size of water units. Water units of small size enjoy sometimes the benefits of closed supervision, intimate monitoring and sincere regulation by the family members themselves. On the other hand, large sized ponds may also have the privilege of initiative and care likely to be taken up by enterprising commercially motivated market oriented fish farmers. Some amounts of business elements sometimes play some role in its operation.

Another interesting feature which might have wider policy implications is that the larger the number of shareholders in a water unit, the lower the level of yield. In Exhibit 5.8, it was shown that there has been a trend towards decline in yields in water units as the number of shareholders increased. Water units cultivated by the solo operator has the yield of 608 kgs. per acre; whereas, the units owned by, for example, 5 or more shareholders, had the yield of 427 kgs. per acre. A large number of water units (ponds and tanks) under multiple ownership are found to be weed-infected and semi-derelict. Because of the recurring deposition of the silt, the bottoms of these water units often dry up during the summer and the water units overspill during the monsoon. Immediate desilting of the tanks, eradication of the excess vegetation and water hyacinths are required to be made in order to provide appropriate conditions for fish cultivations.

In the case of jointly owned water units, it was observed that the shareholders of unequal economic conditions and sometimes-absentee shareholders were, more often than not, found reluctant to take initiatives for renovating water bodies, as their shares of benefits are small; on the contrary, it was observed that in all these cases, there were instances of creating problems by shareholders. Sometimes, familial conflicts among the shareholders have hindered the adoption of modern fish culture practices and ponds and tanks improvements. Different shades of opinion arose among them. All in all, sometimes, age-old water units are eventually remaining in precarious conditions without any efforts for proper maintenance.

From the Exhibit 5.9, it can be safely asserted that the longer the duration of lease period, the higher the yield. The correlation coefficient between yield and duration of lease period is found to be 0.47. This is statistically significant at 10 per cent level of significance. The long duration of lease period provides the fish cultivators incentives and generates a kind of mind-set to undertake different kinds of investment, short run and long run, through adoption of different culture practices. All this might play a positive role in augmenting fish production in a water unit.

Exhibit 5.8: Distribution of Yield by Number of Shareholders

Number of Shareholders	*Yield per Acre (kg)*
Single	608
Joint: 2	510
3	540
4	408
5 and above	427

Source : Field Survey, 2008.

Exhibit 5.9: Yield per Acre by Duration of Lease Period

Duration of Lease Period	*Yield per Acre (kg)*
On annual basis	570
2 years	590
3 years	575
4 years	640
10 years	585

Source : Field Survey, 2008.

5.1 Culture Practices

Fish culture practices include all activities from pre-stocking operations to harvesting of fish through human efforts. The cultural practices may simply be categorized on the basis of major operations like pre-stocking, stocking, input application, applications of supplementary feeds and harvesting.

Pre-stocking refers to those operations prior to stocking in order to clean the pond water by deweeding, netting or other manual activities to eradicate plan weeds, insects, frogs, predatory fish which adversely affect the level of fish production. This would facilitate the better environment for proper growth and movement of fingerlings. Stocking refers to applications of external fish seeds into the pond for the purpose of raising them up to marketable size. There are two important types of fish culture prevailing in the study area which are known as indigenous major carp culture and exotic carp culture. Indigenous major carp culture includes fish species like Rahu, Catla, Mrigal etc.; whereas, exotic carp culture include the culture of exotic species, like Silver Carp, Common Carp and Grass Carp.

Fish thrives well in alkaline water. Lime is used in a pond to maintain the appropriate alkaline nature of the fish-ponds. Toxicants are the substances which are used to eradicate predatory fish, insects, and frogs from the ponds. The most common toxicant is Mahua Oil Cake. Manures are not directly consumed by the fish. It, in fact, enhances the vegetative growth of green aquatic plants and phytoplankton which are ultimately consumed by the phytophagous fish. Dung is one of the most commonly used manure. The purpose of adding fertilizer in the pond is almost similar to that of manure. It also facilitates the growth of micro and macro vegetative plants for an ultimate consumption by the phytophagous fish. The most common fertilizers used are urea and single super phosphate. Farmers very often expressed their unawareness in this matter. All these may be largely due to the inadequate institutional efforts to acquaint them regarding the use and benefits of manure and fertilizers in fish production. Another critical inputs necessary for better and vast growth of fish is the use of supplementary feed like rice bran, mustard oil cake etc. In almost all the ponds, upon enquiry, it was revealed that very few farmers use supplementary feed as per recommended schedule, rather hit and trial method is followed.

5.2 Relationship between Stocking of Inputs—Fish Seeds and Productivity

It is pertinent to note that the stocking rate and the species mix in fish seeds are considered two important determinants for production for fish. Quite a significant proportion of fish farmers used to practise composite fish culture in our study area. This includes major carps, exotic carps, minor carps etc. Fish seed stocked in a sample pond may be categorized into two groups: exotic carps and indigenous carps. The exotic carps include common carp, grass carp and silver carp; whereas, the indigenous carps include major carp, minor carp etc.

Per hectare stocking rate of fish seeds differs among the fish farmers. It is clear from the Exhibit 5.10 that, on an average per acre 15 thousand of fish seeds (amounting to 16 kgs) were stocked. 76 per cent of them constituted indigenous and 24 per cent exotic fish species. Size class-wise variations in the stocking rate of fish seed

Exhibit 5.10: Size Class-wise Distribution of Quantity and Quality of Fish Seed Stocked (Per Acre) in Percentage

Species	*Small*	*Medium*	*Large*	*All Ponds*
Indigenous	70	58	72	76 (12 kg)
Exotic	30	42	28	24 (4 kg)
Total	**16 kg**	**18 kg**	**15 kg**	**16 kg**

Source: Field Survey, 2008.

were also observed. Stocking rate was found highest in the medium sized ponds (18 kgs per acre) followed by small ponds (16 kgs per acre) and large ponds (15 kgs per acre). Small ponds owners used to stock poor quality of fish seeds which were generally collected from natural sources which had high mortality. Large sized pond owners usually used comparatively large sized fish seeds than small and medium pond owners. The medium pond owners stocked fish-ponds by comparatively larger proportion of exotic species of fish seeds (42%) than the corresponding proportion in the small ponds (30%) and large ponds owners (28%).

Attempt was also made to examine the proportion of the different species of fish *vis-à-vis* their recommended proportions for stocking in multi-carp fish culture. There are four major groups of carps like upper level carps (Catla and Silver), middle level (Rohu), lower level (Mrigal and common) and grass eating carps (Grass Carps). In the following Exhibit the proportion of different groups of fish seed stocked in three separate categories of ponds are presented.

Exhibit 5.11: Proportion of Species used in Cultivation

Groups of Species	*Recommended Proportions*	*Small*	*Medium*	*Large*
Surface Feeder	30-40	30	29	21
Column Feeder	10-20	30	18	17
Bottom Feeder	40-50	35	35	40
Grass Eating Feeder	5-15	5	18	22

Source : Field Survey, 2008.

The stocking rate, as it is evident, was not unsatisfactory; but, in most cases, it was found not according to the recommended schedule. The composition of different species of fish seeds in muti-carp culture was mismatched to the recommendation. A large number of sample farmers expressed their complete unawareness about the proper stocking proportion. Stocking of small size of fish seeds, which have high mortality rate, was found predominant. Also, 50 per cent of the fish farmers could get indigenous and exotic carps on ponds, since the traders used to deliver fish seeds on fish pond sites. Even though the fish farmers used to collect fish seeds from different sources (like fish farmers, traders, Fishermens' Co-operative Societies), the fish traders emerge as a most important source, since in our sample about 69 per cent of the fish farmers collected fish seeds (indigenous major carps, exotic carps) from them.

5.3 Sources of Collection of Fish Seeds

While conducting survey, it was also revealed that fish farmers used to change very often the sources of collection of their fish seeds. The reasons identified for this change were higher prices, poor quality, inadequate quantity, distance places, uncertainty about quality, delay in availability, transportation problems etc., poor quality of the fish seeds was the most prominent reason.

Exhibit 5.12: Reasons for Changes in the Sources for Fish Seeds in Order

Reasons	Rank
Poor Quality	1
Higher Prices	2
Distant Place	3
Delay and Uncertainty Regarding Availability	4
Transportation Problems	5

Source : Field Survey, 2008.

Note : Poor quality of fish seeds may be understood in terms of improper size, higher mortality rate, mixed species etc.

Small fish-pond owners tend to stock much higher quantity and large number of fingerlings. It was mainly due to use of locally collected fingerlings from rivers. Poor fish farmers neither had easy access to fish seeds from nursery located at different places nor had funds to purchase better quality of fish seeds.

5.4 Conversion Ratio of Fish from Fish Seeds

Fish seed is one of the most indispensable input for the production of fish. In order to obtain the higher level of fish production, there is a need of use of appropriate number and quantity of quality fish seeds. To understand the production efficiency in fish production, conversion ratio is an important measure. Use of higher potential species of fish would yield higher quantity of fish.

In our study, on an average, the conversion ratio was found to be 64.5, indicating that the use of one kg. of fish seeds would produce 64.5 kg. of matured fish. It has also been observed that, on an average, exotic fish species have comparatively higher conversion ratio (71) than that of indigenous fish species (65). Again, silver carp, one of the exotic fish, have higher conversion ratio (89) than grass carp (81) and common carp (75). On the other hand, Rohu, one of the indigenous major carps, had comparatively higher conversion ratio than Mrigal (66) and Catla (61).

Exhibit 5.13: Conversion Ratio (Fish Species-wise)

Species	Average
Rahu	69
Catla	61
Mrigal	66
Indigenous fish	65
Silver carp	89
Grass carp	81
Common carp	75
Total Exotic Fish	71
All Types of Fish	64.5

Source : Field Survey, 2008.

It was also observed that the medium ponds had much higher conversion ratio for all the species under investigation. This was followed by small ponds and large ponds. The conversion ratio of silver carp of exotic species was found to be higher in all the categories of ponds. This was found true also in the case of Rahu of indigenous carp on all the categories of ponds. In point of fact, it may be stated that the fish farmers are expected to use higher proportion of fish seed species which would have higher conversion ratio. In our study area, relatively a smaller proportion of exotic species of fish seeds like silver carp which used to have higher conversion ratio was used by the farmers of all categories even though larger proportion of Rahu in stocking was used. Upon enquiry, it was also observed that the demand for silver carp may be low due to poor test of this species; hence, the fish farmers are reluctant to this variety. The conversion ratio may not necessarily be a major determinant in the choice of fish species for stocking. Factors like market price, demand and test of a particular variety of seeds may be some other relevant determinants.

5.5 Tenancy Relations and Resource Use Efficiency in Pisciculture

The fish farmers either owned or took on lease the water bodies (tanks and ponds). In the whole of India, 31 per cent of the ponds were owned and 69 per cent were on lease (IIM, 1990). Of course, the proportion varied across the states. It has been observed that in states like Rajasthan, Karnataka, Himachal Pradesh, there did not exist any ownership ponds; whereas in states like West Bengal, Assam, Orissa we witnessed the predominance of ownership ponds. Most of the fish ponds were owned by government agencies like reservoirs, irrigation revenue, Government agencies, fisheries department or village Panchayats. These water bodies were common property resources.

In West Bengal, unlike other states in India, majority of the tanks and ponds are owned by private parties. A significant proportion of these water bodies are found to be leased out to different beneficiaries. The beneficiaries who took the ponds on lease were generally of three types: (a) single individual, (b) two or more individuals and (c) members of co-operatives. The criteria for selecting the leases vary. Some are leased out to working fishermen or persons from fishermen community or unemployed or economically backward rural youth interested in fish farming; some are also sometimes leased out to co-operatives organized by the enterprising individuals with knowledge in pisciculture. On the strength of field data, we have also reason to believe that there are also some cases where the pond owners are interested in leasing out to those lessees who have already proved trustworthy. The number of pond owners covered in our study is 120 in the district of Murshidabad. The total number of ponds studied is 188. Of them, 112 (59.57%) were leased out to individuals.

It was also observed that different kinds of ownership of water units called for different kinds of procedures for leasing. Different owners followed different leasing periods and different criteria for selecting tenants. Absence of uniform leasing period is an important aspect.[1] The uncertainty attached to short duration lease generally dampens the motivations of the lessees. There is no guarantee that the existing lessee would get the same ponds and under the same conditions in the next year also. Automatically, he is worry of taking up productive investment. The reasons for leasing out ponds may be: some have small fragments of ponds which are found convenient to lease out.[2]

A few pond owners do not have adequate manpower or skill or capital and the ability to undertake fish cultivation; and hence are unable to pursue fish cultivation by themselves.

A few others have other occupations which could be profitably pursued otherwise.

All these apart, pond owners belonging to the upper caste have the tendency to shun the harsh life of fish cultivation and hence, the tendency to lease out.

Some pond owners who are sometimes in dire need of cash tend to lease out their ponds to some enterprising relativity affluent lessors.

No other State in India has such a bewildering variety of ponds leasing system as in West Bengal. The modern pisciculture has become gradually more capital intensive in nature and highly profitable. This has made taking the ponds on lease more attractive. Different types of tenancy contracts co-exist in our study area, as in most other parts of West Bengal. At a general level, two forms of tenancy contracts prevail. They are: (1) share contract and (2) fixed rent contract.[3]

Share Contract

This is when rent takes the form of share of the harvest. The amount of rent is a matter of mutual agreement between the pond owners and the tenants. Pond owners and tenants choose among a limited number of standardized contracts. It largely depends upon the location, quality, size of ponds concerned etc.

In our study area, the prevalence of oral lease system mainly in privately owned ponds is observed. Crop sharing tenancy is more prevalent among the small tenants. This is because small tenants find it more difficult to pay the cash rent.

Under crop sharing tenancy system, it was the perception that the tenant would have to part with a part of the surplus, created by his own labour. Even when the hired labour is employed, generally the excess labour costs are borne by the tenants (even though there are instances) where the costs for hired labour are equally shared by the tenants and the pond owners.[4]

Fixed Rent (in cash or in kind)

Rent is paid in cash in most cases at the beginning of the season. Tenants are solely responsible for all the aspects of cultivation. Fixed rent in kind has the same features as the fixed rent in cash except that the rent mutually agreed is paid sometimes at the time of final harvest along with some occasional catch as and when both the tenants and the pond owners mutually desire.

The pond owners are sometimes found an important source of credit to the tenants. Cost sharing is a standard part of the tenancy arrangement. The tenants are found to provide traditional labour intensive techniques and inputs like farmyard manure, mohua oil cake, rice bran, family labour; whereas, modern capital intensive inputs like fingerlings, fertilizers etc. are either wholly or partly provided by the pond owners. The reasons for sharing capital-intensive inputs are quite straightforward on efficiency ground. There are efficiency gains from input sharing since it gives both pond owners and tenants an incentive to equal cost and marginal revenue. Cost sharing has emerged as an adaptation to the requirements of modern pisciculture.

Incidence of production loan is also not insignificant. The pond owners give quite often credit to the tenants and participate in decision-making about the units of those inputs and in general, takes a lot of interest in productive investment on the leased out ponds. Of course, a few cases were observed where the terms and conditions of contracts in tenancy and credit transactions or labour are interrelated. The implications in the relevant factor markets might get re-enforced by such interlinkages. The pond owners may rob his tenants of his freedom in decision making.

In 20 per cent of the cases of the reporting tenants in the sample the pond owners gave advances to the tenants to meet his needs for the purchase of inputs like fingerlings etc. In the rest 80 per cent cases, advances were given without any interest.

The information received would have us believe that the most distinctive aspect in the lease market is the rising incidence of fixed rent tenancy and the entry of some middle-class enterprising individuals as lessors-in. This emergence and growth is a reflection of development of capitalist tenancy as distinguished from subsistence tenancy. This has, of course, reduced the growing tendency for reduction in the access of small/marginal fish farmers.[5]

It is perceived that tenants under cash rents tenancy arrangements have the freedom to utilize the ponds with the objective of production. Cash rent tenancy (fixed) is more profitable; because the whole of economic surplus, after meeting cultivating expenses, is enjoyed by the cultivators. That is why, more resourceful tenants prefer to take ponds on cash rents. Of course, it has been found that sharecropping provides both conflicts and co-operations between pond owners and tenants. It also involved joint provision of many inputs. Exhibit 5.14 summarizes the terms and conditions of different tenancy contracts.[6]

Exhibit 5.14: Types of Tenancy Contracts

Contract	*Proportion of Leased-in Area under Specific Contracts (%)*	*Tenants Share in Output (%)*	*Tenants Share in Inputs (%)*			*Other Features, if any*
			Labour	*Inputs like oil Cake, Rice Bran etc.*	*Cash Inputs Like Fish Seed, Fertili-zers etc.*	
1	2	3	4	5	6	7
Share Contracts	40	50	100	100	100	Cost share shared at the time of occurrence
	15	33.3	100	100	100	
	10	25	100	00	00	
Fixed rent contracts (cash rent)	20	100	100	100	100	Rent is paid sometimes at the beginning of the season or sometimes at different points of time.
Kind rent	15	100	100	100	100	

Source : Field Survey, 2008.

Exhibit 5.14 gives an impression that the highest concentration of ponds is governed by sharecropping. The urban households (or absentee landlords) and the non-labour institutions are generally found to prefer fixed rents. In about 40 per cent of the ponds, output is shared in different proportions between the pond owners and the tenants. Output is shared equally when all the input costs like labour, seed fertilizer etc. are entirely provided by the tenants. There are reductions in the tenant's share to 33.3 per cent or 25 per cent of the total produce when the variable input costs partly or wholly borne by the pond owners. The pattern of association between crop sharing and cost indicates a tendency towards pond owners sharing costs only when they are receiving a larger share of the crop. There are also some cases, where, instead of one tenant and one landowner, there are more than one tenants or owners for one pond owner or one tenant with identical obligations and entitlements. This system generates mainly because of the multiplicity of ownership. In most cases, however, each co-owner or co-tenant provides usually proportionate share of inputs and received proportionate output.

5.6 Profile of the Respondents—Inland Fish Farmers

Human Capital

Nearly all (96%) the respondents were born in the village in which they currently reside and some of them (74%) are Hindus and about 26 per cent belong to the Muslim community. Households are generally large comprising on an average 6.2 family members with males and females in equal proportions. An average of 40 per cent of family members are below 18 years old but only 22 per cent are only in schools. Although primary education is compulsory, not all children attend schools. They often have to work in the home for some households duties. Schooling and its associated costs are sometimes unaffordable.

All the respondent household heads were male. Most (70%) were 31-50 years old. A few were (9%) are younger or older (15%). Of the spouses, 40 per cent are less than 35 years old, 45 per cent more than 50 years old. Overall, the educational status of the households was low.

Exhibit 5.15: Educational Status of Respondent Male Household Heads and their Spouses in the Sample Areas

Educational Status	*Household Heads (% n = 360)*	*Spouses (% n = 327)*
No Education	29	61
Primary (1-4)	19	11
Secondary	17	7
Higher Secondary	15	8
Undergraduate	8	3

Source : Primary Survey Data, 2008.

Exhibit 5.16: Occupations of the Respondent Household Heads and their Spouses

Occupations	*Household Heads (% n = 360)*		*Spouses (% n = 97)*	
	Primary (%)	*Secondary (%)*	*Primary (%)*	*Secondary (%)*
Fish farming	11	26	9	12
Rice farming	38	24	39	24
Sharecropper	13	15	15	18
Livestock	1	3	27	13
Capture fishing	14	18	24	27
Home-maker	0	0	98	53
Rickshaw driver	2	6	0	0
School teacher	7	8	10	16
Vendor/Trader	17	19	18	19
Miscellaneous	10	17	16	19

Source : Primary Survey, 2008

The important primary occupations of the household heads in terms of time spent are fishery, rice farming and some other informal income generating activities (or micro enterprise)(Exhibit 5.16). However, fish farming and rice farming were their two most secondary occupations. Nearly all the spouses (99%) are found home-makers and most had no other job. Some of them (5%) were engaged in fish farming as a secondary occupation.

Respondents had an average of 10.4 years of experience of fish farming. 14 per cent reported up to 2 years of experience and 63 per cent reported 3-5 years. Fish farming activities are found almost male dominated with women significantly involved in feeding the fish only.

Exhibit 5.17: Gender Roles of Responsibilities in Fish Farming Activities

Activity	*Only Males (%)*	*Only Females (%)*
Pond preparation	98	2
Fingerling procurement	97	3
Feed procurement	87	13
Fertilizer procurement	90	10
Feeding Fish	81	19
Harvesting Fish	99	1
Marketing Fish	95	5

Source : Primary Survey, 2008.

Natural Capital

Access to homestead land and water is critical. The surveyed households were either marginal or small landholders with an average of 0.39 acres of homestead land. Most had agricultural land with an average area of 0.31 areas. Almost none had fallow land and 12 per cent of the households leased part their land to others.

The majority of the households (88%) had a single pond and the remainder had two or more ponds. Respondent farmers had to rely on groundwater and rainfall, although most of them did not report significant constraints related to water quality. 43 per cent stated that seasonality influenced the availability of water for fish farming.

Social Capital

The surveyed farmers had not received help from Government directly and most of the farmers used to utilize local indigenous knowledge in their current fish farming practices, from other farmers and also from friends and neighbour. However, technology had started being introduced into the area slowly. Institutions like Fish Farmer's Development Agencies (FFDAs) have become a very important source of finance to the capital-hungry.

Some of the respondent farmers had received training from different agencies of different time duration. It is reported that the government through its local agencies use to disseminate information on the latest technological changes time to time. Farmers reported of their involvement in the cultivation of fish with the available and

Exhibit 5.18: Sources of Information in Fish Farming of the Respondents

Source of Information	*Respondents (%)*
Other farmers	87
Friends or neighbor	54
Government sources	59
Hatcheries	27
Non-government organizations	43
Seed traders	21

Source : Primary Survey, 2008.

affordable technological inputs in their ponds and tanks. Farmers who are situated proximate to the developed parts of the region are relatively utilizing the latest production technology and other facilities extended by government and non-government agencies.

Financial Capital

Two-thirds of the farmers (76%) are relying on their own financial resources for undertaking the fish cultivation. The rest are obtained from various other sources including moneylenders, relatives, friends, banks, co-operatives and other sources. Respondents reported different reasons for not accessing financial assistance from government agencies.

Exhibit 5.19: Reasons for not Acquiring Credit (n = 360)

Reasons	*Respondents (%)*
Complex procedures	75
Do not require credit	60
Credit is unavailable	40
Do not know	48
Fear of misusing credit	25
Cultivators' personel inhibitions	20

Source : Primary Survey, 2008.

Notes

1. Tenants continue to cultivate same ponds without any official record of his cultivating possession over the ponds (i.e. concealed tenancy). Oral lease is a word of mouth agreement between the lessor and the

lessee. In order to evade tenancy legislations, the system of oral leasing is sometimes practiced.

2. The term "reverse tenancy" refers to the situation where large pond owners are leasing in ponds from smaller ones. The phenomenon is not that significant in the case of fish cultivation. In fact, in agriculture this tendency prevails because the landowners are to make full use of some indivisible inputs like pump sets, threshers etc. and hence take recourse to reverse tenancy. But in pisciculture, there does not exist any input indivisible. Hence, the tendency is found to be low.
3. One may encounter some other forms of contract which do not fit in easily with either category.
4. It is sometimes argued that crop sharing leads to misallocation of resources. It is (not) possible to accept that crop sharing arrangement leads to more efficient allocation of resources. Risk is shared between the pond owner and the tenants. In pisciculture, which involves high degree of uncertainty, the incidence of sharecropping is prominent.
5. Like agriculture, pond owners and tenants cannot be described as sharply differentiated class. With conflicting interests, tenants and pond owners are found often in the study area involved in a "co-operative conflict" with many "congruent interests" (like the quantity of fish seeds, fertilizer use etc.) and also many "conflicting interests" (like division of the harvest between the two parties). (*See* Sen, 1990).
6. There are very few cases where the terms and conditions in tenancy and credit transactions or labour are found to be interrelated. The implications are that the imperfections in different factor and commodity markets might get reinforced by such interlocking. The pond owner may have the opportunity of robbing the tenants of the freedom of the tenants in decision making.

6
Measuring Efficiency in Pisciculture

6.1 Measuring Efficiency in Fish Production

It has been observed in past few sections that there was reasonable variation in yield across the farmers in our study area. This may be due to different reasons. One plausible explanation may be the different proportion of inputs used by different farmers. This might create inefficiency in input application by the fish farmers. Against these perspectives, it is pertinent to examine the efficiency in input use by the fish farmers, which is essential for developing an optimal resource management strategy. In this study, the Data Envelopment Analysis (DEA) has been employed to examine the issue.

Based on Farrell's innovative article (1957), several approaches to efficiency and productivity assessment have been developed that can be classified into two broad categories: parametric and non-parametric frontier models. The former (such as regression analysis on the basis of Cobb-Douglas technology) depends, as it is well known, on—the specification of an *ad hoc* functional form; the imposition of certain *a priori* restrictions on the production technology, and then estimation of the parameters of the production or the cost function statistically.

Alternatively, the latter constructs a linear piece-wise function from empirical observations of inputs and outputs, thereby avoiding the need to assume functional relationships between inputs and outputs or to make distributional assumptions regarding the residuals in a regression analysis.

Most of the non-parametric applications are based on the DEA (Data Envelopment Analysis) model as proposed by Charnes, Cooper and Rhodes (CCR) in 1978. In recent years, DEA has become a central technique in productivity and efficiency analysis, applied in different aspects of economics and management sciences. In agriculture, DEA has been applied in comparing organisation ranging from horticulture to aquaculture. Here, attempt has been made to measure the efficiency (or inefficiency) of the fish farmers with the help of Data Envelopment Analysis.

According to Farrell (1957), Technical Efficiency (TE) represents the ability of a Decision Making Unit (DMU) to produce maximum output given a set of inputs and technology (output-oriented) or, alternatively, to achieve maximum feasible reductions in input quantities given input prices and output (input-oriented). The choice between input- and output-oriented measures is a matter of concern, and selection may vary according to the unique characteristics of the set of DMUs under study. In this study, input-oriented DEA seems more appropriate, given that it is more reasonable to argue that in pisciculture, a farmer has more control over inputs rather than output levels, which may often be exogenously bounded. In addition, the inelastic demand of most agricultural products renders cost reduction a better means of increasing profitability than output growth (Coelli, 1996).

Sometimes, it is also observed that farmers produce output more or less than what, with the existing condition, possible to produce. That is, if it is possible for scale his production level up and down, the efficiency level of that farmer will increase. In that case, that particular farm may be called scale inefficient. This information is also important when firms are operating in a region where increasing or decreasing returns to scale exists.

DEA operationalises these efficiency concepts in the context of a set of linear programming problems (Coelli, 1995). It calculates the frontier production function of a set of Decision Making Units (DMUs) and evaluates the relative technical efficiency of each unit, thereby allowing a distinction to be made between efficient and inefficient DMUs. Those identified as "best practice units" (i.e., those determining the frontier) are given a rating of one, whereas the degree of technical inefficiency of the rest is calculated on the basis of the Euclidian distance of their input-output ratio from the frontier (Coelli *et al.*, 1998). That is, if efficiency score of a particular firm appears to be 0.5, say, it implies that he is 50 per cent efficient and can reduce half of its input use.

We consider the situation with 360 fish farms or Decision Making Units (DMUs), each producing output Y from a bundle of 4 inputs. The jth DMU ($j = 1, 2, \ldots, 360$) uses X_k^j units of kth input in the production of Y^j units. A separate Linear Programming (LP) problem is solved for each of the j DMUs ($j = 1, 2, \ldots, 360$) in the sample. The input based technical and scale efficiency for the jth DMU can be obtained by solving the following LP problem—

$$\underset{\lambda^j, \theta^j}{Minimize}\, \theta^j$$

Subject to—

$$\sum_{j=1}^{360} \lambda^j Y^j \geq Y_0^j \text{ (output constraints)}$$

$$\sum_{j=1}^{360} \lambda^j X_k^j \leq \theta^j X_k^0 \text{ (inputs constraints, k = 1, 2, 3, 4)}$$

$$\sum_{j=1}^{360} \lambda^j = 1$$

$$\lambda^j \geq 0, j = 1, 2, \ldots, 360$$

Where,

θ^j = dual of the variable indicating proportional increase in output possible by firm j;

λ^j = weight or intensity variable (or, shadow price) used to derive all possible linear combinations of the sample observations.

Y_o^j = Actual output produced by firm j.

X_k^o = Actual input use by firm j

The DEA problem mentioned above has an important intuitive interpretation. Essentially, the problem takes the jth firm and then seeks to radically contract the input vector, X_k^j, as much as possible, while still remaining within the feasible input requirement set. The inner boundary of this set is a piece-wise linear isoquant, determined by the observed data points (i.e. all the firms in the sample). The radial contraction of the input vector, Xk, produces a projected point, $(X_k^j\lambda^j, Y^j\lambda^j)$, on the surface of this technology. This projected point is a linear combination of this observed data points. The constraints in the above LP problem ensure that this projected point cannot lie outside the feasible set.

6.2 Data and Variables

We consider one output-four input Variable Returns to Scale DEA model. The analysis is based on cross-sectional pond-wise per acre value of output (dependent variable, Y) and the values of all the four independent variables explained as follows—

X_1 = Fish fingerlings used as seed (kg/acre)
X_2 = Supplementary fish feed (kg/acre)
X_3 = Labour (man days/acre)
X_4 = others i.e. aggregated value of Mahua Oil Cake, fertilizers, lime and manures (quintal/acre)

Here, number of inputs has been reduced to four due to two reasons. First, according to the importance of the inputs from the production point of view, fish seed (fingerlings) comes first, followed by fish feed, labour, and others (inputs like mahua oil cake, fertilizers, lime etc.). Second, use of more inputs in DEA model, increases the number of constraints which will in turn increase the efficiency scores of the sample farms as frontier becomes tighter when the number of constraints.

The study is based upon primary data. Data pertaining to output and inputs were elicited from 360 fish farms selected for the study from four districts of West Bengal by administering the questionnaire designed for the purpose. Data are equally distributed among four districts and also among three size classes viz. small (less than 0.49 acre), medium (0.5 to 4.0 acre) and large (more than 4 acre). Summary statistics for outputs and inputs are presented in Exhibit 6.1:

Exhibit 6.1: Summary Statistics of Inputs and Outputs

Inputs, outputs	*Mean*	*Standard Deviation*	*Maximum Value*	*Minimum Value*
Output (qn acre^{-1})	14.32	11.3	15.16	8.26
Inputs				
Seed (Kg acre^{-1})	16.7	18.7	19.2	13.5
Feed (Kg acre^{-1})	17.93	15.4	18.6	14.7
Labour (Kg acre^{-1})	182	137.6	256	113
Others (Kg acre^{-1})	3.82	2.87	4.71	1.97

Source : Field Survey, 2008.

Exhibit 6.2: Distribution of Efficiency Score of Fish Farmers

Efficiency Score	*TE*	*SE*
0.27 to 0.49	196	177
0.50 to 0.69	68	76
0.70 to 0.89	69	71
0.90 to 1.00	27	36

Source : Field Survey 2008.

6.3 Results and Discussion

The DEA model for computing input-oriented technical and scale efficiency was solved by using software DEAP 2.1 (Coelli, 1996). The estimated value of Technical Efficiency (TE) and Scale Efficiency (SE) were shown in Exhibit 6.10 and Diagram 6.3.

The estimated technical efficiency score under CRS technology for the sample farm varies from 0.27 to 1.0, with a sample average of 0.628. It implies, on the one hand, that on an average, the farms can reduce 37.2 per cent of input use and can still produce the same output. The number of farms whose technical inefficiency is greater than 50 per cent (TE score is less than 0.5); that is, the number of farms which can contract more than half of their input use on an average, is 196 (54.4%). The number of farms who are carrying fish production optimally is only 17, which is only 4.72 per cent of the total sample. The difference between maximum and minimum TE score indicates that there is wide variation in the efficiency of the farms.

The interpretation of scale efficiency scores allows for some interesting remarks. Mean scale efficiency scores 0.732, implying that the average size of sample fish farms is far from optimal size.

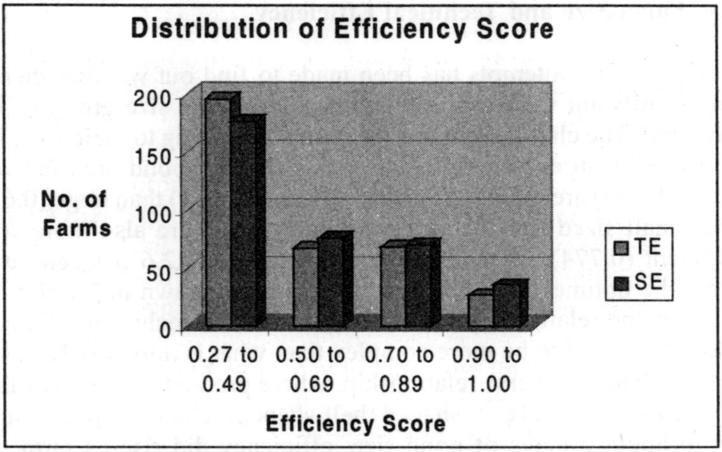

Figure 6.1: Distribution of Efficiency Scores among Fish Farmers.

Assuming no other constraining factor, an additional of 26.8 per cent productivity gain would be feasible, provided they adjusted their farm operation to an optimal scale. Only 27 (7.3%) farms are actually operating at the most productive scale where CRS apply and scale efficiency equals one. The majority of the scale-inefficient fish farms, 236 (65.56%) are operating under increasing returns to scale (i.e. at a point corresponding to the downward portion of the average long run cost curve) and the remaining 124 (34.44%) are under decreasing returns to scale. Efficiency analysis theory suggests that the former are obviously small farms that need to increase their size in order to achieve cost savings, whereas the latter are larger farms that have expanded more than necessary and thus would be better off by reducing their size.

Exhibit 6.3: Summary: Efficiency Score of Sample Farms

	TE_{CRS}	TE_{VRS}	*SE*
Overall Sample Mean	0.628	0.687	0.732
Maximum efficiency	1.0	1.0	1.0
Minimum Efficiency	0.27	0.34	0.42
No. of farms showing efficiency score less than average	221	177	134
No. of "Best Practice" farms (TE = 1)	27	29	36

6.4 Farm Size and Technical Efficiency

In this section attempts has been made to find out whether there is any significant variation in efficiency across the size group of fish farmers.[1] The classification of fish farms according to their size class shows that on average medium farms (having pond area between 0.5 to 4 acre) are more technically efficient (0.651) than large (0.613) and small sized (0.622) farms. Medium farms are also more scale efficient (0.774), as their average size is only 22.6 per cent away from the optimal size. The results have been shown in Exhibit 6.4. Clearly, the relationship between farm size and technical efficiency has been found to be more complex than what is normally believed. Rather than an inverse relationship, where productivity falls as farm size rises, we found a ∩–shaped (bell-shaped) relationship. For farms up to about 5 acres of pond size, efficiency did rise as farm size rises. But beyond this size, it started to fall again. Consequently, it can be argued that the result has crucial implication in the economic viability of the fish farms. Small farms are impeded by greater technical inefficiencies; whereas larger farms usually accept fish farming as their secondary activities. On the other hand, large farms achieve better performance benefiting both from increased technical efficiencies as well as from greater economies of scale. This finding contradicts a popular belief that larger farms are able to capture economies of size and operate at higher efficiency levels than smaller ones. The results also contradict the popular belief of the negative relationship between farm size and productivity and its implication is also quite clear. The pond area of medium farms is limited, though not small, they are likely to put more efforts into maintaining their fish ponds, feeding and monitoring of culture practices. As a result, they tend to be more efficient. The farmer's ability to follow this regular activity decreases both in case of small and large farms.

Exhibit 6.4: Average Efficiency Scores According to Size

Classification of Size	*No. of Farms*	*TE_{CRS}*	*SE*
Small (≺0.49 *acre*)	120	0.622	0.708
Medium (0.5 to 4.9 acre)	120	0.651	0.774
Large (≻5 *acre*)	120	0.613	0.714
Total	**360**	**0.628**	**0.732**

6.5 Size-Efficiency in Fishery Revisited—A Meta-frontier Analysis

One point deserves particular mention here. The efficiency of a farm depends not only on the inputs it uses, but also on several other factors (such as infrastructural facilities, region, level of education and technical knowledge, work culture, monsoon etc.). It is very difficult to incorporate those factors into a production frontier to examine their effects on efficiency, though important. Hence, size-efficiency analysis might reveal more concrete results if it is carried on separately for different region. Also, a definite conclusion can be drawn if it is found that a particular group of farmers are efficient with respect to all the farmers taken together. For that it is important to calculate the group efficiency to reach the final conclusion.[2]

In this section, we employ the concept of meta-frontier production function defined by Hayami and Ruttan (1971, pp. 82) to examine whether there is any systematic difference in the efficiency of the fish farms for different size classes. The meta-production function was first introduced by Hayami (1969) and Hayami and Ruttan (1970, 1971). As stated by Hayami and Ruttan (1971, p. 82), "The meta-production function can be regarded as the envelope of commonly conceived neoclassical production functions." In their discussion of agricultural productivity across various countries, Ruttan *et al.* (1978, p. 46) state, "We now define the meta-production function as the envelope of the production points of the most efficient countries." The concept of a meta-production function is theoretically attractive because it is based on the simple hypothesis that all producers in different groups (countries, regions, etc.) have potential access to the same technology. Following the seminal work of Hayami and Ruttan (1970), Mundlak and Hellinghausen (1982) and Lau and Yotopoulos (1989), we employed the approach to compare agricultural productivity across countries.

6.6 Meta-Frontier Methodology

In Meta-frontier analysis, the performance of each individual fish farm in the sample is measured against two different frontiers—one based on farms from all the different groups in the sample and the other based only on farms from the group to which it belongs. The first can be regarded as the national or *grand* frontier and the other as the *group* frontier.[2] The grand and the group frontiers can be defined as follows. Define the index set $I = \{1, 2, \ldots, N\}$ where each observed data point is an element of I. Now consider a partition $I = \bigcup I_r$ where I_r includes only observations from group r. Then, under the standard assumptions of convexity and free disposability of inputs (x) and outputs (y) the empirically constructed group and grand production possibility sets are

$$S^r = \{(x,y): x \geq \sum_{j \in I_r} \lambda_j x^j;\ y \leq \sum_{j \in I_r} \lambda_j y^j;\ \sum_{j = I_r} \lambda_j = 1\ ;\ \lambda_j \geq 0\ \ (j \in I_r)\}$$

... *(for group r)*

and

$$S^G = \{(x,y): x \geq \sum_{j \in \bigcup I_r} \lambda_j x^j;\ y \leq \sum_{j \in \bigcup I_r} \lambda_j x^j;\ \sum_{j \in \bigcup I_r} \lambda_j = 1;\ \lambda_j \geq 0;\ (j \in \bigcup I_r)\}$$

respectively. It may be noted that while each S^r is a subset of S^G, the latter is bigger than the union of the individual group production possibility sets. This is illustrated in diagram 6.1 for a 1-input, 1-output 2-group example.

Let the points P_1 through P_4 show the input-output bundles of four farms from group P. Similarly, Q_1 through Q_4 are the input-output bundles of farms from group Q. The group frontiers are shown by the broken lines $AP_1P_3P_4C$ for group P and by $BQ_1Q_2Q_3D$ for group Q. By contrast, the grand frontier is the outer envelop of the two frontiers shown by the broken line $AP_1P_3Q_2Q_3D$.

Note that points in the area P_3EQ_2 lie above both group frontiers, but (by virtue of convexity) are below the grand frontier. While judged against their own group frontier the technical efficiency of each the points Q_1, Q_2, and Q_3 equals unity while the corresponding efficiency of Q_4 is $\frac{JQ_4}{JK}$.

When judged against the grand frontier, Q_2 and Q_3 remain efficient. On the other hand, the efficiency of Q_1 falls from unity to $\frac{BQ_1}{BN}$ while the efficiency of Q_4 does not change. Thus, the *group efficiency* of the group Q measured at the points Q_1, Q_2, and Q_3 equals unity (even though point Q_4 is inefficient) while at the point Q_1, the

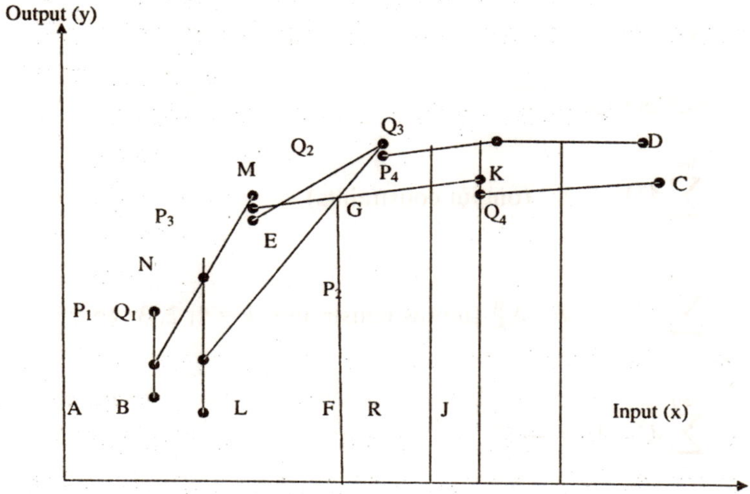

Figure 6.2: Group and Grand Frontiers

group efficiency, measured with respect to grand frontier, is $\frac{BQ_1}{BN}$. The geometric mean of the group efficiency measures at these different points may be used as an overall index of the *group efficiency* of *Q*. From group *P* the points P_1 and P_2 lie both on the group and the grand frontier. The point P_4 is on the group frontier but has technical efficiency $\frac{RP_4}{RS}$. In the case of point P_2 technical efficiency is $\frac{FP_2}{FG}$ relative to the group frontier and $\frac{FP_2}{FH}$ when measured against the grand frontier. Thus, at this point a measure of group efficiency is $\frac{FG}{FH}$. It is interesting to note that point *E* lies on both of the group frontiers but not on the grand frontier. Thus, at this point both groups would have the same level of group (in) efficiency.

6.7 Meta-frontier DEA Model

For the overall or grand efficiency of the fish farms in the sample, we solve the following LP problem, including all 360 farms from all size classes as—

$$\underset{\lambda^j,\theta^j}{Minimize}\ \theta_G^j$$

Subject to—

$$\sum_{j=1}^{360} \lambda^j Y^j \geq Y_0^j \text{ (output constraints)}$$

$$\sum_{j=1}^{360} \lambda^j X_k^j \leq \theta_G^j\ X_k^0 \text{ (inputs constraints, } k = 1, 2, 3, 4)$$

$$\sum_{j=1}^{360} \lambda^j = 1$$

$$\lambda^j \geq 0, j = 1, 2, ..., 360$$

where,

θ_G^j = dual of the variable indicating proportional increase in output possible by farm *j*; or Grand technical efficiency, TE_G^j.

λ^j = weight or intensity variable (or, shadow price) used to derive all possible linear combinations of the sample observations.

Y_o^j = Actual output produced by farm *j*.

Y_o^j = Actual input use by farm *j*

Similarly, the relevant DEA model for size-class *r* with N_r (=120) fish farms in the sample is—

$$\underset{\lambda^j,\theta^j}{Minimize}\ \theta_r^j$$

Subject to—

$$\sum_{j=1}^{120} \lambda^j Y^j \geq Y_0^j \text{ (output constraints)}$$

$$\sum_{j=1}^{120} \lambda^j X_k^j \leq \theta_r^j X_k^0 \text{ (inputs constraints, } k = 1, 2, 3, 4)$$

$$\sum_{j=1}^{120} \lambda^j = 1$$

Where, θ_r^j is the dual of the variable indicating proportional increase in output possible by farm *j*; or the group technical efficiency, TE_r^j.

A point-wise measure of technical efficiency of size class *r* relative to the grand frontier evaluated at the input-output data of farm *j* is—

$$\beta_r^j = \frac{TE_G^j}{TE_r^j}$$

An overall measure of the efficiency of group *r* is—

$$TE(r) = (\prod_{j \in r} \beta_r^j)^{1/N\ r}$$

where N_r (=120) is the number of farms in group *r*.

Clearly, for any fish farms j in a size class *r*, TE_G^j is a measure of its performance relative to other farms within the same size class. On the other hand, β is a measure of its performance compared to all size classes in the state.

6.8 Results and Discussion

Technical efficiency score of each fish farm within each size class was estimated separately based on their individual frontier and also based on the grand frontier comprising all the observations taken together. The summary results were given in Exhibit 6.5. The results examine in the Exhibit below shows the relationship between size of fish farms and technical efficiency. The analysis indicates the following—

At the farm level, the technical efficiency has a mixed relationship with size. While the medium sized farms recorded high technical efficiency, small and big farms recorded slightly high inefficiency. In other words, the size and technical efficiency at farm level is found to be ∩ (bell-shaped). These results coincide with the results obtained on the basis of grand frontier.

Exhibit 6.5: Mean Technical Efficiency of Fish Farms Across Size Class

Size Class	*No. of Fish Farms*	*Technical Efficiency Score*		*Index of Size Efficiency*
		Based on Grand Frontier	*Based on Group Frontier*	
Small	120	0.622	0.736	0.713
Medium	120	0.651	0.753	0.739
Large	120	0.613	0.728	0.702
Total	**360**	**0.628**	**0.749**	**0.714**

The index of size-efficiency of the large farm (0.702) is lower in comparison to lower size farm. It seems that the large farms have failed to capture the economies of scale in the culture practice of fishery.

Though small farms were found to be more efficient than large fishers while evaluated on the basis of all fish farms in the sample, the difference is not quite significant.

Though there is no significant difference in the size-efficiency of the farms, on an average, they can reduce input use by 28.6 per cent (as mean size-efficiency is 0.714) in order to achieve efficiency.

6.9 Inter-Regional Efficiency Difference

West Bengal is a vast state with a number of agro-climatic zones with their distinctive sociological, economic, political and infrastructural features. The intensity of fish culture in coastal and saline region is more than that in any other zones of West Bengal. Easy access to natural resources and other infrastructural facilities helpful in achieving lower cost per unit of output is not evenly distributed all-over the zones of the state. Stability of political power and democratic nature of the overall political environment is also different for different districts.

Exhibit 6.6: Mean Technical Efficiency of Fish Farms Across Region

Region	*No. of Fish Farms*	*Technical Efficiency*		*Area Efficiency*
		Based on Grand Frontier	*Based on Regional Frontier*	
South 24-Parganas (Coastal and Saline Zone)	90	0.648	0.736	0.775
Hoogly (old Alluvial Region)	90	0.623	0.762	0.668
Bankura (Red and Laterite Zone)	90	0.629	0.708	0.789
Murshidabad (New Alluvial Zone)	90	0.612	0.694	0.778
Total	**360**	**0.628**	**0.725**	**0.753**

Different political parties with the varying political and economic agenda form governments in different states. All these factors may have important impact on the performance of a farm. We investigate how far such variation affects the levels of technical efficiency of individual firms. In this section efficiency has been calculated using meta-frontier function techniques to identify whether it is possible to construct a summary measure of the efficiency of a region relative to the state as a whole.[3]

Here also, the performance of each individual fish farm in the sample is measured against two different frontiers—one based on farms from the entire region (West Bengal) in the sample of 360 fish farmers and the other based only on farms from the region in which it belongs—comprising of the sample of 90 fish farms (from each district 90 sample fish farms have been chosen). The first can be regarded as the national or *grand* frontier and the other as the *group* frontier or regional frontier. In our sample, we have four districts as representatives of four agro-climatic zones. The summary results of technical efficiency of each farm evaluated on the basis of grand and regional frontier along with area efficiency (calculated by taking geometric mean of these two magnitudes) have been given in Exhibit 6.6.

The role of each zone in defining the overall efficiency is captured by an overall measure of the distance of individual frontier to the grand frontier and is called as Area Efficiency.[4] The results can be summarized as follows—

The distribution of efficiency scores across the four study regions on the basis of grand frontier indicates that farms in South 24-Parganas districts are the most efficient units (TE score of 0.648),

Exhibit 6.7: Frequency Distribution of Efficient Region of Sample Fish Farms

Region	*Based on Regional Frontier*		*Based on Grand Frontier*	
	Number	*Proportion*	*Number*	*Proportion*
Coastal and Saline Region	5	5.56	7	7.78
Old Alluvial Region	7	10.00	9	10.00
Red and Laterite Zone	7	7.78	7	7.78
New Alluvial Zone	6	6.67	8	8.89
All	27	7.5	31	8.61

followed by Bankura (TE score of 0.629), Hoogly (TE score of 0.623) and Mursidabad districts (TE score of 0.612).

But Hoogly is most efficient district if measured against regional frontier, followed by South 24-Parganas and Bankura.

The area efficiency is highest in Red and Laterite zone (as index of area efficiency of Bankura is 0.789) followed by New Alluvial zone, Coastal and Saline zone and Old Alluvial region.

The variation of area efficiency is significant among the zones. Old Alluvial zone (representative district is Hoogly) showed a sharp drop in efficiency. In other words, low level of area efficiency in this zone clearly demonstrates the high operating costs as compared to their outputs. In addition, these may suggest that the issues like extension services, training of fish farmers or supply of quality fish seed and feed have not been adequately taken care of.

Another interesting observation is that though area efficiency is the lowest in Hoogly district, the number of 'best practice' fish farms (technical efficiency score equals to one) is highest in this region. This is shown in Exhibit 6.7.

It is also important to note that this proportion is quite stable in case of Bankura district. The number of 'best practice' farms remains same irrespective of whether measured against regional or grand frontier.

Interesting is that number of 'best practice' farms have increased while efficiency is measured against the grand frontier.

In fine, it appears that by drawing DEA method over the yield level of individual fish farms, a reasonable degree of variation in efficiency levels has been observed within the region and among the regions. Hence, introduction of systematic policy programmes is called for in removing the inefficiency of the fish farmers and augmenting fish production in the state of West Bengal.

Notes

1. The current relevance of this analysis can be illustrated by the policy issues taken by Government of West Bengal in inland tanks and ponds. Government has recently decided to take up all the derelict and semi-derelict ponds in the state from their owner and lease out those to the large fish farmers in order to augment production in the state. The move is, no doubt, appraisable. But the basic question is whether large fish farmers can be able to augment production more than middle and small farmers. The answer of this question lies on the relationship structure of farm size and productivity.
2. It is a common practice to use production frontiers to assess the level of efficiency of production units or firms. Such frontiers are identified using non-parametric or parametric methods predicated on various non-stochastic and stochastic assumptions. Once a frontier surface is determined, the efficiency of each firm is measured relative to the frontier using radial measures of efficiency that were proposed by Farrell (1957). Frontiers are estimated using cross-sectional or panel data on the levels of inputs used and outputs produced by the firms. While technical efficiencies of firms that are measured with respect to a given frontier are comparable, this is not normally the case among firms that operate under different technologies. Such problems arise when comparisons of firms from different regions are involved. In this section as we want to find out difference in size-productivity relation in inland fish farming across the region to measure the group efficiency relative to its' grand frontier. For this, meta-frontier Data Envelopment Analysis (DEA) has been used.
3. The production function for different regions need not be different if all of the above factors could be taken into account. But most of them are qualitative in nature and unobservable as well, and as a result we couldn't take into them account as factors of production. Hence, it is not wrong to assume that the production technology (defined in terms of the observed inputs and outputs) is itself different for different regions like states for differences in the quality of human capital, work culture and overall working environment, infrastructural facilities etc. Some of them do vary for different ownership as well as organizational pattern.
4. Area efficiency broadly reflects the impact of the social, economic and cultural factors in a particular area on the technical efficiency of a branch. While achievement of high overall efficiency becomes a target at state level, the issues relating to area efficiency call for actions at local/districts level.

7

Constraints for Adoption of Practices

The role of technology in terms of increasing productivity with stability has not received much attention in the fisheries sector in India. General production systems are geared towards meeting the subsistence needs of fish farm families—in good or bad years. The technologies they adopt and practise have evolved over long periods of time to serve subsistence needs. They are characterized by low risk, low cash inputs and low outputs. It is true that adoption of modern technologies requires costly adjustments in production strategies. The recommended technologies usually require farmers to adopt the complete package. They are intended to maximize yields to ensure livelihoods.

Techno-economic efficiency, more often than not, is viewed in an isolated and fragmented manner rather than holistically. Fish cultivation in pond or tank may be uneconomical when viewed in isolation. The farmers are concerned with maximizing net value from all activities and not from one activity alone. Fisheries are maintained by fish farmers not for their economic utility (like fish), but also for social (individual, social prestige, collective orientation, religious and cultural reasons). Economic efficiency as a sole criterion is not sufficient for understanding of sustainable livelihood issue. A holistic framework also encompassing social, cultural and religious dimensions provides for better understanding of sustainability issues.

There is no doubt that the fish production has been a traditional enterprise in our study area. In the past it was practised thoroughly with traditional methods. But during the last few years, precisely after launching of FFDA (Fish Farmers' Development Authority) programmes, certain steps were taken by the fish farmers to adopt modern culture practices.[1] It is of interest now to examine the response of operators to the package of intensive culture practices over time and then to identify the factors that determine the adoption behaviour. In this study, we define adopter-operators as those operators (or fish farmers) who adopt the practices like pre-stocking, stocking, input applications like lime, toxicants, manures, fertilizers, application of supplementary fish feeds, harvesting etc.[2]

Exhibit 7.1 provides an overview of the trend with regard to adoption of practices in the districts by size classes of operators, trained and untrained and receiving and not receiving assistance of any kind from different sources. The percentage of operators of the water units of different size-classes who received training and assistance adopting the package of practices are found to be 37.22 per cent and 38.89 per cent in 2001 and 2005 respectively, indicating thereby that the pace of adoption is not very satisfactory. As against this, only 17.5 per cent and 15.83 per cent of the operators (untrained and did not receive any government assistance) have so far used package of practices in 2001 and 2005 respectively. Again, it is important to note that there has been a marginal decline in adoption behaviour of those farmers who are not trained but received assistance. In other words, the percentage of the fish farmers, adopting culture practices decreases from 3.89 per cent to 3.61 per cent from 2001 to 2005. However, no change was witnessed in the cases of those fish farmers who neither were trained nor received any kind of assistance.

The Exhibit also makes an interesting reading as far as a comparison of the level of adoption by size-class is concerned. An upward movement of the adoption of modern culture practices was also registered by those fish farmers, belonging to small size-class, trained and received assistance from 34.48 per cent to 36.01 per cent to all the small fish farmers surveyed during the year 2001 and 2005. Interestingly enough, there has been also an upward trend in the adoption behaviour even of those small fish farmers who received neither training nor assistance of any kind i.e. an increase from 44.44 per cent to 44.82 per cent during the same period.

Here also, we employ test of association to examine whether training and Government loan-subsidy programme have got any association with the behaviour of the practice of adoption of modern culture practices. Also quite naturally, the degree of association between the attributes—(i) training and adoption, (ii) financial assistance and adoption—are found to be +0.28 and +0.32 respectively.

Certain interesting observations are in order.

One, the package of practices appealed to those fish farmers who are trained and reasonably backed by financial assistance by way of loan/grant with or without any provision of subsidy.

Two, training alone by itself may not necessarily stimulate all the fish farmers, particularly small and medium sized farmers to go in for modern culture practices. Other complementary factors like financial assistance may act as a positive factor.

Three, over a period of time, the fish farmers, particularly the medium sized farmers, tend to practise the modern culture practices through receiving the information/knowledge from the other fish farmers. In our study area, it was also observed that even the small farmers are found to become enthusiastic to internalize the externalities of efficient production system taking place elsewhere in other water units.

It is generally observed that when a technology is introduced in a given area, the choices available to farmers are not just adoption or rejection, as many researchers think. Selection of some parts of a technology or modifications and re-inventions may be options too. Farmers' choice whether to adopt an entire package of a recommended technology or just some parts of a technology is influenced by different factors. They are:

- The availability of household resources such as land, labour, cash income, knowledge and other inputs like fertilizers, water seed. If the above resources are forthcoming from the existing farming systems, farmers are likely to adopt a complete package of a recommended technology. If on the other hand, the resources are insufficient or sufficient but have alternative uses, farmers are more inclined to adopt some parts of a recommended package of a technology.
- The degree to which the technology is appropriate for the farmer's farming environment. If some parts of a technology conflict with the existing environment, there is a likelihood that those parts may not be adopted. On the other hand, if a recommended technology is compatible with the existing farming environment, it is more likely that the entire package will be adopted.

- Economic motivation—If a technology is perceived to be profitable, an entire package of the recommended technology is likely to be adopted. If, otherwise, it is unlikely to be adopted.
- Farmer's characteristics (e.g., belief and gender) Women farmers, unlike men, frequently lack access to both information and technology inputs and this affects their adoption behaviour.
- The farmer's objective to undertake the activity. If a technology is undertaken to spread risk or diversify food and income generation, some parts of a recommended technology are likely to be adopted, contrary to when a technology is adopted for profit maximization. Actions of farmers in managing risk in fish farming include diversification, allocate fewer resources in the activity, operate ponds or tanks in groups and produce fish arbitrarily for meeting domestic requirements only and hence tend to stock at low density.

One important observation in this regard is that most of the fish farmers, even though they tend to adopt, did not use the inputs in accordance with proportions and schedules recommended by the technical experts. They normally chose only those combinations of inputs that suited their resource position best.

It is widely stated that the fish farming involves the use of certain 'cultural practices' to obtain the maximum yield. The tank for fish culture should be neither too deep nor too shallow. If the seasonal tanks dry up during the summer months, lime is required to be applied on the bed. Better results in terms of yield will be achieved if exotic carps like silver carps, grass carps etc. are cultivated along with the indigenous carps like Rahu, Katla and Mrigal. The weed and predatory fishes should be eliminated. Toxicants like Mohua oil cake are normally recommended for use because, by its poisoning effect, it eliminates all undesirable elements and simultaneously acts as manure. Aside from naturally available food chain in the tank, for normal growth, additional food chain in the form of supplementary feeds like rice-bran, wheat-bran, etc. should be given. It follows that intensive composite fish culture involves a high degree of skill.

But it is observed that fish culture is practised in a very neglected and arbitrary manner. Only a small percentage of the adopter-operators in our sample have been found to follow strictly the uses of inputs in accordance with the schedules and doses. In the sample studied, only 7 per cent of the adopter-operators followed preparatory operations like de-weeding, desilting and eradication of predators and weed fishes. Only 4 per cent cultivators used toxicants; 57 per cent of the water had weeds and only 5 per cent of the water units were renovated. The species-mix in seed and the stocking rate—the two major determinants of yield—were not strictly followed. Only 10 per cent of the operators had utilized optimal species-mix in seed and appropriate stocking rate; 28 per cent of the area operated adopted composite fish culture. The operators liberated different species of carps without maintaining right proportions. They could not procure quality fish seed. It was also reported that the average survival from spawn to fry stage is about 30 per cent which is very low. Netting and soil testing were seldom done. It is also to be noted that use of fertilizers and supplementary feed, which indicates the inability of the users to bear higher cash expenses for cultivation and their ability to bear risk, was not made properly. Only 10 per cent of the adopter-operators were found to follow the suggestions made in this regard. Manures for maintaining healthy atmosphere in tank were seldom given. Organic manures were used by about 70 per cent of the operators (the most common being cow dung). Unfortunately, it is also observed that about 95 per cent of the fish farmers in our sample fed their fish irregularly. The most commonly reported fish feed were rice-bran, leftover cooked rice or fresh cow dung, etc. All these findings lend credence to the fact that the level of technology adoption is inadequate, and the input-mix is sub-optimal.

7.1 Constraints behind Unsatisfactory Adoption

As to why fish farmers are tardy in adopting package of practices becomes clear from the information given in Exhibit 7.1. Perhaps the most important reason for non-adoption is the financial difficulties. A sizeable percentage of operators (55%) have reported this problem. Risk factor and failure to provide extension services to provide information also account for the non-adoption. About 64 per cent of the operators consider risk factor as a deterrent for adoption. To sum up, the data reveal that the major causes for non-adoption are the perception of risk factor, cost factor (or financial difficulties) and lack of information.

Risk involved in adopting intensive practices is greater in the sense that it increases proportionately along with an increase in the cost of cultivation. Again, why some operators perceive higher risk in adopting modern practices entailing high costs may be that, in terms of yield, their performance falls much below expectations for various reasons. Consequently, while costs mount up, benefits remain low; the apprehensions about risk and loss thus become real.

Exhibit 7.1: Reasons for Non-adoption of Package of Practices

Financial Difficulties	*Lack of Availability of Quality Fish Seed on Time*	*Plurality of Ownership*	*Risk Factor*	*Lack of Proper Extension Services*	*High Price Spread*	*Percentage Reporting Combination*
1	2	3	4	5	6	7
*	*	*	*	*	*	41
*	*	*	*		*	18
*	*		*			10
*						8
						15
60	15	18	74	5	5	100

Note : Figures indicate percentage of farmers reporting this problem.
Source : Field Survey, 2005-06.

As regards biological and environmental hazards, it is important to note that though initially unwanted predatory fishes or animals can be removed, they may reappear. This poses serious biological hazards. Another serious problem in regard to algal blooms occurring in the ponds is that it creates 'super-saturation' in oxygen levels during day and oxygen 'depletion' during night. This sometimes leads to mass mortality. The 'fear psychosis' of possible occurrence of fish diseases among fish farmers coupled with the lack of fish hospitals is an impediment.

7.2 Ranking of Constraints behind Adoption of Practices

Let us now endeavour to examine the perceptions of the fish farmers about the constraints that hinder higher yield and adoption of modern culture practices. The operators were asked through an open-ended questionnaire to indicate the constraints, which, according to them, were responsible for unsatisfactory yield and low adoption and rank the constraints according to their degree of importance. The constraints ranked 1, 2, 3, 4, 5, 6, 7, 8, 9 and 10 and were given weights 10, 9, 8, 7, 6, 5, 4, 3, 2, 1 respectively. The total rank score for each factor is obtained multiplying the frequency with their respective weightage and adding them up. The constraints were then arranged in ascending order of importance on the basis of total rank score and finally ranked. The total rank score has been given in the parentheses against each item in Exhibit 7.2.

Exhibit 7.2: Constraints According to their Importance

Sl. No.	*Problem Areas*	*Rank (Total Score)*
1.	Lack of easily available and sufficient finance in time	1 (358)
2.	Plurality of ownership: absentee ownership	2 (347)
3.	Erratic supply/inadequate availability of quality	5 (287)
4.	Fish seeds fry/fingerlings in time	4 (307)
5.	High cost of inputs/Adulteration of inputs	6 (275)
6.	Lack of technical knowledge, know-how and training	7 (248)
7.	Lack of contact with extension personnel	9 (198)
8.	Lack of arrangement for soil and water testing at farm level, netting facilities	10 (174)
9.	High price spread	8 (210)
10.	Poaching, theft by unauthorized persons	3 (320)

Source : Compiled from Questionnaire.

It is quite evident from Exhibit 7.2 that non-availability of adequate financial assistance is still the most important deterrent factor perceived by a large proportion of the farmers (ranked 1 by the fish farmers). They were concerned with the sufficient amount of credit to be released on time and available easily. The operators also perceived the assured supply of quality fish seeds and fingerlings at reasonable rates at the time of stocking as an important problem (Rank 5). Multiple ownerships of water units also emerged as a problem. The operators ranked it as second. The phenomena of absentee ownership and location of the water units are also considered as a problem. Ponds situated at varying distances between each other and far from the fish farmers' houses may act as a disincentive.

Poaching is also considered as a major inhibiting factor. Poaching or deliberate poisoning due to rivalry, jealousy or enmity is widespread.[3] Fish lifting is taking place particularly in those water bodies, where there is controversy over ownership rights or situated far from residences. There are also instances that villagers sometimes do not care to understand the proprietary rights or ownership of ponds where they have free access to water units for different purposes. This leads to temptation for poaching where the water units have good stock of quality fish. Other problems which all other operators considered important are lack of training and extension facilities, lack of transport and marketing facilities, non-availability of opportunities for soil and water testing, netting facilities, etc. In short, the fish farmers recognized institutional as well as technological or infrastructural problems as constraints.[4]

The important conclusion to be drawn from the study is that farmers' access to information about a technology, economic motivation and resources endowment are important in adoption of a recommended package of fish farming technology. The results demonstrate clearly that farmers allocate resources to those activities, which meet household needs, more than others. (Wetengere 2010—Deternants of Adoption of a recommended package of Fish farming technology in Advance Journal of Food Science and Technology 2(1) January 2010.

7.3 Case Study

Our field observations reveal the characteristics of the individual family that facilitated or inhibited adoption of technology. From several individual case studies, we are able to decipher that it is the security of the family's livelihood systems as a whole that played in determining role in adopting technology. It is also important to recognize that the livelihood security is to be understood from the farmer's perspective and not from ours. We cannot afford to view things in our own perspective and impose our solutions on the farmers. This realization is crucial as farmer's own perception of livelihood security determines their decision-making behaviour. It provides the one-to-one correspondence between technology adoption and their perception of livelihood security. Therefore, sometimes, it is maintained that livelihood security is a subjective concept. (For example, a fish farmer's perception of food and other security is his/her own assessment of whether he/she will be able to support the family's food and other requirements for a year from the production/income he can earn/controls/manages/monitors. It varies from family to family at a given time and from time to time for a given family. Despite its subjective nature, livelihood security threshold is a powerful indicator that determines who are likely to adopt new technologies and who are not (Hiremath *et al.,* 2004 pp. 95-97).

The case studies were conducted in three villages—Mol Danga (Birbhum), Haripur (Malda) and Rainagar (Bankura), West Bengal. The first two villages are caste-based villages and the third is a tribal village. In each of the villages, there was some development intervention by outside institutions. Selection of individual family case studies were based on, among other considerations, like landholding size, education level, caste, awareness level etc. This would provide diversity of backgrounds in the study of decision making behaviour of fish farmers with respect to technology adoption and farm management.

One

The case study analysis of Rahim Mandal, a fish farmer in the village of Mol Danga in Birbhum District of West Bengal, illustrates the multifaceted considerations of a farmer in arriving at a decision to adopt modern fish farming technology to augment production so as to ensure secure livelihood.

Rahim (56) is the head of a joint family with 11 members. Rahim perceives that his family is above the livelihood security threshold. He has small mud house on one of the elevations. He has also constructed a house for other family members. Rahim is a religious person who encourages the people to speak the truth, avoid superstitions, maintain peace at home and be self-reliant. He did not accept bride price in the marriage. He also propagates not to accept bride price. Like others in the village, he has a strong attachment towards the ancestral land and ponds and tanks. He does not have the desire to leave the village. Rahim owns a small plot of land and two ponds. He owns two bullocks, one cow and 3 goats. He has a small kitchen garden near his house, where he grows vegetables to meet his family needs. Rahim is innovative, open-minded and co-operative by nature. He likes to discuss and analyse the pros and cons of new technology with others in the village before going in for adopting. He believes that joint family is crucial for undertaking the kind of labour-intensive operations that at times fish cultivation warrants. In the event of failure or crisis, Rahim believes, the system is a real cushion to fall back upon.

To have a proper understanding of decision making behaviour of a fish farmer like Rahim, it is pertinent to take care of the background that facilitate in his decision making. Among some other projects, the Fish Farmers' Development Agencies (FFDA) has provided a scope for Rahim to apply different inputs for enhancing production. It appears that before the introduction of this scheme, Rahim was exclusively confined to the production of fish by traditional methods.

Figure 7.1: Factors Contributing to Livelihood Security of Village.

Physical base	*Knowledge and Activity base*	*Emotional base*
Acre of land Lift irrigation Own traditional implements wood lot	Experience with vegetable crops Very few literate mostly 1 crop per year cash crop technology	Attached to traditional customs and value systems
Socio-Economic Base	*Family Base*	*Inner Human Space*
Major income from agriculture, fisheries. Joint family (labour force). Reduced migration.	Ancestral properties inherited food and fodder security	Innovative and open-minded Courageous Co-operative
Collective Orientation	*Family Orientation*	*Individual Orientation*
Prefers village life to city life Desirous to be active members of village co-operative and other local level committees	In love with nature Collective farming Opposed to bride-price Mind-set to try for self-reliant lifestyle	market-oriented adoption Respect family members' attitudes and values

Source : Compiled from Survey Data.

The cultivation was traditional and the use of inputs was minimal. But with FFDAs, certain shifts are observed:

- Adopted semi-intensive technology
- Change towards commercialization
- Increase application of fertilizers and other related inputs.

Precisely, in the case of Rahim, two changes are noticeable which impact positively towards income generation and, so ensure livelihood security. They are one: the interventions have provided job opportunities and two, it enabled to increase production—thus reducing risk and uncertainty and so, vulnerability. So, "Things have changed"—Rahim argues with confidence.

It is important to note that it must be purely economic reason that prompted him to go in for commercial fish cultivation for sustainable kind of livelihood. But if we look more closely, there are some other non-economic and non-physical factors that are more equally important. Economic and market forces are not the only deciding factors.

Two

This case study relates to Buddhhu Mahato (59). He is also the head of the family. He belongs to Nagar Community of Haripur village of Malda district, West Bengal. He explains various changes in the fishery cultivation since the days of his grandfather. Buddhhu has memories of his father. Buddhhu has three sons and two daughters. All the sons and daughters have already got married. His sons separated into nuclear families due to frictions among the brothers and their wives. Buddhhu narrated the history of the practices of fish cultivation followed by his father and grandfather. As a son, Buddhhu recognises his father as the role model and for all practical purposes, he has inclinations to adhere to the practices in traditional form followed by his ancestors in fish farming. Buddhhu's way of utilizing the inputs like fish seeds, fertilizer and chemical and management is predominantly tradition-bound. There was minor departure from the old system of practices. In fact, his attitude to adopt modern practices are very poor. He does not perceive fish production as the only means for livelihood. He has 2.5 acres of land. Buddhhu has one pond of 5.5 acres of water area inherited from his grandfather situated by the side of his homestead. This is used for varieties of purposes like cattle bathing, utensil washing etc. He cultivates varieties of crops on his land. He spends most of the time in this area. Fishery is looked upon as the minor/secondary source of income. Buddhhu is more interested in joint family system. Since fish cultivation involves labour input, he feels, joint family would be more effective. Changes in the physical base of Buddhhu have little effect on adoption of modern system of cultivation. He observed many changes in the commodity and factor markets.

Marketing of fish has become easier and hence, perhaps profitable. Even all these have marginally affected his approach towards fish cultivation. Certain important points are in order. Buddhhu's family is no more joint family. Because of relatively better agriculture, fishery is of less important for ensuring his food security. Economic profitability from fishery does not seem to be that attractive

Figure 7.2: Factors Contributing to Livelihood Security of Buddhhu .

Physical base Has only 2.6 acres of land Fertile land Availability of fertiliser	*Knowledge and Activity base* Use of farmyard manure	*Emotional base* attached to land High value for past practices
Socio-Economic Base No institutional credit delivery system No proper road connectivity	*Family Base* Weak Joint family	*Inner Human Space* desire of free independent attachment to traditions
Collective Orientation Strong community bondage Support when required for social activities Weak interactions with other farmers	*Family Orientation* Mutual support for constructive purpose Members are active	*Individual Orientation* Independent decision making

Source : Compiled from Survey Data.

to Buddhhu. Again, Buddhhu believes that the separation from the joint family provides more freedom in all respects.

Three

Raju Rai (45) is a tribal by caste. He is the head of the family with 2 sons and one daughter, living in a remote village of Bankura district. He is illiterate. But he sent his sons and daughter to the village school. They could not complete even primary education. Raju inherited a small plot of land of size about 1 acre and two small ponds located by the side of his house. His wife, Ramni, is very hard working and cooperative with her husband and other family members. The distinguishing feature of this family is that they all take decision about any kind of activity, including fishery through mutual discussion, Raju talks to his wife very clearly about the programme of activity. He is proud to say that his wife knows many things about fish cultivation. With her by his side, he takes the decision. He believes in nuclear family, true; as it provides more freedom. But he has strong conviction about the supportive role of all in the family. He does not believe in outside interventions; in this sense, he has the spirit of self-confidence and so, he is very courageous. He is honest and sincere.

Figure 7.3: Factors Contributing to Livelihood Security of Buddhhu.

Physical base Only 1 acre of land not that fertile 2 bullocks and 1 cow Some trees in his land	*Knowledge and Activity base* Illiterate Exposure to many ideas	*Emotional base* Freedom for self
Socio-Economic Base No income from other sources No Government interventions Fair law and order condition	*Family Base* cooperative family members very positive cooperative wife interactions with children Mutual respect in the family	*Inner Human Space* tradition bound Belief in work ethics To reciprocate ideas and inputs
Collective Orientation Family ties in village Mutual trust and discussion	*Family Orientation* A nuclear family Wife holds prominent position	*Individual Orientation* Open minded honest Optimism in decision taking To prioritize fishery Self-reliant, hardworking

Source : Compiled from Survey Data.

He believes that agriculture alone could not provide food security to all members in the family. He recognizes fishery as the most viable option to fall back upon in the event of stringent situations arising out of crop failure. Raju along with other family members in traditional customs and values.

7.4 Livelihood system is more than just a set of physical and economic preconditions for survival. It requires psycho-social dimensions of experience of living. As it appears, the livelihood systems are made up of diverse elements which taken together constitute physical, economic, social and cultural universe within which the families live. Livelihood security encompasses food security, social security and psychological security. Each of these has a basic minimum threshold level to be achieved and maintained and each must be pursued in balance with the others. Security of livelihood would then become a notion that has to be understood in a holistic way (Hiremath *et al.*, 2004).

Notes

1. In 2001, an evaluation study was made by the department. Data were available from the CEOs of FFDA of the respective districts. Our survey has been conducted in 2008.
2. Practices considered include de-weeding of ponds, use of fertilizers and fish seed, mohua oil cake, new varieties of seed, extension guidance etc.
3. Ponds are situated at varying distances between each other and far from the cultivator's houses. As the ponds or tanks in the study area have more than one owner, the sum of distances between them and houses will also tend to increase. It poses the problem for effective supervision and increment of time and distance cost. The farmers also seek to ward-off losses and ensure income stability. Under these circumstances, the farmers want to concentrate on those ponds situated nearby. *See* Michael Chislom's "Rural Settlement and Land Use—An Essay on Location", Hutchison's University Press, London (1962) Chapter 4.
4. Unlike any other agricultural crops, where the same is ready for harvesting for a short while, fish is ready for harvesting throughout the period of culture.

8

Evaluating Government Policies

8.1 Government Initiatives in the Past

There is no planning for the development of fisheries immediately after the independence. The State Government was more concerned with the refugee and political problems of the state. But it was almost impossible for government to remain silent about the shortage of foods created through the sudden growth of population in the state. So the Government adopted a policy to increase the food production called "Grow More Food Campaign" (from 1948-49). Under the campaign (1948-52), West Bengal Government had undertaken few schemes to increase the fish production of the state, such as (i) development of beel fisheries, (ii) distribution of capital goods among the needy fishermen; (iii) development of tank fishery; etc. A total cost of 85,55,700 was estimated to be spent within four years (1948-52) with a target of extra production of 10,00,000 *monds* of fish. But the performance of this plan was very much unsatisfactory.

India entered into a new stage of development with the beginning of planned economy in 1952. The first five years plan (1951-52 to 1955-56) for West Bengal had allotted Rs. 154.47 lakhs for the development of fisheries. This plan has stressed on tank fishery development scheme and improvement of tank fisheries with plan provisions of Rs. 22.80 lakhs and Rs. 25 lakhs respectively. Under the inland fisheries development schemes, only 38.27 per cent of total scheme provisions were utilized. In spite of limitation of the first five-year plan and drawbacks in the schemes relating to development of fisheries of West Bengal, considerable amount of water area have been brought under the condition of pisciculture.

Second Five Year Plan (1956-57 to 1960-61) had drastically reduced the total plan provision for the development of fisheries. Only Rs 78 lakhs have been allotted for the development of the fisheries of the state, which was just 50 per cent of the First Five Year Plan. The progress of fishery development under the Second Plan was very slow. It could utilize only 35.37 per cent of the total plan provision. So the new schemes undertaken during the Second Plan were not properly implemented.

In spite of budget curtail in the Second Five Year Plan (1962-63 to 1965-66) had proposed Rs. 204.83 to be spent for the development of fisheries of West Bengal. Total 23 schemes had been taken up during the third plan of which nine were the continuation of the Second Five Year Plan. In this plan, main emphasis was to the co-operative of the fishermen, co-operative farms and co-operative fisheries. Development of large derelict fisheries (19.94 lakh), establishment; establishment of seed farms (12 lakh); setting up of co-operatives of the capture and culture fisheries (19.80 lakhs) were other important areas of investments. It is to be noted that during the plan period, two government corporations have been set up to solve the fish crisis of the state.

Like the previous plans, progress of the third plan was also very much unsatisfactory. Only Rs. 128.41 lakhs had been utilized of which only Rs. 15 lakhs had been spent for the foundation of the Central Fisheries Corporation (CFS) and West Bengal State Fisheries Development Corporation (WBSFDC) respectively. So the actual expenditure under this plan was Rs. 98.41 for the development of the fisheries, which was only 46.21 per cent of the total.

The Fourth Five Year Plan (1969-70 to 1973-74) had proposed a sizable amount of Rs. 295.29 lakhs to be spent for the development of fisheries. Few new schemes were adopted. Development of derelict fisheries, intensive development of fisheries, establishment of quality seed farms, assisting the needy fishermen and establishment of State Fisheries Development Corporation got priority in this plan. But most of the schemes could not reach to their goals because allotted amount had remained unspent.

But it was recognized that the fish crisis of West Bengal could not be solved permanently without long-term perspective. So there was a need of long-term plan both for increasing fish production and development of the social status of the fishermen. Thus, in 1972, West Bengal Government have decided to appoint a committee, which would prepare a master plan for all-round development of fisheries of the state including socio-economic upliftment of the traditional fishermen of the state. By a resolution (no. 2463 fish, dated July 19, 1972) West Bengal Government appointed a "Master Plan Committee" under the chairmanship of Dr. Santi Kumar Dasgupta with total 15 members including two representatives of fishermen communities. The master plan committee submitted its *ad interim* report on December 5, 1973 which identified that the fish produced in the state could only meet 50 per cent of the total demand. The *ad interim* report also recommended that the control of the government over the fisheries is essential for the introduction of the modern pisciculture in order to increase the production of fish. The committee submitted its final report in 1975 with some recommendations for the overall development of the fisheries and fish production. Its major recommendations were—

All freshwater ponds and tanks of the state are to be brought under fish culture. No water could be left fallow or unutilized. This may be brought about by making utilization of water for pisciculture obligatory on the part of pond owners. The ownership of such ponds and tanks where fish culture is not practiced for three successive years may be acquired by the government by equipping itself with suiExhibit legislative powers. Water areas acquired in such a manner may be leased out to deserving fishermen cooperatives, individual entrepreneurs and trained unemployed youths in order of preference. Fish culturists may be given assistance by the State Government for undertaking the development work in their ponds and tanks. Institutional finance may be made available for that purpose.

Organization of village fish farming units was strongly recommended by the committee: (i) to encourage intensive fish culture in all village tanks of all districts; (ii) to give employment to village youths and fishermen; (iii) to supply fish to local markets; and (iv) to popularize fish culture as a profitable profession among unemployed youths and fishermen.

As the success of any intensive fish culture mainly depends on the availability and distribution of high quality seed of all quick growing species like fish, the committee feels the need of setting up of fish seed farms in each block of the state having fisheries potential.

The objectives of such farms will be (i) to raise and supply high quality fingerlings of Indian major carps, and quick growing species exotic fishes; (ii) to maintain a pituitary bank; (iii) to provide extensive service to all fish farmers in their fish culture operation. Each farm has to be organized in such a way so as to provide all necessities, viz., seed, inputs and modern technology of fish culture to all fish farmers of the block.

The committee recommended that changes are to be made in rent fixation, terms and conditions of lease demarcation of leased out waters and so on. The strategy should be lease out water bodies on long-term basis, for not exceeding 10 years particularly.

For the credit facilities and technical assistance for pisciculture, the committee recommended for the establishment of 'Fish Farmers Development Agencies' (FFDA) in each district of the state. This will "integrate and coordinate the relevant activities, viz. (i) to provide training to select persons interested in fish culture; (ii) to assist them in securing suitable water resources for undertaking development; (iii) to assist in securing institutional finances or Government loans for necessary investments, to arrange for technical support; and (iv) to arrange for supply of fish seeds and other inputs.

The recommendations of the Master Plan Committee were no doubt wise and capable to solve the contemporary fish crisis. However, it has also been felt that the plan prepared by the committee required a long time for its proper implementation. In the next Five Year Plans, those recommendations had been tried to be implemented. Following the recommendations, the Fish Farmer's Development Agency (FFDA) had been established in 1989.

8.2 Government Policies during Tenth Plan

Under the macro management approach, various schemes in the fisheries sector were launched under central assistance during the Tenth Plan. The schemes include (i) development of freshwater aquaculture; (ii) development of waterlogged areas into aquaculture estates; and (iii) utilization of alkaline/saline soils for aquaculture. The central assistance of Rs. 135 crore was proposed to various States/UTs to develop inland fisheries and aquaculture across the country. The anticipated expenditure during the plan is 57 per cent. Under the schemes of the Central Government, 1.3 lakh hectare area was brought under improved practices of fish culture and 1.3 lakh fishers were imparted training in aquaculture practices. Through this programme, more than 81 per cent targeted areas have been brought under aquaculture. The lower fund utilization was mainly due to inability of the states to provide their share of allocation. The central assistance pattern of the schemes was examined critically and the utilization levels were assessed along with the factors contributing to the observed levels. The general suggestion is to enhance the central share to 90 per cent, so that the states need to contribute only 10 per cent, instead of present pattern of 75:25.

8.3 Fish Farmers Development Authorities (FFDAs)

In recent years, Government of West Bengal has been extending several facilities for expansion of culture fisheries, such as fish seed supply at cheaper rate, subsidy for renovation of tanks as also some welfare measures like Group Personal Accident Insurance, saving cum-relief scheme, social fishery, river ranching etc.[1] Along with these, FFDAs have been established to help the fish farmers with necessary financial, technological and extension support in order to increase fish production in tanks and ponds by composite fish culture practices. The main objective of the scheme is to provide the much needed field mechanism to popularize composite fish culture among the fish farmers and co-ordinate the activities of different institutionalized agencies in inland fishery development programmes. The focus is basically on creating a demonstration effect through individuals where success of one fish farmer could motivate others to take up fish farming. This called for—

- Progressively bringing all the fallow culture fish resources under optimum fish production in the area of its operation;
- Training and popularizing a new vocation of fish culture;
- Organizing the FFDAs to serve as a nucleus for spreading fish farming in other areas; and
- Strengthening the rural economy by making fish farming economically viable.

Chart 8.1 depicts the broad functions of FFDAs.

According to the data provided by Ministry of Agriculture, Department of Animal Husbandry and Dairing, the FFDAs have been successful so far in bringing some of the derelict/semi-derelict

Figure 8.1: Functions of FFDAs.

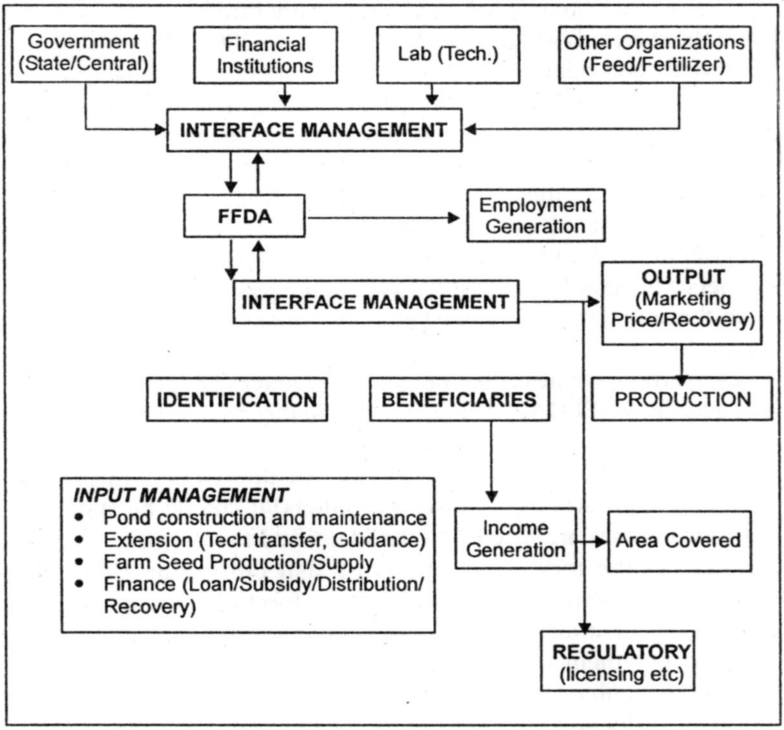

Source : Evaluation Study of FFDAs Programme for Fresh Water Aquaculture, CMA, IIM, Ahmedabad, Dec. 1990, p. 6.

water bodies. A total 18 FFDAs are working in the state, that have brought 2.05 lakh hectare water area under scientific pisciculture and have trained 3.83 lakh fish farmers in the state (*see* Exhibit 8.6). The average productivity of FFDA tanks and ponds in our state is 2685 kg/ha/yr, which is higher than the national average (2216 kg/ha/yr).

Along with this, the micro finance programme in West Bengal has made rapid strides in recent years. Since 2003-04, 1594 SHGs under SGSY have been taken up economic activities in fisheries sector.

It was observed that even though traditional fish culture is still practised in different parts of the State, intensive fish culture technology has started being adopted by quite a large number of fish farmers in the villages.

Some interesting observations are in order from the data collected from the selected fish farmers during the year 2006. In the first place, yields per acre under different types of practices—traditional practices, semi-intensive practices (those who are not FFDA beneficiaries but practise intensive culture) and intensive practices (those who are FFDA beneficiaries and also practise intensive culture) in 2005 are much higher than those in 1989 (The year 1989 is considered, as it was the year of initiation of training for fish farmers under FFDA programme in West Bengal). It is asserted that yield per acre for those farmers who have followed intensive culture practices are much higher than those under semi-intensive or traditional practices in different years. Secondly, yield per acre is gradually increasing at different rates overtime whatever be the type of practices adopted. And, yield per acre under FFDA scheme is much higher than yield under non-FFDA scheme.

The FFDAs deal with a package of approaches to promote intensive fish farming in tanks and ponds. It should be stated that training courses are offered to the identified fish farmers. They are trained on the modern methods of fish culture and fish farm management. Trained farmers' field of information is superior. This superiority of information reduces the risk element in innovation and induces them to adopt new techniques and new inputs. That is, training enhances innovative and allocative efficiency of the farmers to decode information, to evaluate benefit and cost and quickly allocate resources in a cost-efficient manner. Again, in close-knit village communities, fish farmers may have interactions with those farmers who have already received training. The emulation of their methods would be an externality of training. It is true that training in fish farming technologies have induced fish farmers and created employment opportunity. Trained persons have been able to create a new cadre of fish farmers. The changes in the yield, if any, in the water units cultivated by the trained farmers are given in the Exhibit 8.1.

Exhibit 8.1: Practice-wise Distribution of Change in Yield of the Trained Fish Farmers during the years 1989, 1994 and 2005

Year	*Yield Per Acre (in kg)*		
	Traditional Practices	*Semi-intensive Practices*	*Intensive Practices*
1989	458	459	584
1994	582	687	872
2005	609	713	947

Source : Field Survey, 2008.

Note : The year 1989 is considered, as it was the year of initiation of training for fish farmers under FFDA programme in West Bengal.

Yield per acre has significantly increased in the water units of those operators who have received training. The extent to which yields have increased after receiving training may be due, at least in part, to the qualitative improvement in farmer's entrepreneurial ability resulting from the training programme. We have employed the test of association developed by Yule in order to examine whether yield and training programmes are independent attributes. The coefficient of association is found to be positively associated. This exercise leads us to the conclusion that the relationship between training and yield (in other words, use of cultural practices—a proxy for innovations)[2] is quite satisfactory during the period under consideration. Interestingly enough, it is also observed that the idea of adoption of scientific culture has penetrated to and motivated, to some extent, some of those families which did not receive any training whatsoever. It is a reflection of the externality of training.

8.4 Training and Assistance in Culture Practices

But it could also be mentioned that the coverage of training is still not very extensive or adequate and training programme has not taken its roots. Some of the trained fish farmers reported some deficiencies in the system.[3] Exhibit 8.2 states the responses of the respondents in this regard. It transpires that 63 per cent of the trained farmers reported inadequacy of the training programme because of short duration and non-inclusion of practical aspects and course contents being non-comprehensive. At least 15 per cent of the respondents reported the lack of practical demonstration programme in the system.

Another important component of the programme is the extension programme[3]. The extension programme may serve as a catalytic agent in the diffusion process. Extension agents are supposed to preach the benefits of a new farm technology and this promise is expected to be heard and acted upon by most of the innovative farmers. This is instrumental in creating awareness among the farmers to shift from traditional to modern intensive pisciculture. Motivation of the tradition-bound farmers demands a band of well-groomed committed extension personnel. It should be stated that there are few extension employees who are used to propagate the ideas about technology.

Exhibit 8.2: Summary of the suggestions of the Respondents regarding Training Programme

Inadequate Time Period	Course Content should be Revised	Practical Components Like Demonstration should be Included	Percentage Reporting Combination
1	2	3	4
*	*	*	63
*	*	*	15
*	*	*	0
			7
			0.5
50	48	44	100

Source : Field Survey, 2008.

The link between the technologies developed in the research institutes and their exposure to the extension personnel were very week. No systems were developed to facilitate constant interaction between the extension personnel and scientists for the continuous feedback. The extension software was also found inadequate. Most of the extension workers had their training just when they entered the services.

The operational features of the new technology should be examined against the backdrop of prevailing organizational basis of individual water units and pisciculture as a whole. The new technology is scale-neutral, no doubt; but two problems arise with the farmers in this context—one, as a proposition involving higher cost per acre and second, as a proposition involving more working capital than usual. In this context, there arises the question of financial support necessary to internalize the external economies. The Government of West Bengal through FFDA schemes has made arrangements for giving loans and subsidies to adopt modern intensive fish culture.

Exhibit 8.3 gives the distribution of fish farmers for whom assistance is needed by type of assistance.

From Exhibit 8.3, it is found that finance is the most important component of assistance needed in all the years. Technical advice and services are also another important component of assistance, which about 18 per cent of the farmers expressed desire to receive. Another important component of assistance, which the fish farmers desired to obtain, is the regular supply of quantity of inputs and arrangements for different infrastructural facilities.

Exhibit 8.3: Percentage Distribution of the Fish Farmers who needed and Received Assistance

Type of Assistance	*Percentage of the Fish Farmers*	
	Needed	*Received*
Finance	95	8
Technical advice/service	90	16
Supply of fish feed and other inputs	90	55
Others (marketing facilities)	100	2

Source : Field Survey, 2008.

But unfortunately, it is revealed from Exhibit 8.4 that only a small proportion of the fish farmers received a considerable assistance. In the case of finance, most of the fish farmers who were desperately in need of finance are, more often that not, deprived. Technical advice and marketing facilities leave much to be desired. Registered and regulated markets are found to be conspicuous by their absence.

As regards the reasons for the unsatisfactory availability of assistances, it is clear from Exhibit 8.4, for example, that quite a significant proportion of the fish farmers interviewed were not in the know of the programmes, even though twenty five per cent of the respondents applied and did not receive financial assistance respectively. Forty five per cent of the respondents did not even try for technical assistance or extension services, even though fish seed has been received and used by a large proportion of the fish farmers.

Exhibit 8.4: Percentage Distribution of the Fish Farmers—Not Receiving Assistance with Reasons thereof

Reasons	*Finance*	*Technical Advice/Extension Services*	*Quality Seed etc.*	*Marketing Facilities*
Did not know	30	30	30	40
Did not try	30	45	50	36
Tried but failed to receive	25	22	10	15
Reluctant to approach because of cumbersome procedure	35	28	20	19

Source : Field Survey, 2008.

The rest who did not receive was mainly because of the fact that they did not even try (37.5% of those who did not receive). Marketing facilities through appropriate network have not still developed. Again, cumbersome procedure for applying for receiving assistance also acts as a deterrent factor for the purpose of receiving different assistances from the Government agencies.

The study has identified gaps in information for the monitoring of sustainable livelihoods and policy requirements to work towards better management of the inland fishery sources and policy requirements to work towards better management. Government initiatives through policies and programmes for the welfare of the farmers seem to have had very limited impact. The study recognizes that it may have been better to build on the existing assets. When people control assets, whether they are educational, financial or natural resources, they have a sense of ownership, power and hope for the future that profoundly affects the way they conduct their lives.

This SLA focus in this study has helped to identify key strategies that households in pond-tank fish cultivation should follow. However, this research has not been able to cover all the areas that would have been helpful to better understand the complex socio-economic and political dynamics. Future research in this area would help identify policy spaces where interventions can be made through to shape the livelihood outcomes of the fish farmers.

8.5 Evaluation of Governmental Policies

It should be mentioned that there is a prospect of FFDAs in

facilitating intensive fish culture among the fish farmers and obviously, it created a positive impact.[4] Their role in training, demonstrating the attractiveness of pisciculture and arrangements of loans and seeds are found to be instrumental in motivating fish farmers for adoption and hence, increasing the production of fish. The FFDAs are based on decentralized planning ideas. The merits of the FFDAs are derived partly from its ability to discover the dormant resources and skills and endeavour to activate them. Its operative part is being carried out at a very fairly decentralized level—districts, blocks or a cluster of villages. It is true that it is essential to know the fish farmers, understand their social, economic and cultural disabilities and understand their local settings and institutions under which low productivity is generated and sustained before solutions can be conceived of and set into action.[5] The programme is required to be area or community specific, taking into account the different development potentials as well as constraints of each area or community. It is difficult to *tend a flock of sheep from the camel's back*. It is equally difficult to eliminate low productivity from the elevation of the central plan, however 'thorough and earnest'. From these points of view, it is expected that FFDAs would be very much effective. However, it has also been observed that it has left much to be desired. To ensure proper planning, adequate supervision, effective implementation and better monitoring, the FFDAs need to be re-evaluated.

In the first place, it should be stated that this programme, if it is to succeed completely, calls for the real identification of the beneficiaries. It appears from the survey that there exists a great scope for arbitrariness in the selection of beneficiaries. Secondly, the present operational pattern of linking of subsidy with the loan resulted in some unfortunate situation. This has, in fact, resulted in unscrupulous elements taking advantage of the 'subsidy' rather than the real purpose of improving the productivity. Cases of pocketing of subsidy by the bureaucrats, local political leaders and farmers are not infrequent. This needs rigorous monitoring of the schemes at every stage.[6]

Some of the alternative suggestions regarding subsidy may be that an amount may be deposited as fixed deposits in the beneficiaries' account and this could be adjusted after the completion of the repayment by the borrowers. Again, the benefits of subsidy should be linked with the timely repayment. An improvement in the close rapport and co-ordination among the FFDA units, the banks and the local panchayat officers involved in the system is essential.

Thirdly, the cumbersome loaning procedure is normally followed. This causes delays and difficulties in the sanction of loan. The transaction costs of loans, which include informal costs like frequent transportation costs for visiting block and bank officials are quite high. It may be suggested that fishery banks should be established in each block to advance loan well in advance at reasonable rate of interest. It is also observed that the money so borrowed for fish farming has been diverted to other purpose. In this context, it should be noted that if the bottlenecks in the production process dominate, the credit absorptive capacity may go down and the subsidized credit may very well get diverted to consumption purpose. The same consequences may follow here also if the credit does not cover the total requirements of consumption, working capital, etc.

Fourthly, it was also observed that sometimes the flows of credit disbursement are plagued. This is not only due to steadily rising overdue, but also due to, in many cases, faulty loan proposals, laxity in post-credit follow-up, lack of monitoring of end-use, lending without an integrated programme, etc.

In sum, it should be mentioned that credit should be adequate and on reasonable terms there is a need for closer supervision and follow-up to ensure proper end-use of credit; real investment should be backed by adequate infrastructural facilities so that potential income can be translated into actual; and the assets acquired through credit should generate incremental income, (i.e. sufficient to pay back the loan along with interest and still leave reasonable surplus).

Fifthly, FFDAs programmes which have yielded good results in many respects are target-oriented. Being target oriented and in the race to reach the target, benefits are sometimes literally passed on to the ineligibles. It was also observed that the staffs of the development administration were all obsessed with the idea of target achievement. Sometimes, banks are found reactive, instead of proactive. So, it is important to add that target should be fixed, keeping in view the availability of infrastructure and other facilities for optimal utilization of resources.

It is important to note that there has been a proliferation of organizations dealing with development activities like FFDAs, IRDPs, NRY, RLEGP etc. at the grass roots level. This sometime creates the problem of co-ordination, because they emerge as parallel ladders, each operating in its own style and jurisdiction. This also has resulted in certain negative consequences. That is, rural poor are made to go from pillar to post to have access to the benefits that policy offers to them; and agencies sometimes operate at cross-purposes neutralizing the development efforts. Political interferences also seep into every kind of activities here.[7]

On top of all these, the structure of Panchayati Raj or the Government by the local elective bodies began to totter under the heavy weight of political factionalism, scrambles for control over patronage among politicians and bureaucrats etc. A lot of tension was observed in the system due to conflicts and confrontations between politicians and bureaucrats. Again, in the context of rural power structure and week administrative set up, there is a lot of arbitrariness in the different activities. In an atmosphere of scarcity and unequal distribution of local resources, local officials are found to coalesce with rich cultivators. There are a large number of reported instances of bureaucratic malfeasance. Government officials should also learn how to curry favour with the rural elites.[8] It is not only the rural structure but also the behaviour and attitude of the functionaries that determine the performance and outcome of the different programmes like FFDAs. A certain amount of commitment and enthusiasm is required among the officials engaged in the task.

Appendices

Exhibit 8.5: Budget Utilization of Fisheries Sector during Tenth Five Year Plans

Items	*Amount (Rs. crore)*
Outlay	771.00
Expenditure till 2005-06	451.30
Anticipated expenditure 2006-07	157.00
Total expenditure	608.30
Anticipated % utilisation	78.90

Exhibit 8.6: Government Scheme in the Eleventh Five Year Plan

Description of Items	*Current Level of Assistance*	*Proposed Level of Assistance*
Construction of new ponds	Rs. 2 lakh per ha in the plain areas	Rs. 3 lakh per ha in the plain areas
	Rs. 3 lakh/ha in the hill States/Districts and North-Eastern region	Rs. 4.5 lakh/ha in the hill States/Districts and North-Eastern region
Reclamation/ Renovation of ponds/tanks	Rs. 60,000/ha	Rs. 90,000/ha
Cost of inputs	(i) Finfish Culture—-Rs. 30,000/ ha	(a) Finfish Culture—-Rs. 60,000/ha
	(ii) Freshwater prawn culture—Rs 1.2 lakh/ha	(b) Freshwater prawn culture—Unit cost Rs. 1.8 lakh/ha
Running water fish culture in hilly areas as well as in plain areas	Rs. 20,000/unit of 100 m^2. The above cost is inclusive of Rs. 4,000 towards inputs	Rs. 40,000/unit of 100 m^2. The above cost is inclusive of Rs. 8,000 towards inputs
Integrated fish farming	Rs. 80,000/ha	Rs. 1.20 lakh/ha
Aerators/ Pumps	Rs 50,000/unit of two—1 HP aerators/one 5HP diesel pump	Same as earlier
Freshwater fish seed hatchery	Rs. 8 lakh for a fish seed hatchery with 10 million (fry) capacity for the plain areas and Rs. 12 lakh for same capacity in the hill States/ Districts and North-Eastern Region	Rs. 12 lakh for a fish seed hatchery with 10 million (fry) capacity for the plain areas and Rs. 16 lakh for same capacity in the hill States/ Districts and North-Eastern Region

(Contd.)

(Contd.)

Description of Items	*Current Level of Assistance*	*Proposed Level of Assistance*
Fish feed units	Small Units—Unit cost is Rs. 5 lakh with a capacity of 1.2 quintals /day	Small Units — Unit cost is Rs. l0 lakh with a capacity of 1.2 quintals /day
Training of fish farmers	Stipend @ Rs. 100 per day during training period of 10 days and a lump sum of Rs. 100 towards travel expenses/field visits	Stipend @ Rs. 200 per day during training period of 10 days and a lump sum of Rs. 1,000 towards travel expenses/field visits
Establishment of freshwater prawn seed hatchery	(i) Unit cost of Rs. 30 lakh for a large freshwater prawn hatchery with a minimum capacity of 25 million PL/year	(i) Same as earlier
	(ii) Unit cost is Rs. 8 lakh for a small hatchery of 5-10 million PL/year capacity	(ii) Unit cost is Rs. l5 lakh for a small hatchery of 5-10 million PL/year capacity
Establishment of laboratories at State level for water quality and fish health investigations	Unit cost of Rs. 30 lakh (Rs. 25 lakh for the construction of building and Rs. 5 lakh for equipment, glassware and chemicals, etc.)	Unit cost of Rs. 35 lakh (Rs. 25 lakh for the construction of building and Rs. 10 lakh for equipment, glassware and chemicals, etc.)
Provision of soil and water testing kits to each FFDA	Unit cost of each soil and water testing kit at Rs. 30,000. The kits are sanctioned once to each FFDA as one time grant	Unit cost of each soil and water testing kit at Rs. 1,00,000. The kits are sanctioned once to each FFDA as one time grant
Setting up of integrated units, including hatcheries for ornamental fishes	Unit cost is Rs. 15 lakh, which include hatchery of 5-10 m (fry) capacity	Same as earlier
Brood banks for ornamental fishes	Not existing	Rs. 25 lakh per unit including a farm, transport arrangements for dissemination

Ornamental fish seed certification units	Not existing	Rs. 25 lakh per unit including fish holding facilities and disease diagnostic laboratories
Transportation of fish/prawn seed	This will be applicable only for the hill states/districts and North-eastern region	Same as earlier
	Subsidy @ Rs. 20 for 1000 fry transported to all FFDAs. Not applicable to individual fish fanners	Subsidy @ Rs. 50 for 1,000 fry transported to all FFDAs. Not applicable to individual fish farmers
Purchase of vehicle	50 per cent cost of vehicle for each new FFDA and 50 per cent cost for the replaced vehicle (Second vehicle)	Same as earlier

Note: Existing expenditure on all the above items except purchase of vehicles is shared on 75:25 basis by the Centre and States, which is proposed to be on 90:10 basis, respectively barring vehicles. The above assistance under FFDA programme is available only once to a beneficiary. These are Subsidy for the construction of new ponds and tanks. Reclamation/renovation of ponds/tanks and first year inputs to an individual beneficiary up to 5 ha is available with or without institutional finance in the plain areas and 1.0 ha in the hill States/Districts on pro rata basis.

Source: DAHD & F, 2004b & modified.

Exhibit 8.7: Details of Fish Farmers Development Agencies

Sl. No.	State/UTs	No. of FFDAs	Water Area Covered (ha)	Fish Farmers Trained (Nos.)	No. of Benefi-ciaries	Average Producti-vity (kg/ha/yr)
1.	Andhra Pradesh*	22	4,120	11,927	5,805	3,500**
2.	Arunachal Pradesh	2	824	3,500	4,907	1,100
3.	Assam	23	4,522	22,882	13,190	1,750
4.	Bihar	33	25,290	30,459	33,773	2,180
5.	Goa	1	-	-	-	-
6.	Gujarat	21	61,322	25,886	17,583	1,040
7.	Haryana	18	13,948	16,055	17,547	3,730
8.	Himachal Pradesh	2	573	5,560	2,523	2,800
9.	Jammu & Kashmir	2	9,162	4,443	4,614	3,000
10.	Karnataka	18	54,564	15,875	11,161	3,417
11.	Kerala	14	28,177	25,058	83,458	1,465
12.	Madhya Pradesh	38	81,773	40,461	91,984	1,360
13.	Maharashtra	29	27,487	17,076	61,618	1,135
14.	Manipur	8	2,909	4,853	8,773	2,400
15.	Meghalaya	2	798	2,067	2,067	1,500
16.	Mizoram	5	1,310	7,326	5,327	3,000
17.	Nagaland	8	2,998	3,915	16,931	1,800
18.	Orissa	30	37,326	48,552	134,721	2,390
19.	Punjab	17	17,515	22,982	14,493	6,094
20.	Rajasthan**	15	7,637	11,604	7,537	1,447
21.	Sikkim	1	181	1,345	1,634	3,500
22.	Tamil Nadu	17	23,255	7,792	13,690	1,000
23.	Tripura	4	10,023	1,02,678	48,951	2,200
24.	Uttar Pradesh	53	1,11,265	11,3986	107,751	2,550
25.	West Bengal	18	1,16,483	20,5225	383,640	2,685
26.	Pondicherry	2	242	701	1,994	1,410
27.	Uttaranchal	3	134	1,050	1,394	2,240
28.	Jharkhand	16	537	5,759	19,895	1,200
29.	Chhattisgarh	7	5,083	2,767	9,405	2,373
	Total	**429**	**6,49,458**	**7,61,778**	**11,25,366**	**2,216**

*Data as on 1996-97; ** Figures of 2002-03.

Source: Ministry of Agriculture, DAHD & F, Hand Book on Fisheries Statistics, 2005.

Exhibit 8.8: Physical Achievements under Inland Fisheries and Aquaculture Scheme during Tenth Plan

Item/Activity	*Target*	*Achievement*	*% Achievement*
Development of Inland Fisheries and aquaculture			
Area to be brought under Fish cultivation (Lakh ha)	1.6	1.3	81.25
Training of Fish Farmers (lakh no.)	0.67	1.3	135.82

Exhibit 8.9: Initiatives of NABARD to Finance Fisheries Sector

(*Rs. in lakh*)

Year	*Sponsored to Banks*	*Sanctioned by Banks*	*Disbursement by Banks*
2004-05	2124.83	1069.55	691.97
2005-06	3337.17	1987.55	1498.15
2006-07	3845.87	2788.21	2387.83

Source: State Focus Paper, 2008-09, West Bengal, NABARD, 2008.

Exhibit 8.10: Ground Level Credit (GLC) Estimates for Fisheries during Eleventh Plan Period

(*Rs. in crores*)

Sub-Sectors	*2007-08*	*2008-09*	*2009-10*	*2010-11*	*2011-12*	*Total*
Marine	198	227	262	301	346	1,334
Brackish	493	569	654	752	865	3,335
Inland	989	1,137	1,308	1,504	1,730	6,668
Agro- processing	297	341	392	451	519	2,000
Total	**1,979**	**2,274**	**2,616**	**3,008**	**3,460**	**13,337**

Source: Report of the Working Group on Fisheries for Eleventh Five Year Plan (2007-2012), Planning Commission, Government of India, 2006.

Exhibit 8.11: Budget Utilization of Fisheries Sector during Tenth Five Year Plan

Items	*Amount (Rs. crore)*
Outlay	771.00
Expenditure till 2005-06	451.30
Anticipated expenditure 2006-07	157.00
Total expenditure	608.30
Anticipated % utilisation	78.90

Source: Report of the Working Group on Fisheries for Eleventh Five Year Plan (2007-2012), Planning Commission, Government of India, 2006.

Exhibit 8.12: Budget Outlay and Utilization of Fisheries Sector over Various Five Year Plans

Plan	*Central Sector*		*Centrally Sponsored*		*State*		*Total*	
	Outlay	*Expen-diture*	*Outlay*	*Expen-diture*	*Outlay*	*Expen-diture*	*Outlay*	*Expen-diture*
I	1.00	0.38			4.13	2.40	5.13	2.78
II	3.73	1.80			8.53	7.26	12.26	9.06
III	6.72	3.03			21.55	20.29	28.27	23.32
IV	28.00	8.11	6.00	5.17	48.68	40.83	82.68	54.11
V	51.05	39.93	17.00	4.07	83.19	71.11	151.24	115.11
VI	137.10	75.54	36.62	28.80	197.42	182.61	371.14	286.95
VII	156.58	116.93	60.75	53.26	329.19	307.40	546.52	477.59
VIII	139.00	161.01	300.00	268.02	766.39	689.43	1205.39	1118.46
IX	240.00	124.37	560.00	273.18	1269.78	1016.26	2069.78	1413.81
X	175.00	183.15	565.00	485.15	1320.54		2060.54	

Source: Report of the Working Group on Fisheries for Eleventh Five Year Plan (2007-2012), Planning Commission, Government of India, 2006.

Notes

1. The FFDAs are registered societies, envisaging leasing of tanks and ponds owned by government and local bodies to the fish farmers on long-term lease, training of farmers, supply of inputs required, provision of financial assistance in the form of subsidy for fish pond improvement and inputs. The basic organization is the setting up of 58 FFDAs in 58 districts in West Bengal, Bihar, Orissa, M.P., U.P. etc. In addition, extension services were also provided to the fish farmers to spread the technology.
2. Once agents of change appear in the scene in the form of State authorities wanting to change institutions, regulate markets, disseminate research information, it becomes essential for the fish farmers to decode the new information. Ability to decode information depends upon the information field (know what, why where, when, how....) and information field can be expanded by—
   'Learning by doing' method
   State effort in terms of extension and demonstration
   Information received through social interaction
   See, for details, D.P. Chaudhuri, "*Education, Innovation and Agriculture Development*"—Vikash Publishing House, New Delhi,

(1979) and K.J. Arrow, "*The Economic Implication of Learning by Doing*"—Review of Economics and Statistics, Vol. 29, (1962).

3. The training programme is generally followed up with demonstration and extension programmes to combine the fish farmers with the benefit of scientific fish farming. The programme normally includes the principle of fish culture, induced breeding, marketing and management, identification of fish seed, feed and fish disease and its control etc.
4. It has been observed that a large proportion of the rural client, in general, being illiterate, the requirements of complex form filling and documentation have itself limited the access to the bank facilities.
5. A committee headed by the CRAFICARD (the Committee to Review the Arrangement of Industrial Credit for Agriculture and Rural Development) Chairman Mr. B. Sivaraman has documented the pecuniary and non-pecuniary transaction costs associated with the process of getting a loan. Their conservative estimates put the pecuniary cost between 50 per cent and 75 per cent of the subsidy component, which may account to between 15 and 28 per cent of the total investment.
6. See T.N. Chaturvedi, *"Tension in Panchayati Raj, Relations between Officials and non-officials"*, The Economic Weekly, Bombay, 1964, Vol. XVI, No. 22, pp. 146.
7. R.H. Adam Jr., *"Bureaucrats, Peasants and the Dominant Coalition"*—The Journal of Development Studies, Jan 1986, pp. 68.
8. The expectation that the new bureaucracy would have new orientation, new activation, new environment and work-way has been belied in actual practice. S. Kothari's and R. Roy's, "Relations between Politicians and Administrators" in Journal of Public Administration (IIPA, New Delhi, 1999).

9

Conclusions and Policy Options

9.1 Policy Suggestions (for Livelihood)

'Livelihood' is not a common term in economics. In everyday language, it describes the means of living or sustenance. In economic jargon, a livelihood system is nothing but the organization of a household's productive resources to achieve and secure a maximum standard of living. The link between the livelihood systems of the poor and public economic policies is best reflected by two questions. In the first place, what are the most important constraints of the livelihood systems of the poor that keep them in poverty? Second, what measures of economic policy are adequate to overcome these constraints? In positive terms, how can public action create better opportunities for the poor to improve their situation?

(Baumgartner *et al.* 2004)

This chapter provides a summary of the major findings of this study, and highlights the main conclusions that emerged. It also presents the suggestions for improving the applications of the sustainable livelihoods framework in future development plans. The study has investigated the complex and interrelated nature of the factors that led to the unsatisfactory performance in the inland fisheries sector.

The rapid changes at the macro level that India witnessed since the early nineties has contributed to the instability of the livelihood systems of the poorer sections of both urban and rural households. While the benefits of globalization process have largely accrued to the urban sector growth, the rural sector has been left behind.

Slowdown in agricultural growth and productivity, changing cropping patterns, increase in distress migration, changing consumption patterns, government policies favouring industrial houses, among others, have seriously undermined the food and livelihood security of the poorer households. An integrated, multidimensional and holistic approach to poverty reduction efforts is crucial to preserve and enhance the livelihoods of the poor.

It is true that West Bengal has abundant natural endowments, conventional wisdom and human skills in respect of intensified fish farming. But in spite of enormous potentials, much headway has not been made. The levels of production and productivity have not been adequate, leaving a large gap between actual and potential production level. The new technology which seems technically attractive has failed to produce substantial results in real world. The recipients of technology are greatly circumscribed by the constraints like inadequacy of finance, multiple ownership of tanks and ponds, poaching, deliberate poisoning due to rivalry, enmity or even jealousy, inadequate extension work, existence of strong chain of middlemen, shortage of quality fish seeds.etc. As a consequence, it can be stated that present unsatisfactory performance can be attributed to all those problems resulting in the absence of rational management and judicious utilization of the resources. Negative socio-economic factors annoying the fish farmers are at work. Let us suggest some measures which may help solve the problem.

9.2 Major Findings and Policy Options

Most of the impounded water units (tanks and ponds) do not retain water throughout the year. In the post-winter, depth of water becomes less than the minimum requirement. Farmers are forced to harvest juvenile uneconomic varieties belonging to different size-groups. As a result, they could not fetch a commercially viable market price. Hence, our suggestion is that if the source of water is canal irrigation, water should be released at a very nominal rate. Again, since water is also exhausted due to irrigation or seepage problem, measures may be directed towards rain-fed farming on watershed basis or by strengthening the existing canal supplies. The run-off water collected into farm ponds should be used for irrigation. Ponds should be independent of monsoon for assured water supply. Fallow, derelict water bodies, waterlogged areas, beds etc. should be developed for culture of air fishes, breathing fishes, catfishes etc. which have high value of consumer demand.

It is also observed that seasonal tanks dry up during summer months. The tank bed should be thoroughly ploughed and exposed to the sun. This will help remove the marsh grasses from the inner depth of the bed area and increase the fertility of the bottom soil. Desilting should be done in those tanks which do not dry up completely. Mohua oil cake should be used to eradicate all predatory factors and other weed fishes from the perennial tanks.

The adoption of the proper culture practices depends on the research and extension efforts of the FFDAs and fish farmers' commitment. Since both these factors varied a great deal across farmers, the farming community, it was likely that the actual culture practices, the intensity of input use and the yield rates did not follow the same pattern. The actual pattern of input use and culture practices adopted by fish farmers and the corresponding production levels attained by them may be understood by focusing on pond construction and improvement, preparation of pond for culture, pattern and intensity of seed stocking, duration of culture, use of feed, use of manure and also the use of labour inputs.

It was observed that vast majority of water bodies are privately owned, particularly in West Bengal. Leasing arrangements are oral and bipartite matter mainly on short-term duration[1]. This is not congenial for good production. Eviction of lessees is quite frequent. Absence of long-term leasing policy is a genuine hindrance. The uncertainty attached with short duration normally dampens the fish farmer's motivation. Since there is no guarantee that he would get the same size of pond and under the same conditions as in previous years, the fish farmers are likely to be wary of undertaking investment unless the water units are leased for a long period, say seven or ten years. The financial institutions like banks are sometimes found to be hesitant to lend finance for fish culture if the lease tenure is of short duration. Banks are not certain of the fish farmer's repayment capacity. The pond lease should continue to be considered as collateral for the loans by the banks. Now there should be legal policies to safeguard the interests of the lessees by framing suiExhibit tenancy legislations. There should be long-term lease arrangements. Long-term lease arrangements not only increase production but also provide a full time avocation or employment to the unemployed rural youth.[2]

Both individual holdings and multiple ownerships exist in West Bengal.[3] The State Government should enact legislations to the effect that pond improvement work can be carried on with the consent of one of several co-owners. Some amount of business element should be introduced in the management of multi-owned ponds. If a tank or pond is found, wholly or partly, unutilized for a certain period, the Government may take it over and give it to a cultivator who intends to cultivate it.[4,5]

Appropriate technology, keeping in view the regional, environmental and ecological differences, should be developed. Induced breeding technology has an edge over other systems of seed production. The technique involves collection of (pituitary hormone) glands from matured carps. But it has been observed that good quality glands are not available. Attempts should be made to build up pituitary banks (with quality control) necessary for breeding both Indian and exotic carps. It should again be noted that some fish farmers had reported the slow growth of fish from the "machine" seed (particularly of Mrigal variety). The temptation on the part of the seed producers to sell fry with its high mortality rates should be avoided. For this, the rearing space should be enhanced. Again, neither the government machinery nor was any standard feed manufacturer in the country made any effort to come up with a standard feed package. Hence, there is a considerable scope for improving the feed by using formulated feeds. Simple procedures like adding fishmeal will improve the conversion factor. The poultry droppings may be used, as is done in some States like Haryana, to act both as feed and fertilizer.

An organized way of exploitation, transportation and marketing should be evolved so that fishes are harvested at regular intervals and earn optimal revenue by sale of fish throughout the year. Bulk landing of fish at a time should also be discouraged. It is also observed that the fish farmers, sometimes in the districts under consideration, for some reason or other, liberate fish fries three or four times in a year and harvest also three or four times from a particular pond. No doubt, this practice would have augmented the supply of fish of size of different sizes, which is sold at Rs. 30 to Rs. 40 per kg. in the local market. This has naturally, on the one hand, increased the per capita consumption of fish of the rural poor people and on the other hand, generated the decline in the supply of the fish.

It is true that in India the three major carps (Katla, Rahu and Mrigal) together with three other exotic carps (Silver Carp, Grass

Carp and Common Carp) contribute as much as 90 per cent of the freshwater aquaculture production. It should also be considered important to diversify carp culture with other medium carps (Labio Kalbasu, L. Bata, L. Gonius etc.) due to their consumer preference and market price in several parts of the country. This calls for greater R & D back up.

Enhancement of production levels from unit area with due emphasis on environmental upkeep and diversification of culture system are the principal approaches to make the aquaculture a sustainable farming practices.

Strengthening of the marketing structures including storage facilities, ice plants, cold chains, roads and transportations in identified aquaculture areas would ensure higher profit margins to the producers.

Availability of aquaculture inputs to the farmers should receive high priority. Establishment of aqua shop with facilities for soil and water testing the disease diagnosis in addition to availability of material inputs would accelerate the freshwater aquaculture development.

Recent technological advancements have transformed aquaculture to such a status that institutional finance holds the key for the success and growth in this sector.

Mixed farming i.e. pisciculture in the tank proper and other allied activities such as mulberry plantations, animal husbandry, poultry farming etc. on the embankments of the tanks may be considered for better viability of the Pisciculture scheme. The products of piggery or poultry may be utilized for manuring the water of the tanks. These will provide basic nutrients to water, which also help in maintaining the food chain of the fish. No extra expenditure for manure, supplementary feed and supervision, watch and ward will be required.

Co-operative societies are handicapped by socio-economic limitations. Government efforts in the development of fisheries have been confined to rearing and seed distribution, improvement of tanks and training facilities etc.; but no care has been taken to help improve the working of the co-operative societies. As a result, majority of the Primary Fishermen's Co-operative Societies (PFCS) are not working and the existing societies are involved in intra-conflicts which disturb their smooth functioning. More village-based societies should be set up and existing ones are required to be reformed and galvanized. Again, it is important to note that the cases of inter-linkage of credit and commodity markets in the rural areas which have circumscribed the ability of the government to improve the welfare of the fish farmers should be well taken care of.

There is a need for change of attitude and motivation of the development bureaucrats. It is, of course, rightly pinpointed that the ability to set into motion a process of change would critically depend on the support the planners at the block levels or grass roots levels receive from the political leadership at different levels. To what extent such support would be forthcoming is a moot point. In fact, this takes us back to the local socio-political power structure. So, the change in production may be brought about through radical management reform and through changes in the culture of development and bureaucracy.

One point deserves mention. It is that the suggestions or policies imparted to the fish farmers should be economically as well as technically optimal, since most of the fish farmers are in the business of making a living rather than trying to maximize fish production, regardless of the cost. Again, it is worthnoting that being poor, the small fish farmers tend to be risk averse. Their predominant goal is economic survival. They really do trade off lower risk against higher profit or the disutility of increasing risk. Adequate stability of output and income and the avoidance of major short-term losses take precedence over profit maximization. They tend to maximize utility rather than income where utility is the function of the variance of income as well as its average level. It should be rightly noted that some sort of insurance for fish crop might pave the way for stimulating adoption of practices.

In fact, monetized development does not mean only pumping money into the economy, but it entails that supporting facilities are to be provided for its optimal absorption. This involves also public participation in the measure which is conducive not only to their own ultimate benefits, but to the smooth implementation of the programme. For this, an awareness has to be created among the public and this could be achieved only by closer and direct relationship with the beneficiaries.

9.3 Some Emerging Policy Issues

- Fallow, derelict water bodies, waterlogged areas; beels etc. should be developed for culture. Ponds should be independent of monsoon for assured water supply.

- There is a need for effective rapport of fishery development officials with fish farmers in order to take more responsibilities.[6] Efforts should be made to provide institutional support to train fish farmers in order to enrich and motivate them in the field of scientific fish farming.[7]
- Credit institutions should be galvanized to provide appropriate credit. Credit institutions are required to simplify the procedures for disposal of loan applications. For reducing defaults in repayment of loan, an effective post-disbursement monitoring system should be undertaken.[8]
- Subsidy should be need based. It may be extended to inputs for each year.[9]
- A system should have to be organized to facilitate constant interaction between the extension personnel and the scientists for feedback. The extension software should be carefully developed.
- The trainers in the training institutions should also be periodically exposed to new knowledge and skills. The training they impart is then expected to be meaningful.
- It would be appropriate to provide facilities for the supply of fingerlings and evolve locally suiExhibit combinations.
- Steps should be taken to lease out ponds for a longer period, that is, at least ten years or more, to ensure fish pond development activity a financially viable proposition.
- Steps should be taken to help fish farmers in setting up marketing co-operatives with vertical linkage at the terminal and transit markets.
- Aquaculture needs to be integrated with agriculture, piggery, duckery etc.
- Aquaculture needs to be treated on par with agriculture for tax, water supply, electricity and other facilities.[10,11]

Above all, the policy discourse must become less 'donative', begin to build up people's capabilities as citizens, and learn how to respond to the demand they will make. There are no magic 'bullets'. But there are always rays of hope.

The suggestions made here are more general and good as far as it goes. But it may not go really very far. Pisciculture is a case of 'diversity in unity'. So, it calls for detailed individual farm plans in each case.

It is logical for the policy planners to try to stop this downward trend, aiming mainly at the growth of the total production through improvement of fish farming. If fish farming is being developed in order to alleviate poverty, it should be realized that the poor have only small and relatively unproductive ponds. Aiming at fish farming development programme of this group from macro economic point of view is relatively less attractive than aiming at the richer pond owners.

However, for the poor involved, such production has a significant impact as it means only for two months' meals with fish for the family. Therefore, if poverty alleviation is concerned in aquaculture development, instead of using the traditional criteria, such as total increase in production and total financial or economic value of the increased production, more relative parameters such as growth in availability of protein for the rural poor and relative income for rural poor should be used. If the government considers the issue of reduction of poverty, in the true spirit of the term, then they should take the lead in this aspect and should seriously review the objectives of ongoing strategies and further design appropriate planned development mechanism holistically for the fisheries sector.

Notes

1. The Commission has suggested a lease period of fifteen years of ponds with further extension in case of satisfactory progress. Report of the National Commission of Agriculture, Vol. VIII, P. 66, Ministry of Agriculture and Irrigation, Government of India (1976).
2. According to the West Bengal Land Reforms Act, 1965 (amended by an enactment in 1981), all classes of "land" including tanks are to be covered within the purview of ceilings. As a consequence, ponds and tanks in excess of ceiling and its distribution have financial, administrative and legal complications.—S. Paul's "*Infrastructural Base Support Measures for Aquaculture: A Case Study of West Bengal*" in *Fisheries Development in India* by U.K. Srivastava & Reddy (ed.), Concept Publishing Company, New Delhi.
3. It is heartening to note that the West Bengal Inland Fisheries Act, 1984 seeks to tackle the problem of multi-ownership by empowering the State Government to take over derelict ponds and lease them out to a group of fish farmers or co-operatives of genuine farmers.

4. It has been pointed out that the tanks should be leased to a person/persons among the shareholders who will guarantee the production of the targeted optimum; other shareholders will get their shares according to the target. Excess production will be accounted as profits by the person/persons who will take the responsibility for its management as entrepreneurial loss or gain, if any, will be borne by them as a guarantee against negligence.—*See* Susil Kumar Chakraborty's "*Some Problems of Fish Culture in West Bengal: A Case Study*", Indian Journal of Agricultural Economics, Oct-Dec 1968, Vol. XXIII, N. 4, p. 230.
5. In this connection, it may be noted that the private owners of water resources (particularly small) cannot invest in ponds development. They are lacking in resources and they do not have access to the organized money market. It has been observed in the study area that some fish cultivators in the districts are compelled to borrow for meeting consumption requirements and working capital for fish farming. They are found indebted to private financiers like commission agents *aratdars* etc. Again, to secure their access to the fish landings, the commission agents or *aratdars* advance loans against the stipulation that the catch should be disposed of through them. These agents act simultaneously as a lender and auctioneers. The financial dependency of some fish producers on the middlemen sometime robs them of their initiatives, investment and planning. This interpenetration of the credit sphere with the production marketing sphere illustrates the case of interlinkage of product and credit markets.
6. The National Council of Applied Economic Research and World Bank both have found the schemes as the most suiExhibit organizational framework and as a nucleus of growth.
7. It has been observed that a large proportion of rural client, in general, being illiterate, the requirement of complex form filling and documentation have itself limited the access to the bank facilities.
8. Some scholars, taking a cynical view, have termed bribes a useful lubricant for cumbersome administrative machinery. (*See* "*Corruption and Political Development—A Cost Benefit Analysis*", J.S. Nye in American Political Science Review, June 1967, p. 417). It is also stated that corruption in LDCs stems from the power to perform or not to perform acts that results in economic benefits to individuals (in "*Corruption and Development*" by Been Stock, M. in World Development, Vol. 7, January 1979, p. 16.).
9. Mr. A.K. Ghorai has suggested the introduction of different subsidy or privileges for different purposes to different beneficiaries. He also mentioned that in Japan, State subsidy are generally granted only for common facilities. *See* A.K. Ghorai's article "*Modernization of Small*

Scale Fish Seed Units, Quality Control and Marketing", presented in the Second National Fish Seed Congress held at Calcutta, 1986.

10. A Committee headed by the CRAFICARD (the Committee to Review the Arrangement of Industrial Credit for Agriculture and Rural Development) Chairman Mr. B. Sivaraman has documented the pecuniary and non-pecuniary transaction costs associated with the process of getting a loan. Their conservative estimates put the pecuniary cost between 50 per cent and 75 per cent of the subsidy component, which may account to between 15 and 28 per cent of the total investment.
11. Report by the working group on block level planning (Chairman-Professor M.L. Dantwalla), Planning Commission, Government of India.

Annexure A.1

Gross Domestic Product of Agriculture and Fisheries Sector

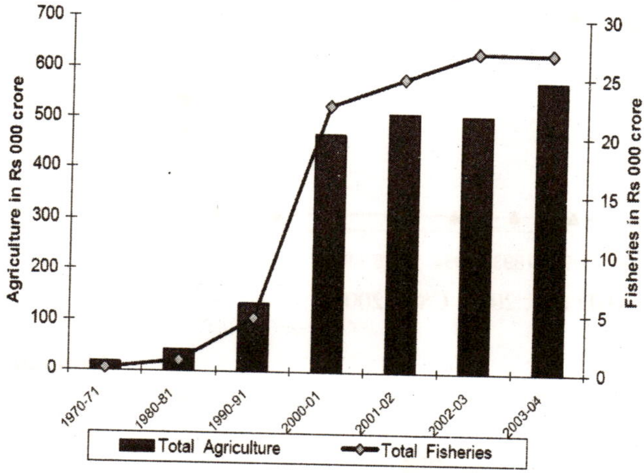

Source: DAHD & F, 2005; CSO, 2005.

Annexure A.2

Percentage Share of Fisheries Sector in Agriculture

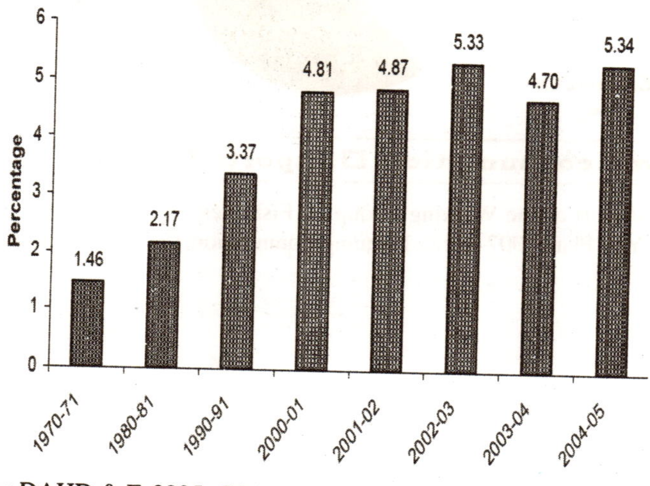

Source: DAHD & F, 2005; CSO, 2005.

Annexure A.3

Global and Indian Fish Exports

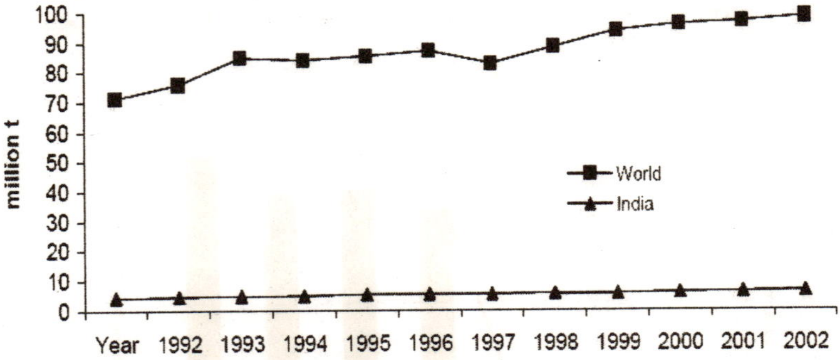

Source: DAHD & F, 2005; CSO, 2005.

Annexure A.4

Percentage Share of Fisheries Sector in Agriculture

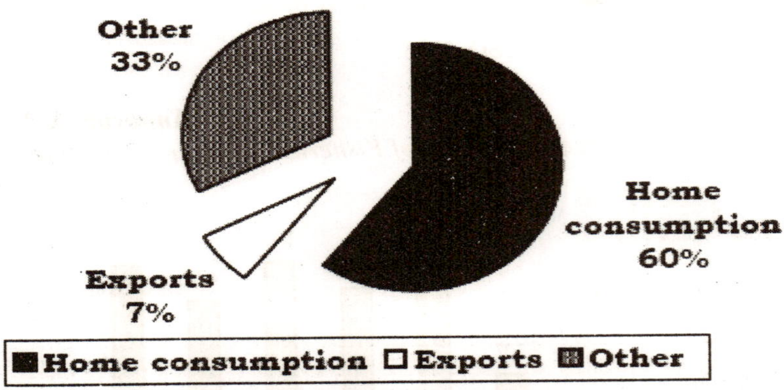

Source: Report of the Working Group on Fisheries for the Eleventh Five Year Plan (2007-2012), Planning Commission, Government of India, 2006.

Annexure A.5

Sector-wise Projected Fish Supply in India by 2011-12

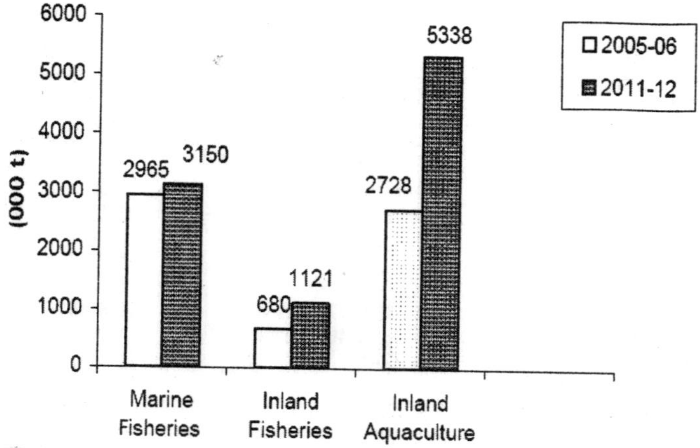

Source: Report of the Working Group on Fisheries for the Eleventh Five Year Plan (2007-2012), Planning Commission, Government of India, 2006.

Annexure A.6

Percentage Share of Inland Fisheries and Aquaculture during the Past Two Decades

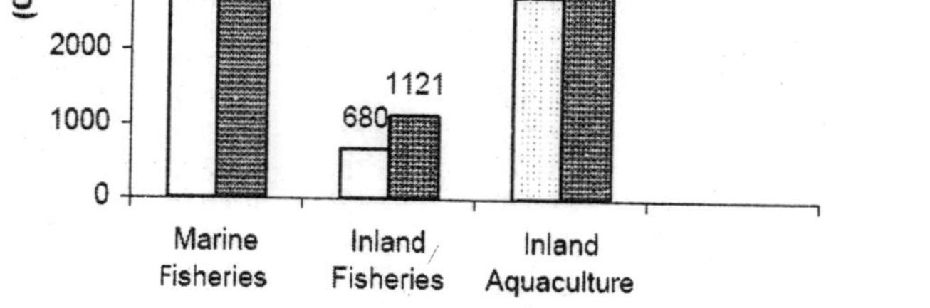

Source: Report of the Working Group on Fisheries for the Eleventh Five Year Plan (2007-2012), Planning Commission, Government of India, 2006.

Annexure A.7

Growth in Fisheries Exports and Integration with International Market

(million t)

Area	*Present Production (2006)*	*Projected Production (2012)*
Marine capture	2.958	3.1
Mariculture	0.007	0.05
Inland capture	0.68	1.12
Coldwater fisheries	0.0003	0.001
Coastal aquaculture	0.113	0.25
Freshwater aquaculture	2.6145	5.088
Total	6.3728	9.609
Exports (Quantity)	0.46	1.06
Exports (Value in Rs. crores)	7245	15.000

Source: Fisheries Division, ICAR, 2006.

Annexure A.8

Contribution of India to World Fish Production

(000 't)

Year	*World Production*			*Contribution of India*		
	Total	*Marine*	*Inland*	*Total*	*Marine*	*Inland*
1950	19,755	17,521	2,234	730	520	210
1955	28,642	24,968	3,673	839	596	243
1960	36,691	32,665	4,026	1,161	880	282
1965	51,229	46,141	5,088	1,331	824	507
1970	67,279	61,277	6,003	1,759	1,086	673
1975	68,341	61,481	6,860	2,267	1,482	785
1980	75,585	67,953	7,633	2,445	1,555	891
1985	91,553	80,888	10,665	2,839	1,747	1,092
1990	1,03,590	88,997	14,593	3,875	2,300	1,575
1995	1,24,152	1,02,801	21,351	4,998	2,786	2,212
1996	1,28,648	1,05,252	23,396	5,353	3,016	2,337
1997	1,30,882	1,05,770	25,112	5,477	3,024	2,453
1998	1,17,790	92,593	25,197	5,275	2763	2,512
1999	1,26,651	99,468	27,183	5,592	2848	2,744
2000	1,30,433	1,01,831	28,602	5,689	2852	2,837

Source: Hand Book on Fisheries Statistics, 2005.

Annexure A.9

Growth in Fisheries Exports and Integration with International Market

Five Year Plan	Average Annual Exports		Average Annual Production		% Exports of Production	
	Quantity ('000 t)	Value (Rs. crores)	Quantity ('000 t)	Value (Rs. crores)	Quantity	Value
VIII	287	3094	4819	12359	5.95	25.03
IX	379	5536	5595	24558	6.78	22.54
X	463	6716	6301	32327	7.35	20.78

Source: Estimates based on MPEDA, 2006, CSO, 2000 & 2005.

Annexure A.10

Physical Achievements under Inland Fisheries and Aquaculture during Tenth Five Year Plan

Item/Activity	Target	Achievement	% Achievement
Development of Inland Fisheries and aquaculture			
Area to be brought under Fish cultivation (Lakh ha)	1.6	1.3	81.25
Training of Fish Farmers (lakh no.)	0.67	1.3	135.82

Source: Report of the Working Group on Fisheries for the Eleventh Five Year Plan (2007-2012), Planning Commission, Government of India, 2006.

Annexure A.11

Capital Formation and Output of Fisheries Sector during Past Three Five Year Plan

Five Year Plan	Average Annual Gross Fixed Capital Formation (GFCF) (Rs. crores)	Average Annual Output		GFCF/Output Ratio
		Quantity ('000 t)	Value (Rs. crores)	
VIII	1561.80	4819.06	12566.40	12.43
IX	3210.60	5594.60	24558.00	13.07
X	4896.00	6299.50	31682.50	15.45

Source: Estimates based on CSO, 2000 & 2005.

Annexure A.12

Financial Achievements of Different Schemes during Tenth Five Year Plan

(Rs. Crores)

Sl. No.	*Scheme*	*Outlay in Tenth Plan*	*Expenditure till 2005-06*	*Anticipated Expenditure 2006-07*	*Total Expenditure*	*% Utilisation*
1.	Development of Inland Fisheries and Aquaculture	135.00	67.94	9.0	76.94	56.99
2.	Development of Marine Fisheries	125.00	74.34	14.0	88.34	70.67
3.	Marine Infrastructure and Post-Harvest Operations	125.00	60.16	31.0	91.16	72.93
4.	Strengthening of Database and IT Scheme	45.00	11.62	5.0	16.62	36.93
5.	Welfare of Fishermen and Training & Extension	135.00	99.09	22.0	121.09	89.70
6.	Fisheries Institutes	175.00	138.15	45.0	183.15	104.66
7.	NFDB	31.00	-	31.00	31.00	100.00
8.	**Total**	**771.00**	**451.30**	**157.00**	**608.30**	**78.90**

Source: Report of the Working Group on Fisheries for the Eleventh Five Year Plan (2007-2012), Planning Commission, Government of India, 2006.

Annexure A.13

Annual Fish Seed (Fry) Requirement during Eleventh Five Year Plan

Water Resource/Fish	*Area (million ha)*	*Stocking Rate (Fry/ha)*	*Requirement (million fry or PL)*
Ponds & tanks (Carps)	2.00	12,000	24,000
Reservoirs (Carps)	3.00	3,000	9,000
Wetlands (Carps)	0.35	4,000	1,400
Sea bass	-	10,000	2
Scampi farming	2.00	4,000	8,000
Brackish water (Shrimp)	2.50	40,000	10,000

Source: Report of the Working Group on Fisheries for the Eleventh Five Year Plan (2007-2012), Planning Commission, Government of India, 2006.

Annexure A.14

Annual Fish Feed Requirement during Eleventh Five Year Plan

(million t)

Freshwater Aquaculture	*Grow-out Systems*	*Seed Production*
Total feed requirement**	3.05	0.1
Rice bran/wheat bran requirement @ 70% of the total	2.14	
Oil cake requirement @ 30% of the total	0.91	0.1
Brackishwater Aquaculture	0.23	

** Considering 20% of fish to be produced @ 6 t/ha with FCR 2.5 and 20% of fish to be produced @ 4 t/ha with FCR of 1.5. and rest from fertilizer-based systems

Source: Report of the Working Group on Fisheries for the Eleventh Five Year Plan (2007-2012), Planning Commission, Government of India, 2006.

Annexure A.15

Inland Fishery Resources in India

Sl. No.	States/UTs	Rivers & Canals (km)	Reservoirs (million ha)	Ponds & Tanks (million ha)	Beels, Oxbow Lakes & Derelict Water Bodies (million ha)	Brackish Water (million ha)
(1)	(2)	(3)	(4)	(5)	(6)	(7)
1.	Andhra Pradesh	11,514	0.23	0.52	-	0.06
2.	Assam	4,820	0.002	0.023	0.11	-
3.	Bihar	3,200	0.06	0.10	0.01	-
4.	Goa	250	0.003	0.003	-	Neg
5.	Gujarat	3,865	0.24	0.07	0.01	0.1
6.	Haryana	5,000	Neg	0.01	0.01	-
7.	Himachal Pradesh	3,000	0.04	0.001	-	-
8.	Jammu & Kashmir	27,781	0.01	0.02	0.01	-
9.	Karnataka	9,000	0.44	0.29	-	0.01
10.	Kerala	3092	0.03	0.03.	0.24	0.24
11.	Madhya Pradesh	17,088	0.23	0.06	-	-
12.	Maharashtra	16,000	0.28	0.06	-	0.01
13.	Manipur	3,360	0.001	0.01	0.004	-
14.	Meghalaya	5,600	0.01	0.002	Neg	-
15.	Nagaland	1,600	0.02	0.05	Neg	-
16.	Orissa	4,500	0.26	0.11	0.18	0.43
17.	Punjab	15,270	Neg	0.01	-	-
18.	Rajasthan	*5290	0.12	0.18	-	-
19.	Sikkim	900	-	-	0.003	-
20.	Tamil Nadu	7,420	0.57	0.06	0.01	0.06
21.	Tripura	1,200	0.005	0.013	-	-
22.	Uttar Pradesh	28,500	0.14	0.16	0.13	-
23.	West Bengal	2,526	0.02	0.28	0.04	0.21
24.	Arunachal Pradesh	2,000	-	0.28	0.04	-
25.	Mizoram	1,395	-	0.002	-	-
26.	A & N Islands	115	0.001	0.003	-	0.12
27.	Chandigarh	2	-	Neg	Neg.	-
28.	Delhi	150	0.004	-	-	-
29.	Lakshadweep	-	-	-	-	-
30.	Pondicherry	247		Neg	0.001	Neg
31.	Dadra & Nagar Haveli	54	0.01	-	-	-
32.	Daman & Diu	12	-	Neg	-	Neg
33.	Chhattisgarh	3,573	0.08	0.06	-	-
34.	Uttaranchal	2,686	0.02	0.001	-	-
35.	Jharkhand	4,200	0.09	0.03	-	-
	Total	1,95,210	2.916	2.407	0.797	1.24

* Provisional.

Source: Hand Book on Fisheries Statistics, 2005; Report or Working. Group on Fisheries for the Tenth Five Year Plan, MoA, 2001.

Annexure A.16

Fish Production over the Plan Period in India

Plan Period	*Fish Production at the End of the Period ('000 t)*			*Growth (%) During the Plan Period*			*Average Annual Growth Rate*
	Marine	*Inland*	*Total*	*Marine*	*Inland*	*Total*	
(1)	(2)	(3)	(4)	(5)	(6)	(7)	(8)
Pre-Plan Period (1950-51)	534	218	752		-	-	-
1st Plan (1951-56)	596	243	839	11.61	11.47	11.57	2.31
2nd Plan (1956-61)	880	280	1.160	47.65	15.23	38.26	7.65
3rd Plan (1961-661)	824	507	1.331	6.36	81.07	14.74	2.95
Annual Plans (1966-69)	904	622	1.526	9.71	22.68	14.65	4.88
4th Plan (1969-74)	1,210	748	1.958	33.85	20.26	28.31	5.66
5th Plan (1974-79)	1,490	816	2.306	23.14	9.09	17.77	3.55
Annual Plan (1979-80)	1,492	848	2.340	0.13	3.92	1.47	1.47
6lh Plan (1980-85)	1.698	1,103	2.801	13.81	30.07	19.70	3.94
7th Plan (1985-90)	2.275	1.402	3.677	33.98	27.11	31.27	6.25
Annual Plan (1990-91)	2.300	1.536	3.836	1.10	9.56	4.32	4.32
Annual Plan (1991-92)	2.447	1,710	4.157	6.39	11.33	8.37	8.37
8th Plan (1992-97)	2.967	2.381	5.348	30.42	69.83	45.44	6.49
9th Plan (1997-02)	2.830	3,126	5.956	4.62	31.29	11.37	2.27
10th Plan (2002-03)	2.990	3,210	6.200	5.65	2.69	4.10	4.10
10th Plan (2003-04)	2.941	3.458	6.399	1.64	7.73	3.21	3.21
10th Plan (2004-05)	2.780	3.520	6.300				

Source: Central Marine Fisheries Research Institute, Kochi for the period up to 1970-71, State Governments/Union Territory Administrations since 1970-71; Hand Book on Fisheries Statistics, 2005.

Annexure A.17

Fish Seed Production over the Plan Period in India

Year	Production (million fry)
1973-74 (End of IV Plan)	409
1978-79 (End of V Plan)	912
1984-85 (End of VI Plan)	9,639
VII Plan	
1985-86	6,322
1986-87	7,601
1987-88	8,608
1988-89	9,325
1989-90	9,691
Annual Plans	
1990-91	10,332
1991-92	12,203
VIII Plan	
1992-93	12,500
1993-94	14,239
1994-95	14,544
1995-96	15,007
1996-97	15,852
IX Plan	
1997-98	15,904
1998-99	15,156
1999-2000	16,589
2000-01	15,608
2001-02	15,758
X Plan	
2002-03	16,333
2003-04	19,231
2004-05	20,811

Source: Hand Book on Fisheries Statistics, 2000.

Annexure A.18

Fishers' Population of India

(Hundreds)

Sl. No.	State/Union Territory	Total No. of Members				Number of Family Members Engaged in Fishing Operations	
		Males	Females	Children	Total	Full time	Part time
1	Andhra Pradesh	2,494	2,509	3,931	8,934	1,175	1,507
2	Arunachal Pradesh	16	14	14	44	–	19
3	Assam	1,313	980	1,611	3,904	1,057	664
4	Bihar	13,912	12,667	23,014	49,595	371	583
5	Chhattisgarh	6,216	5,297	7,601	19,114	76	466
6	Goa	55	49	36	140	22	17
7	Gujarat	1,345	1,299	2,289	4,933	837	370
8	Haryana	59	33	73	165	27	14
9	Himachal Pradesh	15	14	27	56	6	6
10	J&K	96	76	132	305	33	20
11	Jharkhand	5,779	5,716	7,814	19,309	52	214
12	Karnataka	558	529	502	1,590	144	99
13	Kerala	2,240	3,178	2,061	7,478	1,148	327
14	Madhya Pradesh	2,139	2,006	3,025	7,170	54	179
15	Maharashtra	634	466	619	1,718	196	497
16	Manipur	250	241	214	705	30	41
17	Meghalaya	5	5	14	24	-	5
18	Mizoram	55	53	71	179	1	14
19	Nagaland	58	55	36	149	-	-
20	Orissa	710	483	607	1,800	353	388
21	Punjab	22	19	51	91	16	13
22	Rajasthan	26	17	30	73	7	10
23	Sikkim	99	83	86	268	11	3
24	Tamil Nadu	1,720	1,561	1,485	4,766	693	431
25	Tripura	160	132	176	467	35	56
26	Uttar Pradesh	704	439	598	1,791	145	158
27	Uttaranchal	.32	.23	.35	1	.52	2
28	West Bengal	5,872	2,052	1,192	9116	2,679	4,465
29	A & N Islands	99	77	0	176	26	72
30	Chandigarh	2	1	2	5	2	1
31	D & N Haveli	–	–	–	–	–	–
32	Daman & Diu	76	78	101	255	41	–
33	Delhi	5	5	15	25	2	3
34	Lakshadweep	104	26	0	130	42	38
35	Pondicherry	124	128	128	380	47	26
	India	**46,962**	**40,340**			**9,331**	**10,721**

Note: Data of the year 2002-03.

(Contd.)

Annexure A.18 (contd.)

(Hundreds)

	State/Union Territory	*Family Members Engaged in Fishing Related Activities other than Actual Fishing*			
		Marketing of fish	*Repair of fishing nets*	*Processing of fish*	*Other activities*
1	Andhra Pradesh	1,121	504	219	260
2	Arunachal Pradesh	420	–	–	–
3	Assam	132	113	26	–
4	Bihar	331	167	56	167
5	Goa	20	6	3	7
6	Gujarat	147	116	34	637
7	Haryana	–	–	–	38
8	Himachal Pradesh	2	1	–	–
9	Jammu & Kashmir	39	11	1	–
10	Karnataka	114	47	16	26
11	Kerala	254	135	81	426
12	Madhya Pradesh	152	103	23	18
13	Maharashtra	650	272	184	45
14	Manipur	–	–	–	–
15	Meghalaya	–	–	–	–
16	Mizoram	1	–	–	–
17	Nagaland	–	–	–	–
18	Orissa	132	113	4	9
19	Punjab	–	–	–	–
20	Rajasthan	–	1	–	–
21	Sikkim	–	–	–	–
22	Tamil Nadu	221	237	48	69
23	Tripura	13	4	–	1
24	Uttar Pradesh	246	89	50	376
25	West Bengal	613	320	95	394
26	A and N Islands	5	5	5	1
27	Chandigarh	3	–	–	–
28	Dadra & Nagar Haveli	–	–	–	–
29	Daman & Diu	–	–	–	–
30	Delhi	–	–	–	–
31	Lakshadweep	–	–	6	2
32	Pondicherry	31	13	24	89
	India	**4,647**	**2,257**	**875**	**2,562**

Source: Indian Livestock Census-2001. Summary Table Volume-I; Hand Book on Fisheries Statistics 2005.

Annexure A.19

Structure of Fisheries Cooperatives

Sl. No.	*State*	*State Federation (17)*	*Central Societies (108)*	*Primary Societies (11,440)*	*Membership*	*Total Fishermen*
1	Andhra Pradesh	1	10	3,646	3,59,021	4,96,731
2	Arunachal Pradesh	–	–	4	300	5,716
3	Assam	1	–	456	3,909	4,75,000
4	Bihar	1	5	532	40,000	11,13,018
5	Delhi	–	–	2	239	16,430
6	Goa	1	–	10	1,000	18,836
7	Gujarat	1	4	385	80,000	1,40,208
8	Haryana	–	–	59	1,005	16,034
9	Himachal Pradesh	–	1	28	7,096	8,455
10	Jammu & Kashmir	–	–	–		13,000
11	Karnataka	1	3	296	76.136	8,10,468
12	Kerala	1	16	292	2,00,000	7,10,502
13	Madhya Pradesh	1	7	1,001	62,570	1,30,982
14	Maharashtra	1	21	2,024	2,08,273	4,25,652
15	Manipur	1	–	181	9,182	32,350
16	Meghalaya	–	–	58	2,569	11,097
17	Mizoram	–	–	36	808	,600
18	Nagaland	–	–	168	4,285	1,85,350
19	Orissa	1	4	482	1,20,000	2,02,112
20	Punjab	–	–	4	60	4,200
21	Rajasthan	1	–	107	4,624	13,557
22	Sikkim	–	–	–	–	550
23	Tamil Nadu	1	10	675	4,44,866	2,67,309
24	Tripura	1	–	129	14,225	50,955
25	Uttar Pradesh	1	5	110	41,000	1,60,823
26	West Bengal	1	20	1,072	1,60,000	5,97,180
27	A & N Islands	–	–	45	3,812	3,678
28	Chandigarh	–	–	1		250
29	D & N Haveli	–	–	–	–	130
30	Daman & Diu	–	–	6	2,993	31000
31	Lakshadweep	–	–	2		6000
32	Pondicherry	1	2	36	28,754	10971
33	Chhattisgarh				31,427	
34	Jharkhand				9150	
	Total	**17**	**108**	**11,847**	**19,17,305**	**59,59,144**

Source: Hand Book on Fisheries Statistics 2005.

Annexure A.20

State or Union Territory-wise Total Fish Production in India

Sl. No.	State/Union Territory	2003-04		2004-05		2005-06	
		Inland fish production	Percentage	Inland fish production	Percentage	Inland fish production	Percentage
1.	Andhra Pradesh	648.70	19.00	642.32	18.25	672.25	17.901
2.	Arunachal Pradesh	2.65	0.08	2.70	0.08	2.754	0.073
3.	Assam	181.00	5.30	186.31	5.29	188.01	5.006
4.	Bihar	266.50	7.80	267.51	7.60	279.53	7.443
5.	Goa	3.60	0.11	4.23	0.12	4.04	0.108
6.	Gujarat	45.48	1.33	50.43	1.43	69.936	1.862
7.	Haryana	39.13	1.15	42.05	1.19	48.2	1.283
8.	Himachal Pradesh	6.56	0.19	7.81	0.22	7.295	0.194
9.	Jammu & Kashmir	19.75	0.58	19.90	0.57	19.15	0.510
10.	Karnataka	70.00	2.05	95.00	2.70	120.6	3.211
11.	Kerala	76.18	2.23	76.45	2.17	77.98	2.076
12.	Madhya Pradesh	50.81	1.49	62.06	1.76	61.077	1.626
13.	Maharastra	127.00	3.72	129.40	3.68	135.2	3.600
14.	Manipur	17.60	0.52	17.80	0.51	18.23	0.485
15.	Meghalaya	5.15	0.15	5.64	0.16	4.118	0.110
16.	Mizoram	3.38	0.10	3.68	0.10	3.75	0.100
17.	Nagaland	5.56	0.16	4.90	0.14	5.5	0.146
18.	Orissa	190.00	5.56	193.66	5.50	203.24	5.412
19.	Punjab	83.65	2.45	77.70	2.21	85.64	2.280
20.	Rajasthan	14.30	0.42	16.93	0.48	18.5	0.493
21.	Sikkim	0.14	-	0.14	0.00	0.015	0.000
22.	Tamilnadu	101.14	2.96	151.73	4.31	155.04	4.128
23.	Tripura	17.98	0.53	19.84	0.56	23.871	0.636
24.	Uttar Pradesh	254.00	7.44	277.00	7.87	289.58	7.711
25.	West Bengal	988.00	28.93	1035.60	29.42	1090	29.025
26.	Andaman & Nicobar Islands	0.09	–	NA	NA	0.043	0.001
27.	Chandigarh	0.08	–	0.08	0.00	0.087	0.002
28.	Dadra & Nagar Haveli	0.05	–	0.05	0.00	0.048	0.001
29.	Delhi	2.10	0.06	1.41	0.04	0.7	0.019
30.	Pondicherry	5.20	0.15	5.50	0.16	2.181	0.058
31.	Chhattisgarh	111.00	3.26	120.07	3.41	131.75	3.508
32.	Uttaranchal	2.56	0.07	2.57	0.07	2.789	0.074
33.	Jharkhand	75.38	2.21	NA	NA	34.27	0.913
Total		**3414.72**	**100.00**	**3520.46**	**100.00**	**3755.4**	**100.001**

Source: Extracted from the Agenda Note of TMC meeting (December 7-8, 2006) for centrally sponsored scheme on 'Strengthening of database and information networking for the fisheries sector', DAHD, Ministry of Agriculture, GoI.

Annexure A.21

Area Covered under BFDA in West Bengal

Year	Total Area (in ha)
1990-1991	157.40
1991-1992	131.86
1992-1993	202.04
1993-1994	274.25
1994-1995	301.53
1995-1996	400.57
1996-1997	316.59
1997-1998	327.47
1998-1999	496.40
1999-2000	531.68
2000-2001	499.70
2001-2002	460.75
2002-2003	403.03
2003-2004	333.85
2004-2005	240.76
2005-2006	278,13
2006-2007	325.25

Source: ME & MS Wing, Department of Fisheries and Fishing Harbours, Government of West Bengal.

Annexure A.22

Number of Boats and its Registration in West Bengal

No. of Boats Licensed for Operation in Sea in the Coast of West Bengal

Year	Mechanised			Non-Mechanised		
	Purba Medinipur	South 24-Parganas	West Bengal	Purba Medinipur	South 24-Parganas	West Bengal
2002-2003	174	1015	1189	2	240	242
2003-2004	395	1908	2303	9	295	304
2004-2005	843	1761	2604	72	609	681
2005-2006	754	1279	2033	146	341	487
2006-2007	830	1490	2320	43	222	265
Total	**2996**	**7453**	**10449**	**272**	**1707**	**1979**

(Contd.)

Annexure A.22 (contd.)

Registration of Boats in West Bengal

Year	*Mechanised*			*Non-Mechanised*		
	Purba Medinipur	*South 24-Parganas*	*West Bengal*	*Purba Medinipur*	*South 24-Parganas*	*West Bengal*
1998-1999	-		-	-	-	-
1999-2000	411	259	670	144	114	258
2000-2001	405	1357	1762	558	512	1070
2001-2002	372	806	1178	131	1404	1535
2002-2003	434	956	1390	203	1252	1455
2003-2004	407	922	1329	83	778	861
2004-2005	413	631	1044	161	855	1016
2005-2006	182	438	620	166	444	610
2006-2007	216	349	565	60	293	353
Total	**2840**	**5718**	**8558**	**1506**	**5652**	**7158**

Source: ME & MS Wing, Department of Fisheries and Fishing Harbours, Government of West Bengal.

Annexure A.23

Reservoir Fishery Resources in West Bengal

Sl. No.	*District*	*River*	*Canal/Khal*	*Beel/Baor*	*Total Area*
1.	Coochbehar	13095.82	1664.58	1168.11	15928.51
2.	Jalpaiguri	16006.44	562.29	504.38	17073.11
3.	Siliguri	3395.63	683.94	683.94	4763.51
4.	Uttar Dinajpur/ Dakshin Dinajpur	4032.08	1774.30	3548.59	9354.97
5.	Malda	6497.60	2511.42	4551.55	13560.57
6.	Murshidabad	36283.23	10013.88	3790.69	50087.80
7.	Nadia	4191.28	2771.75	4271.61	11234.64
8.	24-Parganas (N)	14299.00	8712.00	8861.19	31872.19
9.	24-Parganas (S)	17704.98	13492.47	5749.47	36946.92
10.	Howrah	107.36	2019.82	118.28	2245.46
11.	Hoogly	4358.74	3714.94	3884.76	11958.44
12.	Purba Medinipur/ Paschim Medinipur	12774.12	8766.07	404.01	21944.20
13.	Bankura	15960.15	11711.04	1973.00	29644.19
14.	Purulia	3707.29	–	–	3707.29
15.	Burdwan	11316.64	5991.36	1939.91	19247.91
16.	Birbhum	795.63	5695.85	632.16	7123.64
	Total	**164525.99**	**80085.71**	**42081.65**	**286693.35**

Source: ME & MS Wing, Department of Fisheries and Fishing Harbours, Government of West Bengal.

Annexure A.24

Employment Generation in Fisheries Sector in West Bengal

Employment generation in Fisheries Sector (Plan schemes only) Mandays - Unit: in '000s			
Sl. No.	*Name of Sector*	*2005-06*	*2006-07*
1.	Inland Fisheries	2688380	2827740
2.	Brackish water	518490	541200
3.	Marine Fisheries	10458000	10548000
4.	Extension wing	368000	384000
5.	Welfare Scheme	1240700	1240700
6.	Co-op Society	1634140	1654140
7.	Others	128000	159500
	Total Man Days	17035710	17355280
	Total Man Year	70982	72313

Source: ME & MS Wing, Department of Fisheries and Fishing Harbours, Government of West Bengal.

Annexure A.25

Details of the Training Programme in West Bengal upto 2005-06

Fish Farmers Trained		*Fish Farmers Trained*	
Men	222116	Gen	153390
Women	12906	SC	74569
Total	**235022**	**ST**	**7063**

Source: ME & MS Wing, Department of Fisheries and Fishing Harbours, Government of West Bengal.

Annexure A.26

Fish Seed Production in West Bengal

(*Unit in Million*)

Year	*Target*	*Achievement*
1991-1992	8000	8150
1994-1995	8100	8126
1995-1996	8150	8180
1996-1997	8400	8435
1997-1998	8500	8500
1998-1999	8610	8610
1999-2000	8700	8725

(*Contd.*)

Annexure A.26 (contd.)

Year	Target	Achievement
2000-2001	8850	8850
2001-2002	9000	9000
2002-2003	9100	9100
2003-2004	10000	11890
2004-2005	12500	12200
2005-2006	12500	12500
2006-2007	13000	13200

Source: ME & MS Wing, Department of Fisheries and Fishing Harbours, Government of West Bengal.

Annexure A.27

Production of Fish in West Bengal

(*Units in MT*)

Sl. No	District	Inland Fish Production			Marine Fish Production		
		Fish	Prawn	Total	Fish	Prawn	Total
1.	Darjeeling (DGHC)	395	0	395	0	0	0
2.	Darjeeling (Siliguri)	1450	0	1450	0	0	0
3.	Jalpaiguri	21724	0	21724	0	0	0
4.	Coochbehar	20426	0	20426	0	0	0
5.	Uttar Dinajpur	16005	0	16005	0	0	0
6.	Dakshin Dinajpur	32992	0	32992	0	0	0
7.	Malda	29288	5	29293	0	0	0
8.	Murshidabad	83582	10	83592	0	0	0
9.	Nadia	68993	20	69013	0	0	0
10.	Birbhum	67518	0	67518	0	0	0
11.	Burdwan	89995	0	89995	0	0	0
12.	Hoogly	67009	60	67069	0	0	0
13.	Howrah	47600	58	47658	0	0	0
14.	North 24-Parganas	130541	40516	171057	0	0	0
15.	South 24-Parganas	180815	9900	190715	46989	6848	53837
16.	Purulia	39135	0	39135	0	0	0
17.	Bankura	52682	0	52682	0	0	0
18.	Paschim Medinipur	58868	0	58868	0	0	0
19.	Purba Medinipur	108547	12871	121418	114581	9680	124261
	Total	**1117565**	**63440**	**1181005**	**161570**	**16528**	**178098**

Source: ME & MS Wing, Department of Fisheries and Fishing Harbours, Government of West Bengal.

Annexure A.28
Year-wise Export of Fish through Kolkata and Haldia Port

Year	*Quantity (in ton)*	*Value (in Crore Rs.)*
1983-1984	4766.00	44.120
1984-1985	4308.00	34.030
1985-1986	3538.59	36.780
1986-1987	4334.78	49.050
1987-1988	4093.31	48.170
1988-1989	4851.37	65.720
1992-1993	9562.00	183.670
1993-1994	121.33	262.290
1994-1995	13023.00	325.650
1995-1996	13361.00	330.060
1996-1997	16111.00	420.440
1997-1998	14450.00	416.690
1998-1999	15060.00	457.910
1999-2000	16348.00	511.700
2000-2001	18553.00	595.400
2001-2002	17647.37	503.909
2002-2003	17502.96	575.228
2003-2004	18201.09	560.282
2004-2005	17580.91	502.108
2005-2006	18778.30	550.166
2006-2007	20560.00	617.000

Source: ME & MS Wing, Department of Fisheries and Fishing Harbours, Government of West Bengal.

Annexure A.29
Short-Term Credit Programme for Fish Farmers in West Bengal

Name of Districts	*2005-06*		*2006-07*	
	Area Involved (ha)	*No. of Beneficiaries*	*Area Involved (ha)*	*No. of Beneficiaries*
(1)	(2)	(3)	(4)	(5)
Darjeeling (DGHC)	15 J.U	15	62 unit Jhora	60
Darjeeling (Siliguri)	6.91	23	6.31	21
Jalpaiguri	51.21	216	68.20	163
Coochbehar	18.57	80	56.27	42
Uttar Dinajpur	51.10	90	11.00	18
Dakshin Dinajpur	44.48	29	53.31	35
Malda	33.39	26	22.02	5
Murshidabad	62.16	54	52.16	45
Nadia	36.55	18	74.97	22
Birbhum	185.20	216	107.36	137

(Contd.)

Annexure A.29 (contd.)

(1)	(2)	(3)	(4)	(5)
Burdwan	374.50	789	301.7	354
Hoogly	114.58	163	128.88	155
Howrah	29.39	16	57.07	120
North 24-Parganas	744.30	339	696.26	295
South 24-Parganas	407.27	1000	522.66	1134
Purulia	40.50	50	100.44	33
Bankura	95.73	65	28.02	23
Paschim Medinipur	33.50	73	148.47	224
Purba Medinipur	698.61	930	945.82	1429
Total	**3027.95**	**4192**	**3380.92**	**4315**

Source: ME & MS Wing, Department of Fisheries and Fishing Harbours, Government of West Bengal.

Annexure A.30

Fisher Folk Population in West Bengal

(Units in number)

Name of District	*No. of Fisher Folk Family*		*Fisher Folk Population*					
	Inland	*Marine*	*Male Inland*	*Marine*	*Female Inland*	*Marine*	*Total Inland*	*Marine*
Darjeeling	956	-	1677	-	1282	-	2959	-
Jalpaiguri	26000	-	41125	-	39905	-	81030	-
Coochbehar	28542	-	75085	-	61224	-	136309	-
Uttar Dinajpur	14210	-	36452	-	33648	-	70100	-
Dakshin Dinajpur	10957	-	30600	-	25277	-	55877	-
Malda	13857	-	46347	-	42327	-	88674	-
Murshidabad	46684	-	121674	-	100376	-	222050	-
Nadia	51252	-	146000	-	110000	-	256000	-
Birbhum	49751	-	113526	-	87221	-	200747	-
Burdwan	35000	-	98000	-	42000	-	140000	-
Hoogly	18718		41223	-	33650	-	78873	-
Howrah	17494	2442	51236	7123	38582	4978	89818	12101
North 24-Parganas	50897	4103	134877	10873	119607	9643	254484	20516
South 24-Parganas	52917	25443	145522	69969	119063	57248	264585	127217
Purulia	4528	-	18050	-	16662	-	34712	-
Bank Lira	22860	-	64010	-	50292	-	1 14302	-
Paschim Medinipur	11629	-	35586	-	34190	-	69776	-
Purba Medinipur	8620	17081	26378	52267	25345	50217	51723	102484
Total	**464872**	**49069**	**1227368**	**140232**	**980651**	**122086**	**2212019**	**262318**

Source: ME & MS Wing, Department of Fisheries and Fishing Harbours, Government of West Bengal.

Annexure A.31

District-wise Status of Fisherman Co-operative Societies in West Bengal

Sl. No.	Name of the District	No. of CFCS	Primary Fisherman Co-Operative Society				
			Category-A	Category-B	Category-C	Total	No. of Ornamental Co.op.
1.	Darjeeling	1	1	0	1	2	-
2.	Jalpaiguri	1	13	1	2	16	1
3.	Coochbehar	1	61	4	0	65	-
4.	Uttar Dinajpur	1	15	19	0	34	11
5.	Dakshin Dinajpur	1	13	4	0	17	8
6.	Malda	1	88	2	0	90	13
7.	Murshidabad	1	14	64	18	96	9
8.	Nadia	1	27	28	18	73	1
9.	Birbhum	1	3	6	12	21	9
10.	North 24-Parganas	1	41	17	31	89	1
11.	South 24-Parganas	1	36	28	38	102	21
12.	Howrah	1	13	2	7	22	5
13.	Hoogly	1	14	6	15	35	-
14.	Burdwan	1	25	12	17	54	-
15.	Purba Medinipur	1	54	0	0	54	6
16.	Paschim Medinipur	1	21	0	2	23	-
17.	Bankura	1	23	5	34	62	7
18.	Purulia	1	15	10	23	48	-
19.	Purba Medinipur (Marine)	1	25	0	75	100	-
20.	South 24-Parganas (Marine)	1	4	7	39	50	-
	Total	**20**	**506**	**215**	**332**	**1053**	**93**

Source: ME & MS Wing, Department of Fisheries and Fishing Harbours, Government of West Bengal.

Annexure A.32

Fish Based Industries in West Bengal

Sl. No.	*Name of the District*	*Ice Plant*		*Feed Plant*		*Fish Meal Plant*		*Net Making Centre*	*Fish drying Centre*	
		No.	*Capacity (Ton)*	*No.*	*Capacity*	*No.*	*Capacity t/Day*	*No.*	*No.*	*Capacity (T)*
(1)	(2)	(3)	(4)	(5)	(6)	(7)	(8)	(9)	(10)	(11)
1.	Darjeeling	5	380.8	-	-	-	-	-	-	-
2.	Jalpaiguri	4	22.2	-	-	-	-	-	-	-
3.	Coochbehar	-	-	-	-	-	-	-	-	-
4.	Uttar Dinajpur	20	16.5	1	27.5	-	-	-	-	-
5.	Dakshin Dinajpur	13	20.7	-	-	-	-	-	-	-
6.	Malda	4	37	-	-	-	-	-	15	131.1
7.	Murshidabad	8	30	-	-	-	-	-	-	-
8.	Birbhum	-	-	-	-	-	-	-	-	-
9.	Barddhaman	3	16	-	-	-	-	-	-	-
10.	Nadia	33	217	-	-	-	-	-	-	-
11.	North 24-Parganas	14	100	-	-	-	-	1	-	-
12.	Hoogly	4	40	2	-	-	-	3	-	-
13.	Bankura	4	1703	-	-	-	-	-	-	-
14.	Purulia	9	11	-	-	-	-	-	-	-
15.	Paschim Medinipur	8	61	1	50	-	-	-	-	-
16.	Purba Medinipur	73	989.5	6	21.5	29	257	2	41	12191
17.	Howrah	15	25.3	2	-	2	-	-	-	-
18.	South 24-Parganas	71	1571	-	-	3	32	-	296	601.6
	Total	**288**	**5241**	**12**	**99**	**34**	**289**	**6**	**352**	**12923.7**

Source: ME & MS Wing, Department of Fisheries and Fishing Harbours, Government of West Bengal.

Annexure A.33

District-wise Different Types of Hatcheries in West Bengal

Sl. No.	*Name of District Hatchery*	*Carp Hatchery Plant*	*Macro-Brachium Hatchery*	*Demonstration Centre*
1.	Darjeeling	1	0	5
2.	Jalpaiguri	7	0	0
3.	Coochbehar	15	0	0
4.	Uttar Dinajpur	16	0	1
5.	Dakshin Dinajpur	7	0	0

(Contd.)

Annexure A.33 (contd.)

(1)	(2)	(3)	(4)	(5)
6.	Malda	4	0	7
7.	Murshidabad	20	1	40
8.	Nadia	10	0	10
9.	Birbhum	7	0	5
10.	Burdwan	13	0	101
11.	Hoogly	14	1	2
12.	Howrah	8	2	1
13.	North 24-Parganas	90	2	0
14.	South 24-Parganas	11	0	14
15.	Purulia	4	0	1
16.	Bankura	97	0	0
17.	Paschim Medinipur	11	0	2
18.	Purba Medinipur	13	4	0
19.	ADF, Marine, Diamond Harbour	2	0	0
	Total	**350**	**10**	**189**

Source: ME & MS Wing, Department of Fisheries and Fishing Harbours, Government of West Bengal.

Annexure A.34

Number of Hatcheries in West Bengal

Sl. No.	*District*	*Private Hatcheries*	*Govt. Hatcheries*
1.	Coochbehar	12	1
2.	Jalpiguri	8	0
3.	Darjeeling (Karshiang)	0	1
4.	Darjeeling (Siliguri)	0	0
5.	Uttar Dinajpur	6	1 (CADC)
6.	Dakshin Dinajpur	9	0
7.	Malda	1	1
8.	Murshidabad	22	0
9.	Nadia	7	1
10.	24-Parganas (N)	200	0
11.	24-Parganas (S)	0	0
12.	Howrah	8	0
13.	Hoogly	51	0
14.	Purba Medinipur	7	2
15.	Paschim Medinipur	4	1
16.	Bankura	200	0
17.	Purulia	5	0
18.	Burdwan	19	1
19.	Birbhum	5	0
	Total	**564**	**9**

Source: ME & MS Wing, Department of Fisheries and Fishing Harbours, Government of West Bengal.

Annexure A.35

Outlay in Eleventh plan for West Bengal Fishery

(Rs. in Lakh)

Sl. No.	Major Heads/Minor Heads of Development	Projected Outlay for 11th Plan	Allocation for Annual Plan				
			2007-08	2008-09	2009-10	2010-11	2011-12
1		2	3	4	5	6	7
1.	2405-00-001 -Direction and Administration 001-Augmenting supervisory and administrative staff both in the field and headquarters	165	5	40	40	40	40
2.	002-Acquisition and management of properties for administrative unit	485	85	100	100	100	100
3.	2405-00-101-Inland Fisheries 001-Projects on brackish water fish farming through brackish water fish farmer's development agency	230	30	50	50	50	50
4.	002-Introduction of cold chain system & supply of insulated boxes for preservation of fish and fish by-products	325	5	80	80	80	80
5.	003-Distribution of minikits,water conditioners etc. and development of social fisheries	170	10	40	40	40	40
6.	005-Subsidy for fishing nets and fishery requisites in inland fisheries sector	80	0	20	20	20	20
7.	006-Subsidy on short-term credit to the small fish farmers, fish venders and entrepreneurs in the development of pisciculture, door to door vending, setting up of small fish markets and fish-meal plants.	1000	0	250	250	250	250

8. 007-Administrative cost to operate state project units and improvement and management of training centre (formerly World Bank Project)	0	0	0	0	0	0
9. 008-Construction and management of hatcheries for ornamental fish endangered species and fresh water prawn in different districts of the State	410	10	100	100	100	100
10. 009-Development of reservoir fisheries, sewage-fade fisheries and air breathing fish culture	81	1	20	20	20	20
11. 010-Dev. of aquaculture (FFDA) and introduction of aerators for enhanced fish production	780	60	180	180	180	180
12. 012-State grants to SFDC/WBFC for pisciculture operation	500	100	100	100	100	100
13. 015-Setting up of district level and state level laboratories for conducting research activities related to aquaculture	83	3	20	20	20	20

Source: ME & MS Wing, Department of Fisheries and Fishing Harbours, Government of West Bengal.

Annexure A.36

State/Union Territory-wise Inland Fish Production

Year	Budget Estimate	Actual Expenditure	Percentage
2002-03	Rs. 3508.95 lakh	Rs. 1619.13 lakh	46.14
2003-04	Rs. 3032.39 lakh	Rs. 2715.29 lakh	89.54
2004-05	Rs. 3210.00 lakh	Rs. 3710.14 lakh	115.58
2005-06	Rs. 3310.00 lakh	Rs. 3788.26 lakh	114.45
2006-07	Rs. 4732.00 lakh	Rs. 4150.16 lakh	87.70
Total	**Rs 17793.34 lakh**	**Rs 15982.98 lakh**	**89.83**

Source: Annual Report: 2006-07, Department of Fisheries, Government of West Bengal.

Appendix I

Ensuring Food Security in India Today: Some Emerging Issues and Challenges

> "Social security was both a private and state matter. The primary responsibility for maintaining the family—wife, children, parents, minor brothers and unmarried or widowed sisters—lay with the head of the family; no one could become an ascetic without first providing for his wife and children.... However, the state had the obligation to provide a safety net and maintain children, the aged, childless women and the helpless."
>
> —*The Arthashastra: Kautilya by L.N. Rangarajan*

There is no denying the fact that improving food security should be an issue of considerable importance for a country like India where more than one-fourth of the population is estimated to be absolutely poor and one-half of the children malnourished in one way or another[1]. In recent years, there have been many emerging issues in this context of food security. These are (a) economic liberalization in the 1990s, (b) establishment of WTO, (c) the phenomenon of hunger amidst plenty: accumulation of million tonnes of food stocks; while 200 million or so people still live below the poverty line, (d) the introduction of targeting in the PDS, (e) the Right to Food etc. Ail these have provided opportunities and challenges for the food and nutrition security of the country. This will also provide some insights into how food security crisis can be associated with the development of Inland fish cultivation in India.

The concept of food security has undergone considerable modifications/paradigmatic shift in recent years. Food availability and stability were considered good measures of food security till the seventies and the achievement of self-sufficiency accorded high priority in the food policies of developing countries. But in spite of food self-sufficiency, some countries could not solve the problem of chronic household food insecurity. This necessitates a change in approach.

Again, the nutritionists argue that mere energy intake is not necessarily an effective measure of nutritional status. In fact, it depends not only on the nutrient intake but also on non-nutrient food attributes, privately and publicly provided inputs and status. The non-food factors which influence "biological absorption" are also considered as important for food security as food factors.

It is well known that other things remaining the same, higher level of malnutrition would lead to a higher burden of diseases in a society and *vice versa*. So, there is a growing consensus to the need to widen the definition of food security. Calorie norm, at best, can provide a threshold but not the standard for food security at the household level. However, it is a different matter that nowhere, in developing as well as developed countries, this notion of access to nutritionally adequate diet is operationalised.

There are some serious lacunae of the calorie norm. In the first place, calorie adequacy cannot be equated to a healthy and active life. More and more people are able to access adequate calories; but this is not reflected in a sizeable reduction in malnutrition. Even if we assume that adequate calories are available to every member of the households, there is no certainty that available calories will meet the requirements of protein energy and micro-nutrients, such as iron, iodine and vitamin A. Within an assurance of nutritional adequacy, food security has very little meaning (United Nations, 2000). Again, from the policy point of view, it is useful to distinguish between growth-mediated and support-led food security system. India has been following both growth-led and support led policies and has been using short and long term measures for improving food security.

The food security policy pursued since Independence may be considered as a success story in some aspects. It is true to say that famines have been largely eliminated since independence. The overall food production has substantially increased from 50 million tonnes in 1950-51 to 235 million tonnes in 2008-09. The level of procurement and the reach of the PDS have increased considerably over time. Food/cash for work programmes have also helped the poor raising their purchasing power. Nutrition programmes have contributed to the welfare of pregnant mothers, pre-school children and school-going children. With the advent of economic liberalization and globalization, some new challenges have also emerged.

Despite the implementation of different programmes, there are certain concerns about calorie intake and malnutrition. Poverty levels remain high, despite a significant reduction in poverty in recent years. The calorie intake of the bottom 30 per cent is low. The problem of malnutrition is acute and widespread and is extremely serious among women and children. The pregnant women with anaemia is as high as 70 per cent. At the all-India level, more than 50 per cent of the children under the age of five were underweight in 2003-04. Currently, the present nutrition-related public health problems are (a) chronic energy deficiency and undernutrition and (b) micro-nutrient deficiencies such as anaemia due to iron and folic acid deficiency, vitamin A deficiency and iodine deficiency disorders. (GoI 2005) (Box 1).

Box 1: Still a Long Road to Fight Hunger

Access to food is still a mirage for many in India despite high GDP growth. Even after two decades of India embarking on the path of new economy, the nation struggles to pull out its vast chunk of population below the poverty line and those staring into the nightmare of hunger everyday. The Global Hungry Index has rated 84 countries on the basis of three leading indicators, namely the prevalence of child malnutrition, rate of child mortality and the proportion of people who are calorie deficient. India's ranking is way below neighouring countries like China, Pakistan and Sri Lanka. China is rated much ahead of India at the ninth place, while Pakistan is at the 52nd place. Sri Lanka was at the 39th position and Nepal ranked 56 by index; while Bangladesh was just one position lower than India at 68th. The Report also stated that India alone accounted for a large share of the world's undernourished children as India is home to 42 per cent of the world's underweight children, while Pakistan has just 5 per cent......The world is nowhere near to meet the first Millennium Development Goal of halving the proportion of hungry people between 1990 and 2015 and for India the country would miss the target for sure.

—by Sangita Jha in *Sopan*, November, 2010

Understanding the significance of diverse agencies and various forms of economic inequality in framing social policies forms a driving force in widening the concept of social security in developing countries like India. The genesis of such an understanding can also be traced to the conflict between the traditional notions of social security and the newer approaches to the analysis of insecurity and vulnerability brought out by the contemporary development theory.

The members of society have already reached an acceptable standard of living and the main aim of social security is to protect them from a fall in their standard of living. Implicit in this is the understanding of social security as a concept whereby the core of income and welfare through regular participation in work and production leaving only specific contingencies to be tackled through public policy. The need for a broader concept of social security began to be articulated by communities living in the developing countries as it was gradually established that the reigning western notion of social security does not take into account the high degree of deprivation and vulnerability of the majority of the population.

Taking cognizance of the fact that social security is defined in terms of protection against human deprivation, any attempt towards human development may be conceived as a social security measure. Though social security mechanisms aim at human development, at the operational level, a clear distinction has to be made between human development measures and social security mechanisms. Social security measures primarily aim at removing vulnerability by preventing a decline in the living standards, in general, and promoting basic living standards, in particular, during economic contingencies. In sum, "public action can play a role in reducing human deprivation and removing human vulnerability in a developing country. The focus is on the use of a class of means—" (Ahmad *et al.,* 1990). This is reasonable, because many of the developing countries have large shares of employment in unorganized/informal sectors and the workers do not have access to the benefits of traditional social security measures. It is also argued that human development is a prerequisite for the effective implementation of social security measures, for it builds the capabilities of individuals so that they are entitled to security gains. And social security mechanisms provide a safeguard against the risk of individuals relapsing to a below minimum standard of living during economic crises and contingencies. Hence, in this context, the pivotal role of the state emerges.[2]

For most of its history, social security theories have focused on developed countries with an emphasis on growth-mediated social policies. Thus, depending on the level of a country's economic development, different packages of social security measures were initiated. But the universality of growth-oriented measures has been questioned. Growing awareness of the successful experiences of countries like China, Chile, Costa Rica, Cuba and Jamaica followed Public support/action-led security measures rather than rapid income growth under conditions of lower growth rates (Dreze and Sen, 1989). Impressive performance in countries like Sri Lanka or the state of Kerala amply demonstrate that economic growth has followed rather than preceded wide-ranging measures of public support; their successes do not lie in the size of financial allocation to particular public provision, but increasing the political, social and economic conditions for ensuring the efficiency and spread effect of social security measures to the deprived sections of the population. The need for a broader concept of social security began to be articulated by the communities living in the developing communities and as such, it was gradually established that the western notion of social security does not take into account the degree of deprivation and vulnerability of the majority of the population in the country.

Of course, there is a symbiotic relationship between economic growth and social security—growth mediated and support-led. The significance of economic growth cannot be overlooked since the public resource-base needs to be augmented for supporting security measures. At the same time, equitable growth cannot be ensured unless vulnerability of large sections of the population is reduced through social security mechanisms.

Another issue is also relevant here. Some economists like Dreze and Sen (1989) recognized social security measures as comprising promotional and protective measures[3]. The conventional social security comprising only protective social security measures is inappropriate for countries like India. This is because less than 8 per cent of the workforce is engaged in regular employment in the organized sector. The informal sector provides the bulk of employment. But, generally, the incomes accruing to people from such employment is inadequate. Quite a significant proportion of total population in India are still below the poverty line.

Income deprivation is an important cause of deprivation in nutrition, health and basic education. The poor also suffer from unexpected contingencies; so, if social security is to be meaningful for the poor, the provision of such security has to include promotional as well as protective measures. Moreover, the provisions of social security cannot be treated in isolation from the goal of attaining higher levels of human development in the country. Social security, in fact, provides the necessary conditions for human development to take place. There is a need for a balanced package of promotional and protective measures. Protective social security is not sufficient. Promotional social security measures are related to investment in human capital and social capital which build the social capabilities of the individual.

Social security is a term that has traditionally been used to denote protection against economic and social distress caused by the stoppage or fall in income resulting from death, old age, sickness, employment injury, maternity and temporary unemployment. Dreze and Sen (1989) regard social security as an objective to be pursued through public means rather than narrowly defined particular set of strategies. One concept is aimed at providing relief in the event of specific contingencies, whereas Dreze and Sen's concept views social security as comprising, in addition, promotional and protective components, such as measures that aim at improving endowments, exchange entitlements, real incomes and social consumption. Social security measures in India have gained much attention in the wake of increasing informalisation of the economy consequent upon the introduction of economic reforms in the early 1990s. The concern is "the direct role that public action can play in reducing human deprivation and eliminating vulnerability in a developing country with the use of a class of means is to pursue a category of objectives, broadly reduction of deprivation and vulnerability "(Ahmad *et al.*, 1990). It is pertinent to design a comprehensive social security regime that can capture and account for the major systems and different patterns of insecurity. It is widely feared that this will result in a rise in deprivation and poverty as the people lack minimal security mechanisms necessary for social and economic upliftment.

The concept of food security is interpreted in a variety of ways. However, physical and economic access to food at the household level, at all times, to ensure healthy and active life is the crux of food security (In practice, food security is generally equated with the absence of hunger, or at best, provisions of predetermined number of calories at the household level. This notion of food security and the resultant policies and programmes have failed to achieve the principal goal of food security, i.e., enabling households to lead a healthy and active life.

Trends in food production/cereal consumption/food consumption

The planning for security must be done on these two broad parameters: whether the country would be able to produce what would be required to feed the growing population in coming years? And whether we can ensure access to food to vulnerable sections through PDS or any other targeted mechanism?

Let us take the issue of availability or production of foodgrains. The demand supply projections carried out by the National Centre for Agricultural Economics and Policy Research (NCAP) has estimated that the country would require 296 million tonnes of foodgrains (cereals and pulses) during 2020-21 period as against 238 million tonnes produced at the end of 2005-06 provided the country grows at the rate of 7 per cent during this period. This means the country would have to produce about 42.3 per cent more foodgrains by 2020 to keep at peace with varying consumption basket of the country that arises from rising incomes and growing pace of urbanization.

Considering the obvious constraints of land availability and the need of growing population, meeting these projected targets is no means a task. The demand and supply projections for the years 2011-12 and 2020-21, thus underlines the need of ramping up the current rate of growth of all foodgrains from 0.7 per cent to 2.21 per cent to meet the increasing demand of food, feed and processed food requirements.

In this context, the NCAP assessment points out an urgent requirement of ramping up the productivity rates for these foodgrains to meet these productivity target considering the cultivation area being roughly constant.

Meeting these targets would mean raising the wheat productivity levels by about 23 per cent and the rice productivity levels by about 44 per cent. While these productivity levels for cereals may seem modest, the productivity jump required for pulses is more than 100 per cent which is going to be major area that would require government's serious attention.

What adds to the complexity of achieving these projected food production targets is the serious limitation involved in area expansion.

An area expansion in one crop, say, wheat, would require crop substitution reducing the area reduction in the other crop. This would mean a gain for one crop resulting into the loss of another crop, which the government cannot afford keeping in view the total demand of individual crops. Thus, a gain in area for wheat may translate into a loss in area for pulses or some other crops. This leaves government with no option but to look for productivity jumps to meet these targets.

Over the years, India has made rapid progress in the production of food. India achieved near self-sufficiency in the availability of foodgrains by the mid-seventies. The annual growth rate of food production including non-cereal food increased from 2.1 per cent during the 1960s to 3.0 per cent in the subsequent decade and further to 3.8 per cent during the 1980s. There seems to have been some diversification in food production in the 1980s on account of the impressive growth of output of oilseeds and livestock products. The diversification of food production more or less conforms to the growth patterns of domestic demand. The annual fluctuations in the per capita availability of foodgrains declined in the eighties and nineties when compared to the previous period (Rao and Radhakrishna, 1997) and there was a decline in the seasonal and regional variations in the prices of foodgrains (Bhalla, 1994). What is particularly noteworthy is that the up-trend in foodgrains production has barely kept pace with population growth. Ironically, even at the slow growth rate of foodgrains production, the supply has outstripped the effective market demand and the nineties has seen a rapid increase in the stock of foodgrains held by the government (Radhakrishna, 1998).

Inter-state comparisons reveal a weak correlation between nutritional status and per capita SDP as well as between nutritional status and per capita calorie consumption. The state level mismatch between the food intake and nutritional status could be attributed to the differences in education, health, availability of safe drinking water and environmental status. The improved nutritional status at a comparatively lower level of consumption of food energy as observed in Kerala and Tamil Nadu could be due to better health care and nutritional intervention. It is not clear as to how much of the malnutrition is due to an inadequate diet or how much due to environment.

The declining trend is visible across all the states with the exception of Kerala, West Bengal and Orissa. It is very prominent in Punjab and Haryana. The absolute fall, for example, of about 4 kg.

per capita per month in the rural areas of Punjab and Haryana and about 2 kg. in urban areas occurred mainly due to a reduced consumption of coarse cereals. What is striking is the low per capita intake of cereals in Punjab. This is partly due to the diversification of the food basket in Punjab in favour of non-cereal food, particularly milk, milk products, egg and fish, vegetables and fruits etc. It merits mention that cereal price induced inflation would hurt the poor of the backward regions most.

The nineties witnessed an increase in cereal price. This has significantly reduced the calorie intake of the poor. This is clearly brought out by available food price elasticity estimates which show that for the poor, the food (calorie) price elasticity is numerically large. The counter-intuitive result could be attributed to the changes in the consumer preferences (Suryanarayana, 1995; Meenakshi, 1996). The upward trend in the real price of cereal in the nineties had coincided with a slowdown in the decline of poverty. (Ravi, 200) Despite this moderate increase in food expenditure, the nutrition intake did not improve between 1972-73 and 1993-94; the per capita calorie intake declined at 0.25 per cent per annum in rural areas and 0.08 per cent in urban areas. The stagnancy or marginal decrease in the food energy intake despite improvement in income was due to the decline in the consumption of cereals, which is the cheapest source of calories. For the lowest 30 per cent of the population, there has hardly been any increase in the per capita cereal expenditure at constant prices in the rural as well as urban areas. It seems, the improvement in economic access to food made possible by income. (The per capita cereal consumption of the poor remained the same despite a significant improvement in their per capita expenditure and a decline in the relative cereal price.) Of course, the saturation in cereal consumption would not be a major cause of concern if the food energy intake levels of the poor were nutritionally adequate. The per capita calorie intake in 1993-94 was 1,678 kcal per day in rural areas and 1,682 kcal per day in urban areas. This section of the population was deprived of an adequate diet that would provide the required food energy. There has also been a substantial diversification of the consumption basket of the poor in favour of non-cereals, particularly non-food items.

It has already made substantial progress in terms of overcoming transient food insecurity by giving priority to self-sufficiency in foodgrains and through public procurement and distribution of foodgrains, employment programmes etc. However, despite a significant reduction in the incidence of poverty (from 55 per cent in 1973-74 to 28 per cent in 2001-02), chronic food insecurity persists as a large proportion of India's population is still below the poverty line. While India could achieve some success in combating transient food insecurity, caused by droughts or floods, it has failed to make much dent in chronic food insecurity, reflected in the low energy intake and high incidences of malnutrition. India is overcoming one of the worst crises it faced since independence. However, it originated as an appendage of green revolution whose chief concern was with a quick breakthrough in foodgrains production—which necessitated concentrating on rice and wheat—and not with food security of the poor or increase in the production of staples consumed by them. As the upsurge continued, the surpluses became an embarrassment. At the same time, the mere presence of food in the economy or in the market does not entitle a person to consume it (Dreze and Sen, 1989 p. 9). Simultaneously, the poverty and the deprivation suffered by the poor—particularly their foodgrains needs—assumed a prominent role in Indian policies.

Public Distribution System

India is one of the few countries in the world which has experimented with a broad spectrum of programmes for improving food security. Even the ability to buy may not guarantee food security, unless there is an efficient distribution system (Suryanarayana, 2000, p. 80). The outcome was the coming into being of a countrywide network of Public Distribution System (PDS) as a social safety net. "The PDS aims at insulating the consumers from the impact of rising prices of these commodities and maintaining the minimum nutritional status of our population. The PDS supplies have a stabilizing effect on open market prices by increasing availability, removing scarcity psychosis and deterring speculative tendencies (GoI 1991-92, Part II, p. 53). The PDS has remained a major instrument to execute the Government of India's economic policy to protect the poor. Public interventions in the foodgrains market aims at procurement of foodgrains for public distribution and maintenance of buffer stocks to ensure not only short-term but also long-term stability of prices of essential commodities and protect the interest of the consumers. Procurement of foodgrains also ensures remunerative returns to the farmers and provides them incentives to invest more on agriculture and to ensure that in the event of any overproduction and due to any other reason, the market prices do not fall below the support prices.

But the system reflects certain flaws. Foodgrains distribution among the targets under this scheme remained at a low level and full coverage of target households was never achieved. The problems of relatively better-off sections of farmers receive far more attention in policy making than deprivations suffered by the poor. A notable development is the widening gap between allocation and offtake. The areas which are relatively backward are not receiving adequate care. The system is not found to be congenial setting for progress towards decentralisation, debureaucratisation and depoliticisation. The system is inherently costly as it is based on surpluses of two superior cereals—rice and wheat—generated in a few green revolution pockets. These surpluses have to be procured, stored and distributed all-over the country. The system is far too centralized, hierarchical and bureaucratic to achieve cost-effectiveness to respond quickly to the areas and to distinguish those in real need for assistance from those who do not need it. Judged by the yardsticks of coverage of vulnerable groups, quality of food security provided and impact on the conditions of beneficiaries, the performance of the system is poor. The system is practically absent in some of the hard core poverty areas.

Physical access to PDS for the poor is quite difficult. The poor people have to fight at every stage to get a ration card, obtain the entitlement to supply, to retain their cards and so on. Life for the poor is a daily struggle. The malfunctioning and non-functioning of the PDS is only a part of the wider problem of the nature of the function of the state. While the system is ostensibly for the benefit of the poor, it is not targeted on the poor and has shown little concern to extend its reach to areas where food distress is widespread among the poor. The delivery mechanism works better in urban rather than rural areas.

The present food security system viewed as a safety net for the poor needs to be assessed in relation to the broader context of changing agricultural and poverty scenario in India. It seems to suggest that what is urgently required is a thoroughgoing restructuring of the system rather than piecemeal improvements in it. In reality, political economy considerations are important in designing sustainable food transfer programmes. Too much fine tuning in targeting may lead to erosion of political support for food subsidies.

There is a strong case for including a significant section of the population who are neither rich nor poor. It is narrowly focused one and, therefore, runs into a number of problems. Such a programme will entail less errors of exclusion of the poor than a targeted PDS, which is narrowly focused for those below the poverty line in the strict sense of the term. This is because poverty line is a methodologically driven one and may not be suitable for purposes of programme implementation. For example, it will be easy to include a household just "below" the poverty line but very difficult to exclude another which is just "above" the poverty line. Further, there are additional costs of enforcements in implementing a targeted PDS. Again, the poverty line is an unsatisfactory criterion. If one goes by the intake of calories, then around 53 per cent of the population is deficient in terms of calorie intake. If one goes by the nutritional status of the children, then again more than half the population is nutritionally poor. The Kerala PDS which highlights the advantages of universalisation has got institutionalized and became an integral part of public policy. If social security measures have to target essentially these vulnerable groups who are disadvantaged, basic needs obviously assume priority. Accordingly, individual capabilities have to be essentially built up *vis-à-vis* basic needs for ensuring an effective participation of these groups in the workforce, market and political processes.

Some Emerging Issues

There are several emerging issues at the national and global levels in the context of food security in the country like (a) climate change, (b) production of bio-fuel and (c) introduction of bio-technology which have significant bearing on food security.

Climate change, a reality of today, is one of the most important global environmental challenges facing humanity (with implications for production, natural economic systems, fresh water supply etc.). Climate change cuts across boundaries. India is one of the countries recognized to be most vulnerable to climate change. The IPCC 2007 concludes that the impact would be particularly severe in the tropical areas, which mainly consist of developing countries including India. India with 70 crore rural population depending on climate sensitive sectors (like agriculture, forestry and fisheries) and natural resources for their subsistence and livelihood will be hard hit. The adaptive capacity of dryland farmers, forest dwellers, fisher-folk and nomadic shepherds is very low. Recent IPCC Report and a few other global studies indicate a probabilities of 10-40 per cent loss in crop production in India within temperature. Global warming in most terms is likely to favour negatively tropical crop production and favour positively in temperate region. This is likely to have consequences on international food prices and hence, on food security (Misra, 2010).

Various studies have indicated a probability of 10 to 40 per cent loss in crop production in the country due to the anticipated rise in temperature by 2008-2110. Studies conducted by IARI has pointed to a possible loss of 4 5 million tonnes in the overall wheat production with every one degree centigrade increase in temperature throughout the growing period of the crop. Though agriculture's share in green house gas emission in India is relatively small, it will be a consequence of climatic change. The policy implications for climatic change impacts in agriculture are multidisciplinary and include possible adaptation in food security policy to account for changing crop yield as well as shifting boundaries for crops.

Another area of concern is bio-technology. The tools of bio-technology have infused a new round of technology into Indian agriculture at a time when the green revolution technologies have lost steam. A few scholars have apprehended that a sort of 'scientific apartheid' can well develop with bio-technology. The diffusion of transgenic crops has been rapid. It reached 125 million hectares in 2008 from a very small base. The implications of bio-technology are important. The locus of agricultural research has changed to the domain of the private sector. The advent of bio-technology facilitated by the intellectual property rights changed the scenario completely and now it is the private sector which is undertaking private research. The research spillovers from the developed countries could not be possible now in view of the IPR protection. There is also wide asymmetry in the research expenditures apart from privatization. The share of the developing countries is a mere 8-9 per cent in bio-technology research and the private sector in the developed countries is a major player in bio-technology research expenditures. In fact, many of the seed companies in the country resort to purchase of seed licence rather than any innovative research and discovery. This can perpetuate the dependency syndrome for a long time to come unless the public sector steps in to undertake the basic research in this field. There are some more concerns regarding the privatization of bio-technology research in India.

The political economy issues in the cases of bio-technological research organization and product development resemble the green revolution technologies, albeit in a slightly different manner. The acquisition of seed companies by biotech companies across the globe has been responsible for concentration in the seed market, where a few multinationals dominate the market. The spending in India on total agricultural research per annum is around $500 million and bio-tech research may not account for more than $50 million. The international public agricultural research represented by the CGIAR network is also on the decline and the spending on bio-technology is around $85 million comprising 7 per cent of the total research expenditure per annum. On the other hand, the largest agro-tech multinational company invests $490 million in bio-technological research per annum. This asymmetry in investment is likely to lead to unfavourable outcomes for the resource-poor farmers and for the poor in general in countries like India.

It is true that a wide range of traits in all the crops can be developed by means of modern bio-technology. But the pattern of commercialization in the last few years shows that the profit motive limits it to those that can be lucratively marketed. The traits of importance to the developing countries like drought tolerance, and higher genetic potential are not developed, though that is possible. The commercialized transgenics are limited to only four crops, viz. soyabeans, maize, cotton and mustard accounting. What is more worrying is the fact that not even a single research experiments is being carried out on "orphan crop" like minor millets, pulses and oilseeds. If this pattern of commercialization continues neglecting staple crops like paddy, wheat, minor millets pulses and oilseeds, there can be serious problems by way of distortions in the crop-mix of the country. The availability of the green revolution technologies is responsible for the diversification in favour of paddy and wheat and away from crops like coarse cereals, which provide food with higher calorific value. This has helped in achieving self-sufficiency in food production; but several other problems like sustainability and environmental degradation have emerged due to the ways in which those technologies are applied. If better varieties with higher productivity and profitability are applied to only commercial crops, then the cropping pattern may shift in their favour and food security may suffer. The present pattern of product development driven primarily by the profit motive of the multinational companies can wreck havoc with the country's agriculture. Unless efforts are made to develop varieties that can increase the genetic potential of these crops in dry land situations, poverty reductions could not be achieved.

Bio-fuel is now viewed as a strong future source of energy. In the context of shrinking crude oil reserves, rising demand and the resultant rise in prices of petroleum, as well as the concerns about global climate change and energy security, bio-energy is becoming increasingly relevant as a possible and potential alternative to fossil fuels (Raju et al., 2009). Currently, India's bio-fuel production accounts for only 1 per cent of the global production. The Government of India is in the process of firming up various policies to encourage the use of bio-diesel in its energy sector. The present strategy of the government is to utilize the wastelands for bio-diesel plantations so as not to affect the food security of the country. However, *jatropha* cultivation are slow to take off due to lack of good quality of planting materials etc. so far, nearly five lakh hectares of lands in the country is only put under *jatropha* cultivation. Chhattisgarh is leading with around 0.84 lakh hectares followed by Rajasthan 0.33 lakh hectares, Tamil Nadu 0.20 lakh hectares etc. There is another point of view that diversion of forest and wasteland for cultivation of energy plantations may cause a conflict with pastoral livelihoods. Any large scale bio-fuel programme has to ensure that it does not compromise with the nation's food and nutritional security.

The role of the state, market and civil society in this context is quite pertinent. Ensuring nutritional security requires that the vital institutions—the state, the market and the civil society—each should recognize own role and responsibilities in warding off hunger and ensuring food security.

The state's role in strengthening food security is more prominent in ensuring availability of food and ensuring its access by the households, particularly the poor households. State interventions are of direct as well as indirect nature. Investment in research and development in agriculture or the investment in infrastructure or institution of land reforms will have an indirect but significant impact on the availability of food. This is what Dreze and Sen have called "growth mediated security." The widespread move towards globalization, on the one hand, and secular decline in the food prices at the international level on the other, have been advanced as the arguments to forsake food self-sufficiency as a national objective and organize production on the basis of comparative costs, security. But advocacy of unrestricted exposure to international markets ignores the fact of the dependence of a large majority of rural producers on foodgrains production as their main source of livelihood. It overestimates the resilience of the system to compensate these producers from heavy and sudden dislocations. To take a doctrinaire approach on 'free' trade in foodgrains would amount to jeopardizing one of the essential attributes of food security and will compromise the prospect of livelihood for those who are inherently food insecure. At the same time, food self-sufficiency should not be interpreted as an invitation to autarky. It connotes a trade strategy which would not expose the vulnerable sections of producers as well as consumers to avoidable shocks from external trade. More often than not, it is the poor whose interests are sacrificed in the pursuit of fiscal discipline. The policy makers take the easy options of raising foodgrains prices for the producers, lowering issue prices for the poor and subsidizing the gap between the high procurement prices and low issue prices.

If foodgrains markets function efficiently, the prospect of annihilating food insecurity will brighten. There is an increasing degree of market integration in recent years in the case of rice and wheat, but that is not true for *jowar* (sorghum) which is the poor man's crop. In the unorganized markets in remote areas. Physical access itself is a problem. Market efficiency ignored two ground level realities i.e. high transaction costs to be incurred by the poor and discriminatory prices faced by the poor, especially in areas where markets are not developed. The factors responsible for imperfections in the markets faced by the poor are unequal bargaining power of different economic agents, asymmetry of information and moral hazards. Another factor leading to imperfection is the high transaction costs. The poor face all these handicaps. Weak bargaining power of the poor producers and the poor consumers is a fact of life, whether one subscribes to the notion of interlocked markets or not. In any case, the poor and sell in small quantities and intermittently and as a result, the transaction costs are higher which thwart competition Removing imperfections in the markets can contribute to food security and their prevalence exacerbates food insecurity (Vyas, 2006).

While the role of the state in providing and upholding legal framework and in strengthening market infrastructure is recognized, role of civil society to correct market distortions is not fully appreciated. The civil society's proactive role in ensuring food security is an ethical role. There is another aspect of the role of the civil society institutions which imparts true meaning to food security i.e. influencing consumption in the direction of healthy and productive life[5].

Policies: Towards a Food Secure India

There has been a paradigmatic shift in the concept of food security from food availability and stability to household food insecurity and from assessment of input measures like energy intake to output indicators such as anthropometric measures and clinical signs of malnutrition. This shift calls for an intensive analysis to understand the nature and extent of food insecurity and nutrition deprivation at the household level. It is true that food security is not confined only to production, availability and demand for food. Ultimately, the question is that of the ability of the people to access food and utilize it effectively at all times to lead a healthy and active life. Nutrition security is an important dimension of food security.

There is no doubt that in the post-independence period, India has several achievements on the food fronts. Successive Five-Year Plans have laid considerable emphasis on policies and strategies aimed at raising the level of nutrition and standard of living of the people. The production of foodgrains has increased more than four-fold since Independence—From 50 million tonnes in 1950-51, it has increased to about 210 million tonnes in 1999-2000. As a result, India has moved from a stage of chronic food shortages to self-sufficiency in food production, and has built-up substantial buffer stocks. The level of procurement and the reach of PDS has also increased considerably, overtime. Again the Government has introduced several nutrition programmes, such as the Integrated Child Development Services providing supplementary nutrition for pre-school children and expectant or nursing mothers. All these have contributed greatly towards improving the availability of food and level of nutrition in the country.

But all is not well with the food security policy. With the advent of liberalization and globalization, some new challenges have also emerged. Despite the implementation of several programmes, there are concerns regarding calorie intake and malnutrition. Poverty levels remain high. The calorie intake of the bottom 30 per cent is low. The problem of malnutrition is acute and widespread and is extremely serious among the women and the children. Even in states where the poverty ratio has fallen, unemployment has increased, suggesting that a significant proportion of the population is still threatened by a lack of access to a means of livelihood and is potentially vulnerable to food insecurity.

While the PDS provides a degree of food security to some sections of the population, there are doubts whether the benefits are commensurate with the costs of running the system. What demands scrutiny is whether the PDS is an efficient mechanism. There is no alternative but to revamp the PDS, if need be gradually, so as to make it reach and serve the poor better.

The validity of the growth-oriented measures, however, has been questioned in the context of developing countries, characterized by low growth rates and high growth rates of population combined with rampant poverty and illiteracy. Moreover, the majority of their population lives outside the mainstream of development and has little or no access to any form of social security. Such a dismal scenario underscores the need for a broader interpretation of social security which accounts for a high degree of deprivation and vulnerability in the developing countries. Given this broad perception of social and economic security, state and social institutions do have a pivotal role to play in providing social security to the weaker and marginalized sections.

The ineffectiveness of the promotional security measures often portrays the state as an agency with merely a progressive face bereft of any real intention of providing a secure present or future for its citizens.

India has made impressive progress in the reduction of the problem of hunger. But, the reduction can be achieved through the intake of cereals; whereas, the latter demands other non-cereal food as well as access to safe, better sanitary conditions, quality of care etc. The overcoming of the problem of hunger is not the same as elimination of malnutrition. For enhancing the capabilities of the vulnerables, a proper blend of different policies is extremely desirable. The experiences across world show that skill development and training are the most important factors.

It is ironical that India witnesses such acute forms of food insecurity as it accumulates stocks of foodgrains in public warehouses in unprecedented levels—more than 60 million tonnes in 2005-06. (Box 2).

Box 2: Rotting Grains, Rotting State

At a time when the Union Government is hell-bent on pushing through the Food Security Bill, several million tonnes of foodgrains rot, thanks to the criminal apathy and neglect of the powers that be. Rogues that rule the roost show contempt for the poor. Food Corporation of India disclosed that it has a stock of 57.8 million tonnes of foodgrains in its godowns on August 1, 2010 fulfilling the buffer stock stipulation of 31.9 million tonnes as on July 1. According to FCI, 1,83,000 tonnes of rice, 22,000 tonnes of wheat, 1,10,000 tonnes of maize were damaged between1997 and 2007. Sadly enough, the FCI has not disclosed the value to State Governments did not show interest in questioning the deceptive act. There is a distant endorsement of disappointment about PDS in the latest Report of the CAG on the dealings of FCI till date and the storage loss was being accounted for on actual basis as the difference between the receipt weight and the issue weight. The CAG indicted for irregular disbursement of Rs. 786 crores in 2007 in regard to incentive bonus. There is no data to ascertain whether the farmers had actually received the amount

—*Foodgrains going waste in Sopan* by Sankar Ray Kolkata, September 2010

Democracy may have averted famines but it cannot claim to have averted food insecurity. Achieving freedom from hunger still remains one of the biggest challenges of a democratically free India. (Dev *et al.*, 2003) It is recognized that food availability at the macro level cannot be equated with the food security at the household or micro level.

To ensure food security, the household should have 'entitlement' to access adequate food. At the same time, it is also pertinent to recognize that the concept of food security should go beyond the availability of a given quantity of calories for the individuals in a household. It should also meet nutritional requirements. Against this background, the concept of food security comprises four elements: (a) availability of food, (b) household's entitlement to food, (c) stability in the supply of food throughout the year, and (d) protection against malnutrition.

The issue of food security needs to be seen in a holistic perspective taking into account both the macro and micro aspects and hunger and nutrition. In such a comprehensive food security system, the state is responsible for ensuring that every needy person has economic access to nutrition and food. So, there is a need for strengthening and effective implementation of various schemes and programmes, such as PDS, Annapurna, Mid-day meal scheme and ICDS and extending Antyodaya Anna Yojana to all the destitutes in the country. In the holistic scheme of food security, gender aspects of food security should be given due importance in realizing every person's rights to food. Women's economic and social empowerment not only improves intra-household food distribution and health-related matters, but also the implementation of food and nutrition programmes. The access of the poor to employment will help greatly promote food security through increased purchasing power.[6]

In order to improve the food and nutrition security in the country, the present programmes such as PDS, Antyodaya Anna Yojana, nutrition programmes and public works programmes have to be strengthened. Employment security is crucial for achieving food security. Economists like Amartya Sen have argued that food availability is not a major problem at the national or local level. It is the economic access at the household level which is responsible for the low accessibility of food. In this context, creating purchasing power through employment is crucial.

In point of fact, it may be noted that at the all-India level, the poorest 40 per cent have only diversified their consumption basket, with the improvement in their economic status (to the neglect of nutritional considerations), to the extent required by the principle of complementarity among food items. As a result, though their calorie intake has increased consistently, the calorie levels fall short of the normative minimum. This emphasizes the need for formulating policies with reference to both poverty and nutritional deficiency considerations. The average level of calorie intake is so low and the incidence of calorie deficiency is so high across states that there is little scope for eradicating the incidence of calorie deficiency by pursuing a targeted policy uniformly across regions. However, it is not suggested that the PDS alone would be enough to protect the poor. In fact, the poor must be helped to reach a critical minimum level of income through the expanded network of employment programme so that their economic access to the PDS would be ensured.

In the race between population growth and foodgrains production, even when the income-induced demand for foodgrains is slackening, improving food productivity would improve food security. In this regard, economic agenda is clear. It would call for encouraging production by investment in infrastructure and promoting scientific research and extension, by (a) strengthening supportive institutions of credit and marketing, (b) providing appropriate subsidies and fixing fair procurement prices, (c) regulating market to foster competition and discourage exploitation and (d) mitigating or at least minimizing uncertainty by introducing measures such as crop insurance, establishing forward markets and fixing minimum support prices. The time has come to encourage our farmers to diversify into areas such as horticulture, floriculture and oilseeds. Again, in rural areas, over-dependence on land has resulted in high levels of disguised unemployment, although the proportion of the rural population dependent on agriculture is declining. Enhancing rural non-farm employment by removing bottlenecks faced by village industries should be the cornerstone of any poverty alleviation scheme.

The public works approach to unemployment would make sense if it is so organized that there will be progressively less and less reliance on it, so that it ultimately becomes redundant. It is true that they may not necessarily increase the skills of workers. But it is expected that in future, skill-based workers are going to get much higher wages and the wage employed people continue to get lower wages. The difference between the unskilled and the skilled workers would widen further, particularly after the introduction of economic reforms in the country.

Notes

*** Reprinted from the Proceedings of the International Seminar organized by the Department of Environmental Sciences, Visva-Bharati, Santiniketan, India in 2010.

1. Malnutrition among children is in fact more widespread in India than in Sub-Saharan Africa, notorious for famines and poverty. Undernourishment is a problem which has serious long-term implications for daily activities so much so that Pacey and Payne (1985) define undernutrition as unacceptable penalties in terms of hunger, illness, dysfunction and risk of dysfunction The nutritional status has

a bearing on efficiency and productivity of labour, the only asset of the poor and hence, their wages and incomes too.

2. On the effectiveness of social security measures, Dreze and Sen (1993) maintains that the distinction of China and Kerala or Sri Lanka does not lie in the size of financial allocation to particular provisions. According to them, the real success lies in creating political, social and economic conditions for implementing the public programmes effectively with determination.
3. Public action is not just a question of public delivery and state initiative. It is also a matter of participation by the public in the process of social change. Public policy in India has been sporadic, fragmented across departments and ministries.
4. On this, see Dev, S. Mahendra (2003).
5. Impact of self-employment *vs.* wage-employment programmes because they have a self-targeting nature and other secondary benefits. Again, self-employment programmes like IRDP is better because they increase the skills of the workers An employment programme/policy which does not enhance the skill of the participant is, at best, a relief measure. The poor need work immediately and cannot afford to wait for skill acquisition. This situation cannot be ignored. Hence, the need is for Employment Guarantee Scheme type of programmes which are not skill demanding. But equally, they are not skill promoting. This type of employment of the poor and their self-reliance leaves the country unprepared to face the challenge of the technological revolution which we cannot arrest at our frontiers. Is there a way through which the needs of today can be reconciled with the challenge of the future? (Dantwala, 1996 p. 56). The EGS of Maharastra is that it provides employment on public works projects on demand. The public works fit into the ideas of Nurkse (1957). This guarantee was created. But this programme provides only short-term relief and supplementary income and are not useful for long-term benefits.
6. However, much of the authority of civil society institutions at the grass root level has been eroded with the increase in penetration of the market and explosion of wants. Some of these institutions still wield moral force and appeal to the basic goodness of the human being. The moralization that the society can exercise will be any time more effective than the regulations imposed.

Appendix II

Role of Indigenous Fish Species in Aquaculture Production and Rural Livelihood

Freshwater aquaculture in India has been increasing at a rate of 11 per cent per year, contributing 95 per cent of the total aquaculture production. Polyculture of Indian major carps and Chinese carps is the main aquaculture technology practiced in the country and carps alone contribute 87 per cent of the total aquaculture production (Ayyappan and Jena, 2003). But, as part of the pond management in this culture practice, fish poisons from organic and inorganic origin have been prescribed to the pond aquaculturists to eradicate Small Indigenous Fish Species (SIFS) from the fish ponds (Wahab *et al.*, 2003). Polyculture technologies focused on large carps only, in this way, have deprived the members of the farming households, especially the children and women, because large carps are grown for cash crop, not for family consumption. Even the large carps seldom used for family consumption often are not distributed evenly in the family, rather the male senior members consume the largest share depriving the women and children (Amilhat *et al.*, 2009; Garaway, 2005). On the other hand, small fish, which are eaten whole and constitute a rich source of vitamins and micronutrients, if available for consumption are distributed evenly among all family members. The low intake of vitamin A and other micronutrients has caused an increase in night blindness, anemia and stunted growth, which can be mitigated by providing vitamin A rich small fishes like mola (A. mola), calcium rich punti (P. sophore) and other micronutrient rich fishes (Ahmed, 2009; Rooas *et al.*, 2003, 2007; Wahab, 2003). As a consequence, along with the recommended six species of silver carp, grass carp, common carp, and three Indian Major Carps, many fish growers are currently culturing even more than ten species in the composite fish culture (Jena *et al.*, 2005; Katiha *et al.*, 2006). Continuous refinement and modification undergone by the research institutes regarding carp culture have led the fish farmers to culture even predatory or weed SIFS like *Channa triatus*. (Sol), *Anabus testudineus* (Koi), *Mystus vittatus* (Tangra) and *Ompok pabda* (Pabda), *Amblypharyngdon mola* (Mourala), *Colisa fasciatus* (Kholse).

Side by side, it is also true that, carp culture through SIFS without any supplementary feed, quality seeds have always been discouraged by scientists (Mazid and Kohinoor, 2003). They have also discouraged introduction of predatory species without recommended adoption package of practices. But stark reality is that fish farmers, caring only for profit, have introduced mola, bata or some other SIFS in their polyculture practices without following scientific advice, resulting in frustrating outcome in terms of fish production (Neiland and Bene, 2004; Allision and Ellis, 2001). It is, therefore, important to locate these efforts within specific socio-economic contexts and to formulate relevant strategies, as appropriate. The objective of this paper is to find out whether introduction of such small fish species can necessarily increase pond fish productivity or not. A field study was conducted in West Bengal during 2007-08 and meta-frontier technique using non-parametric Data Envelopment Analysis (DEA) has been followed to measure the levels of technical efficiency in carp-cum SIFS culture at the firm (pond) level. Both a grand frontier applicable to all firms and a group frontier specific to firms practicing carp-cum-SIFS culture and only-carp culture have been used in order to evaluate their efficiencies. This permits one to separately identify how diversification of carp culture through SIFS can affect the overall pond fish production.

1. Materials and Methods

The study has been based on primary source of information obtained through field survey from representative respondents in 2007-08. Excluding hill and terai region, one district has been selected from each of the rest four zones (like old alluvial region, red and laterite zone, new alluvial region and coastal and saline zone). At the second stage, three blocks from each district have been randomly chosen. At the final stage, a comprehensive list of pond or tank owners from each village in the selected blocks has been prepared and then those villages in which farmers are growing SIFS with carp polyculture have been purposively chosen. In case of non-fulfilment of this condition in a particular village, a nucleus of villages with two or more contiguous villages was constituted. From each village, five fish farmers each from small (having pond of size less than 0.5 acre), medium (having pond of size between 0.5 to 5 acre) and large (having pond of size more than 5 acre) group have been randomly selected. In this way, the total number of 30 household pond owners from each block has been chosen. The number of sample pond owner from each district is 90 and the total number of ultimate unit of analysis for the state as a whole is, therefore, 360.

The study has been performed on the basis of an open-ended and exploratory research design. Observations are made according to the administered pre-designed structured questionnaires to all the fish farmers selected. The data pertaining to yield during the period, type and extent of water resources, adoption behaviour, information on fish seed, feed, labour as also some other inputs, information on fish outputs produced and some other micro-details are culled for one production year. It has been found that among those 360 fish farmers interviewed, only 138 have introduced SIFS along with carp polyculture, details of which have been presented in Exhibit 1. In this paper, fish farmers practishing SIFS along with carp are termed

Exhibit 1: District-wise Sample Farmers Practicing Carp Culture with or Without SIFS

District	*No. of Fish Farmers*	*Progressive Farmers (Culturing carp with SIFS)*	*Traditional Farmer (Culturing only Carp)*
24-Parganas (S)	90 (25.0)	51 (56.67)	39 (43.33)
Hoogly	90 (25.0)	42 (46.67)	48 (53.33)
Murshidabad	90 (25.0)	26 (28.89)	64 (71.11)
Bankura	90 (25.0)	19 (21.11)	71 (78.89)
Overall	360 (100.0)	138 (38.33)	222 (61.67)

Note: Figures in the parentheses indicate percentage to the respective totals.

Source: Field Survey, 2007-08.

as "progressive" farmers. Those, who are culturing only carps (not diversifying with SIFS) are termed as "traditional" farmers.

Fish polyculture typically involves the production of several fish species or outputs using several inputs, including seed or fingerlings, feed, manure and fertilizers, labour, etc. In practice, fish farmers produce different types of fish species using seeds of different species of each category (SIFS and carps). Here, output for carp and SIFS is expressed as the aggregated nominal value of total fish output, of each category, of all species taken together, instead of each species from the group individually. Aggregation has been done because of the inability or unwillingness on the part of the fish farmers to provide detailed information about the use of different species of fish seed or fish output of carps and SIFS.

2. Analytical Framework

Data Envelopment Analysis (DEA) models operationalizes the concept of efficiency in the context of linear programming problems that calculates the frontier production function of a set of Decision-Making Units (DMUs) and evaluate the relative technical efficiency of each unit, thereby allowing a distinction to be made between efficient and inefficient DMUs. Those identified as "best practice units" (i.e., those determining the frontier) are given a rating of one, whereas the degree of technical inefficiency of the rest is calculated on the basis of the Euclidian distance of their input-output ratio from the frontier (Coelli *et al.*, 1998).

Technical Efficiency (TE) represents the ability of a DMU to produce maximum output given a set of inputs and technology (output-oriented) or, alternatively, to achieve maximum feasible reductions in input quantities given input prices and output (input-oriented), thereby producing fish optimally (Farrell, 1957). In this study, input-oriented DEA seems more appropriate, given that it is more reasonable to argue that in the agricultural and its allied sector a farmer has more control over inputs rather than output levels, which may often be exogenously bounded (Sharma *et al.*, 1999). Also, from utility-maximization point of view, most of poor farmers tend to be risk averse in nature. Their predominant goal is economic survival. They really do trade off lower risk against higher profit or the disutility of increasing risk. Adequate stability of output and income and the avoidance of major short-term losses take precedence over profit maximization. As a result, rational use of inputs, rather than output maximization, appears more rational strategy for the fish farmers. Again, since both input- and output-oriented measure give the same numerical figure for technical efficiency score, the same interpretation will follow the same result (Fare *et al.*, 1994; Kumar *et al.*, 2004).

The efficiency of a firm depends not only on the inputs it uses, but also on several other factors (such as infrastructural facilities, region, level of education and technical knowledge, work culture, size etc.). It is very difficult to incorporate those factors into a production frontier to examine their effects on efficiency, though important. Hence, group-efficiency analysis might reveal more concrete results if it is carried on separately for different groups. Also, a definite conclusion can be drawn if it is found that a particular group of farmers are efficient with respect to all the farmers taken together. For that, it is important to calculate the group efficiency to reach the final conclusion.

In this section, the concept of meta-frontier production function has been employed to examine whether there is any systematic difference in the efficiency of the fish farms for different aquaculture diversification strategy (Hayami, 1969; Hayami and Ruttan, 1970). The concept of a meta-production function is theoretically attractive because it is based on the simple hypothesis that all producers in different groups have potential access to the same technology.

In Meta-frontier analysis, the performance of each individual fish farm in the sample is measured against two different frontiers—one based on farms from all the different groups in the sample and the other based only on farms from the group to which it belongs. The first can be regarded as the *grand* frontier and the other as the *group* frontier. The grand and the group frontiers can be defined as follows. Define the index set $I = \{1, 2, ..., N\}$ where each observed data point is an element of I. Now consider a partition $I = \bigcup I_r$ where I_r includes only observations from group r. Then, under the standard assumptions of convexity and free disposability of inputs (x) and outputs (y) the empirically constructed group and grand production possibility sets are

$$S^r = \{(x, y) : x \geq \sum_{j \in I_r} \lambda_j x^j;\ y \leq \sum_{j \in I_r} \lambda_j y^j;\ \sum_{j = I_r} \lambda_j = 1\ ;\ \lambda_j \geq 0\ \ (j \in I_r)\}$$

(for group r)

And

$$S^G = \{(x, y) : x \geq \sum_{j \in \cup I_r} \lambda_j x^j;\ y \leq \sum_{j \in \cup I_r} \lambda_j x^j;\ \sum_{j \in \cup I_r} \lambda_j = 1;\ \lambda_j \geq 0;\ (j \in \cup I_r)\}$$

respectively. It may be noted that while each S^r is a subset of S^G, the latter is bigger than the union of the individual group production possibility sets.

3. Mathematical Presentation

For the overall or grand efficiency of the fish farms in the sample, we solve the following LP problem, including all 360 farms from observation as—

$$\underset{\lambda^j, \theta^j}{Minimize}\ \theta_G^j$$

Subject to—

$$\sum_{j=1}^{360} \lambda^j Y^j \geq Y_0^j \text{ (output constraints)}$$

$$\sum_{j=1}^{360} \lambda^j X_k^j \leq \theta_G^j X_k^0 \text{ (inputs constraints, k)}$$

$$\sum_{j=1}^{360} \lambda^j = 1$$

$$\lambda^j \geq 0, j = 1, 2, ..., 360$$

Where, θ_G^j is the dual of the variable indicating proportional increase in output possible by farm *j*; or Grand technical efficiency, TE_G^j.

λ^j = weight or intensity variable (or, shadow price) used to derive all possible linear combinations of the sample observations.

Y_0^j = Actual output produced by farm *j*.

X_k^0 = Actual input used by farm *j*

Similarly, the relevant DEA model for group *r* with N_r (=138 or 222) fish farms in the sample is—

$$\underset{\lambda^j, \theta^j}{\text{Minimize}} \ \theta_r^j$$

Subject to—

$$\sum_j \lambda^j Y^j \geq Y_0^j \qquad \text{(output constraints)}$$

$$\sum_j \lambda^j X_k^j \leq \theta_r^j X_k^0 \qquad \text{(inputs constraints, } k\text{)}$$

$$\sum_j \lambda^j = 1 \qquad \lambda^j \geq 0,$$

Where, θ_r^j is the dual of the variable indicating proportional increase in output possible by farm j; or the group technical efficiency, TE_r^j.

A point-wise measure of technical efficiency of group r relative to the grand frontier evaluated at the input-output data of farm j is—

$$\beta_r^j = \frac{TE_G^j}{TE_r^j}$$

An overall measure of the efficiency of group r is—

$TE(r) = (\prod_{j \in r} \beta_r^j)^{1/N\,r}$ where N_r is the number of farms in group r.

Clearly, for any fish farm j in a group r, TE_G^j is a measure of its performance relative to other farms within the same group. On the other hand, β is a measure of its performance compared to all groups in the study.

Technical efficiency score of each fish farm within each group was estimated separately based on their individual frontier and also based on the grand frontier comprising all the observations taken together. Index of intensification efficiency broadly reflects the social, economic and cultural factors in a particular group on the technical efficiency of a fish farm.

Analysis of such group efficiency relationship in pond fishery in West Bengal appears relevant, especially from the point of view of recent policy issues taken by Government of West Bengal in Inland tanks and ponds. Resource diversification has already been taken up by the government. Many small indigenous species are already bred and successfully cultured at various places in the state. The Directorate is also pushing for the creation of aqua-sanctuaries to build up a bank of SIFS and indigenous fish species of the State, towards *in situ* germ-plasma conservation. The move is, no doubt, appraisable. But the basic question is that whether fish farmers can be able to augment production more than carp farming through introduction of such species.

4. Results and Discussion

The livelihoods of a large number of small and marginal farmers are associated with fish farming in the study area. The peak fish farming season is from April to December, a culture period of around nine months. Fish fry are stocked in April to June and harvested primarily from October to December. Culture period is limited to one crop annually. Fish Culture practices in the study area include all activities from pre-stocking operations to harvesting of fish through human efforts. Their cultural practices may simply be categorized on the basis of major operations like pre-stocking, stocking input application, application of supplementary feeds and harvesting.

The average size of fingerlings was 5-7 cms. in length and 10-12 gms. in weight. Farmers did not attempt to stock any specific ratio of different carp species. Even, recommended schedule of stocking have not been followed by huge number of farmers (253 out of 360 farmers studied). However, along with carp, farmers also stocking SIFS like mola (*Amblypharyngodon mola*), bata (*Labeo bata),* puti (*Puntius sophore*), koi (*Anabas testudineus*) and also some economically important small cat fish like, pabda (*Ompok pabda)* in their ponds to enhance total fish production. Average stocking density per acre was 5,779 fingerlings for carp and 8243 for SIFS. Usually, carp fingerlings were stocked from local *aratdars* (33.6%), or hatchery (66.4%). Natural sources, such as old perennial ponds, floodplains and rice fields are the sources of seed for SIFS.

Lime is used in a pond to maintain the appropriate alkaline nature of the fish ponds. The most common toxicant is mohua oil cake. Dung is the most commonly used manure. Apart from such organic fertilization, inorganic fertilizers, like urea, single super phosphate are also used by some of the operators in the study area. Rice bran, white bran, mustard oil cakes are most common among the supplementary feeding applied by the farmers (Lorenzen, K., 2008). In almost all the ponds, upon enquiry, it was revealed that very few farmers use supplementary feeds as per recommended schedule, rather hit and trial method followed. Forty two per cent of the farmers generally employed commercially manufactured improved feeds. The most common feeding frequency in extensive farming system was once per day. The average annual yield of carp and SIFS were estimated at 974 and 154 kgs per acre, respectively. There was a significant difference in fish yields between different farming systems.

4.1 Variations in Technical Efficiency according to Diversification

At the farm level, the technical efficiency has a mixed relationship with carp diversification strategy of the farmers. While the progressive farmers practicing carp culture along with SIFS recorded slightly more technical efficiency, both on the basis of group and grand frontier; farmers culturing only carp have been found as slightly inefficient. This is evident from Exhibit 3. Taking all observations into consideration, grand technical efficiency has been found as 0.651 and 0.642 for progressive and traditional farmers respectively. Implication is that, progressive farmers can be able to minimize its input use by 34.9 per cent and can still produce the same output. Alternatively speaking, progressive farmers can enhance its production by 34.9 per cent by using its existing inputs optimally. Side by side, using existing inputs, traditional farmers can increase fish production by 35.8 per cent. Hence, traditional farmers are 0.9 per cent less efficient than progressive farmers.

The index of intensification-efficiency (signifying farmers' capability to cultivate fish in appropriate manner) of the "progressive" farms (practicing SIFS with carp) is 0.723, which is higher than that of "traditional" farms (0.714). Clearly, result indicates that introduction of SIFS with carp polyculture increases technical efficiency of farmers only marginally.

In order to find out regional variations in such kind of efficiency, if any, average technical efficiency score has been computed for each region and depicted in Exhibit 4. The result, in this case, appeared ambiguous. In case of coastal and saline zone (South 24-Parganas is the representative district) and red and laterite region (Bankura is the representative district), the results are the same as derived earlier. That is, intensification of carp culture through introduction of SIFS

Exhibit 2: Mean Technical Efficiency of Fish Farms across different Culture Practices

Diversification Group	*No. of Fish Farms*	*Technical Efficiency Score*		*Index of intensificatic Efficiency*
		Based on Grand Frontier	*Based on Group Frontier*	
Farmers Culturing carp with SIFS	138	0.651	0.742	0.723
Farmer Culturing only Carp	222	0.642	0.727	0.714
Total	**360**	**0.646**	**0.734**	**0.713**

has increased technical efficiency of the farms. But, the "traditional" farmers, producing only carps, in Old Alluvial Region (representative district is Hoogly) and New Alluvial Region (Murshidabad is the representative district) are found more technically efficient than "progressive" farmers.

Also, judging by Coefficient of Variation (CV) in the group efficiency levels, progressive farmers of Bankura had much higher degree of variation (more than 154%) than other. Highest mean along with highest variability in the levels of efficiency, the progressive fishers in Bankura did not necessarily appear to have performed in superior fashion. It may be, few of the progressive farmers had outperformed in this district, which uplift their group technical efficiency. On the other side, traditional farmers in the district of Hoogly had the mean group technical efficiency level 0.767 with variability of only 24 per cent. Highest mean along with lowest variability in the levels of efficiency, the traditional fishers in Hoogly appear to have performed in superior fashion. However, high variation in technical efficiency had been found in the district of Murshidabad.

Clearly, the relationship between diversification of aquaculture through SIFS and technical efficiency has been found to be more complex than what is normally believed. Rather than an direct and positive relationship, where productivity increases along with diversification, mixed relationship had been found. Hence, in order to find out the effect of diversification on the technical efficiency score, regression analysis has been adopted. The dependent variable is the measured level of (grand) technical efficiency of an individual farm. Diversification as dummies has then been regressed on the technical efficiency score. Those who adopted local species along with carp (thus diversified their culture) have been given the value of 1, while other has been valued as 0. The relationship between diversification and technical efficiency appeared as positive and significant. The result is depicted in Exhibit 5. The model is significant because of high F value. The high value of R^2 shows that the independent variables together account for 47 per cent variations in the technical efficiency score. The regression coefficient for diversification through SIFS is 0.212 and it is positive and statistically significant at one per cent probability level. The inference is that the (grand) technical efficiency score increases by 11.41 per cent when there is one per cent increase in SIFS in carp polyculture.

Exhibit 3: Mean Technical Efficiency of Different Culture Strategy for Different Region

Region	*Criterion*	*Class Culturing Carp*	
		With SIFS	*Without SIFS*
South 24-Parganas (Coastal and Saline Zone)	% of farms	56.67	43.33
	Grand TE	0.657	0.632
	Group TE	0.752	0.734
	CV (in %)	35.25	56.23
Hoogly (Old Alluvial Region)	% of farms	46.67	53.33
	Grand TE	0.577	0.631
	Group TE	0.713	0.767
	CV (in %)	81.36	24.35
Bankura (Red and Laterite Zone)	% of farms	21.11	78.89
	Grand TE	0.705	0.711
	Group TE	0.797	0.736
	CV (in %)	154.20	44.0
Murshidabad (New Alluvial Region)	% of farms	28.89	71.11
	Grand TE	0.609	0.623
	Group TE	0.682	0.729
	CV (in %)	68.29	139.71
Overall	% of farms	100	100
	Grand TE	0.651	0.642
	Group TE	0.742	0.734

*CV indicates coefficient of variation in individual technical efficiency score within the respective group.

Exhibit 4: Regression Results Explaining (Grand) Technical Efficiency Score using Diversification Dummies

Independent Variables	*Regression Coefficient*
Diversification dummies	0.212* (-1.015)
Constant	122.08
R^2	0.472
F	12.990*

Note: Figures in the parentheses are *t* values.
* indicates one per cent level of significance.

Overall, an ambiguous relationship between technical efficiency and diversification strategy through SIFS has been found. While, Meta frontier DEA model, used in this paper are drawing no concrete conclusion, regression results are suggesting for introduction of SIFS in polyculture system to enhance production and efficiency. More sophisticated economic models may suggest a different set of explanatory variables which may in turn give different results. Also, influence of some other dummies in the regression model may reveal clear picture. Nevertheless, the theoretical and empirical results in the paper show that ambiguity is always a part of the efficiency-diversification puzzle.

4.2 Constraint behind Non-adoption of SIFS

It is almost clear from the above discussion that more clarity is needed on the issue of aquaculture diversification through SIFS. Farmers are found tardy regarding its adoption because they are not quite convinced about the feasibility of introducing such species in culture system. As to why fish farmers are tardy in adopting SIFS becomes clear from the information given in Exhibit 6. Perhaps the most important reason for non-adoption is the financial difficulties. A sizeable percentage of operators (more than 77%) have reported this problem. Almost half of the operators are facing problems regarding multiple ownerships. Risk factor and failure to provide extension services to provide information regarding feasibility of SIFS also account for the non-adoption. About 56 per cent of the operators consider risk factor as a deterrent for adoption. To sum up, the data reveal that the major causes for non-adoption of SIFS are the perception of risk factor, cost factor (or financial difficulties) and lack of information.

Exhibit 5: Reasons for Non-adoption of SIFS

Questions Regarding Nature of Constraints	*Yes*		*No*	
	Frequency	*%*	*Frequency*	*%*
Are you facing financial difficulties	280	77.7	80	22.3
Is there lack of availability of quality seed	161	44.7	199	55.3
Is plurality of ownership a problem	178	49.4	182	50.2
Is risk factor acting as fear-psychosis	201	55.8	159	44.2
Is there lack of Proper Extension Services	139	38.6	221	61.4
Is High Price Spread a problem	65	18.1	295	81.9

Source: Field Survey, 2007-08.

Also, fishers in the study region have no proper idea about the biological and environmental hazards of introducing wild SIFS in polyculture system. They use to believe that unwanted predatory fishes can hamper the natural growth of carp. More than six species culture, according to some of them, creates 'super-saturation' in oxygen levels during day and oxygen 'depletion' during night. This sometimes leads to mass mortality of fish. The 'fear psychosis' of possible occurrence of fish diseases, specially in case of bata have also accounted for low applicability of SIFS in carp ponds.

The operational features of the new diversification strategy should be examined against the backdrop of prevailing organizational basis of individual water units and pisciculture as a whole. The new technology is scale-neutral, no doubt; but two problems arise with the farmers in this context—one, as a proposition involving higher cost per acre and second, as a proposition involving more working capital than usual. In this context, there arises the question of financial support necessary to internalize the external economies. The Government of West Bengal through FFDA schemes has made arrangements for giving loans and subsidies to adopt modern intensive fish culture. But, the success behind such arrangements are not quite satisfactory. There is wide gap between farmers who want to receive assistance and those who actually received it.

Sometimes, good stock of quality fish in the water units in diversified carp polyculture system had led to temptation for poaching. Other problems which all other operators considered important are lack of training and extension facilities, lack of transport and marketing facilities, non-availability of opportunities for soil and water testing, netting facilities, etc. In short, the fish farmers recognized institutional as well as technological or infrastructural problems as constraints.

5. Conclusion

In empirical application of the model, taking 360 fish farms from all-over West Bengal, the contributions of small indigenous fish species to the overall fish production, productivity and efficiency have appeared inadequate. Though the nutritive and livelihood importance of local fish species in carp polycultue is widely accepted, proper package of practice, with seed production technology and supply chains should be developed. Since, natural water bodies (and not government hatcheries) are still the source of SIFS; those resources should be protected and galvanized. For that, National Rural Employment Guarantee Scheme (NREGS) can be integrated to clear ponds of water hyacinth, to enhance fish production and in the ultimate analysis, local livelihoods. Such packages could also be implemented under the Rashtriya Krishi Vikas Yojana (RKVY). Along with these, keeping in view of consumer's preferences and market demand, some particular SIFS should be prioritized and government should strengthen their market linkages.

Another point deserves particular mention. The fish farmers practise their own indigenous technology as a common practice through natural resource management. The close and intimate observation of farmers through their age old practices has developed the expertise of acquiring knowledge and skills possessed by local people. This may substantially contribute to productive efforts and endeavours. For example, some small farmers, in the study area, use to immerse banana logs in their pond by cutting into pieces. According to them, banana plant cell helps in increasing pH of the pond water through their alkaline secretion. Such activity helps to minimize protozoan disease and worm of fish. Some farmers would be able to minimize mass mortality of *bata* species in this way. Unfortunately, scientific attitude to these indigenous technologies of the farmers are yet to be generated. Conventional extension system is no longer able to address effectively grassroot level reality. All these call for different extension approaches like participatory extension approaches including dissemination of success stories of technology adoption, indigenous innovation by different farmers, community based management systems. The financial assistance required for progressive farmers, is to be area or community specific, taking into account the different development potentials as well as constraints of each area or community. From these points of view, it is desirable that development plans at the district level would be very much effective.*

* This part has been prepared in collaboration with Dr . Gayden Mishra, Research Scheme. Dept. of Economics, Visva-Bharti, India

Appendix III

Diversifying beyond the Farm towards Rural Livelihood

There is no denying the fact that diversification is a core strategy of contemporary rural livelihood systems. Inland fisheries sector may be characterized by a dwindling asset base, human welfare deterioration, and the consequent household level response of poverty driven by low-return from non-fisheries engagements. These may have been caused by different reasons which may pose serious threats to fisheries' household viability livelihood status.

It is true that income growth from the fishery units has been very slow. This is arguably the most important contextual fact to be kept in mind while looking at the rural livelihood features. (Farrington *et al.,* 2006). Almost all of the respondents engage in diverse income generating and livelihood activities including fishing, fish marketing, fish culture and labour regardless of their primary occupation.

Occupational diversification is considered to be a positive phenomenon, as it constitutes an important component of the growth process. This concept is viewed from two perspectives. The first is the "development perspective". This is argued that the forces of economic growth and changes have created new opportunities, resulting in the emergence of a diversified occupational structure. The second perspective is the "deterioration trajectory" (Shylendra *et al.,* 2004). This is caused by factors inimical to growth and prosperity, all forcing livelihood diversification of a distress nature. Distress diversification has been put forward as a residual sector hypothesis (Vaidyanathan, 1986).

Since the number of ponds is inequitably distributed across different sections and most of them are small in number, the extent of livelihood

Exhibit 1: Occupational Structure, 2008 ($n = 360$)

No. of households	*Proportion in total Occupations*
Fisheries	128
Agriculture	168
Agricultureal labour	218
Animal husbandry	52
Artisans	64
Services**	16
Trade and commerce	9

* A household may have one or more than one alternative occupations. So there is an overlap in the number of households in column 2.

**Services include office jobs in different organizations, private or public

Source: Primary Survey 2008; Compiled from Survey Data 2010.

support from fish cultivation in terms of income, employment and food varies significantly. Roughly, 24/360 percentage of households depend largely on fish cultivation. Other occupations which are found significantly important to the respondents are agriculture and agricultural labour as the dependable occupations (Shylendra *et al.*, 2004). It is observed that an overwhelming proportion of households, therefore, depend, directly or indirectly, on agriculture. There are a number of non-agricultural occupations, being pursued by the fish farmers. Some such occupations are traditionally associated with specific caste. Of course, in course of time, many new or modern occupations emerged. It appears from the data obtained through the Survey that there are three major alternative categories of occupations (non-farm): artisans, trade and business and services. About 52/360 households consider animal husbandry as the important area of occupation which provides security and the farmers may fall back upon it. There are 24/360 households who are engaged profitably in various activities like pottery, carpentry and embroidery etc. It is found that mostly in some community, the women refrain from engaging in activities outside the household. To them, pottery has proved quite handy to supplement their family income, especially during the lean season. Another category of non-farm occupation is the service sector. In recent time, certain modern occupations have emerged; teachers, clerks, drivers, automobile servicing. Roadside restaurants, tea stalls, grocery shops sweepers, and attendants etc. There are some other occupations like foodgrain trade, tailoring shop, flour mills etc. which are mainly carried out by fish farmers who are relatively financially better-off.

The analysis of the occupational structure reveals that quite a significant proportion of the fish farmers have diversified their occupation, though in varying degrees, depending upon the socio-economic (resource) endowments. As a result, the impact of the process on the livelihood is of varying nature. Again, small and weak farmers who are found inefficient in resource utilization have tried to broaden their livelihood base by way of pursuing different kinds of non-fishery activities. There is a continuity in certain traditional occupations like carpentry, blacksmithy etc. It is also evident that in the case of those fish farmers, the nature of diversification of traditional occupations demonstrates a picture for their struggle for survival and consolidation in the face of strong forces of change. They try to secure their livelihood through these occupations.

To sum up, in our study area, we witnessed a significant diversification of occupations. This is of a significant nature and magnitude, but with variations both in the form and impact across different sections of the fish farmers. The main driving force behind this variation is either to supplement the earnings from the fisheries units or traditional occupations or to pursue economic consolidation. Of considerable significance are the introduction of modern production technology and commercialization. It is observed that irrespective of form, diversification seems to help the bulk of households to supplement their income from fish farming. It enables them to overcome risk and vulnerability arising out of production failure or income depletion. Surplus earnings sometimes act as a source for investment in various production activities. It also acts as a cushion for any expansionary activities being taken up. Or for the weaker, diversification is certainly helping in sustaining their livelihood. In point of fact, it may be noted that the fish farmers have been trying to establish market linkages. The market has become the most important determinant that governs their life and livelihoods. However, many respondents interviewed voiced their concern with losses in local traditional knowledge and traditional occupational skills as a consequence linked to the transformation in the production system. Technology played a major role in transforming the local livelihood strategies and options. Technology is found to be an asset that helps enhance the livelihoods; opportunities to access it were limited to those who have already financial and human capital. Another important finding of the study is that the fish farmers have been adaptive to the need for formal education which is found to be a key element of human capital asset that helps them improve their livelihood by way of engaging in some form of other additional income generating activities.

References

Ahmed, M. (1997). Socioeconomic and policy issues in the floodplain fisheries of Bangladesh. In *Open water fisheries of Bangladesh.* Edited by C.f. Tsai and Y. Ali, University Press Limited, Dhaka: 89-98.

Ahuja, Vinod (Editor) (2004), *Livestock and Livelihoods: Challenges and Opportunities for Asia in the Emerging Market Environment*, National Dairy Development Board of Indian and Food and Agriculture Organization of the United Nations. 372p.

Ahuja, Vinod and Arindam Sen (2007), Viability and future of small scale commercial poultry production in developing countries, paper presented at *International Conference on Poultry in the 21st Century: Avian Influenza and Beyond*, Bangkok, November 5-7, 2007.

Ashley, C., and Carney, D. (1999). Sustainable livelihoods: lessons from early experience. Department for International Development, London.

Bailey, C. and Jentoft, S. (1990). Hard choices in fisheries development. Marine Policy July: 333-344.

Baland, J.M., and Platteau, J.P. (1999). The ambiguous impact of inequity on local resource management. World Development 27(5): 773-788.

Barbier, E., Burgess, J. and Folke, C. (1994), *Paradise Lost? The Ecological Economics of Biodiversity*. Earthscan, London.

Bardhan P.K. (1984), *Land Labour and Rural Poverty: Essays in Development Economics.* New York and Oxford: Columbia University Press and OUP.

Behnke, R. (1994). Natural resource management in pastoral Africa. Development Policy Review 12: 5-27.

Bello W. and J. Collins (1987). 'Cory's Cop-out'. New Internationalist. Issue 177, November 1987.

Bernstein, H., Crow, B., and Johnson, H. (1992). Rural livelihoods: crises and responses. Oxford University Press and the Open University, Oxford.

Biribudo, W. (1995), "Women in fisheries development programme in Papua New Guinea" in Regional workshop on the role of women in fisheries development, 17-21 July 1995, Iloilo City (Philippines).

Bradstock, A. (2005a), Land Reform and its Impact on Livelihoods. Evidence from eight reform groups in the Northern Cape Province of South Africa. Farm Africa, September 2005.

Bradstock, A. (2005b), Supporting Land Reform: Participatory planning experience in the Northern Cape Province. Farm Africa, July 2005.

Breemer (van den) J.P., Drijver, C.A., and Venema, L.B. (Eds.) (1995). Local resource management in Africa. John Wiley and Sons, Chichester.

Campbell, D.J. (1990). Strategies for coping with severe food deficits in rural Africa: a review of the literature. Food and foodways 4(2): 143-162.

Carney, D. (1998), 'Implementing the Sustainable Rural Livelihood Approach' in Carney, D. (ed). *Sustainable Rural Livelihoods: What contribution can we make?* Papers presented at the Department for International Development's Natural Resources Advisers' Conference, July 1998, UK Department for International Development, London.

Carter, M.R. (1997). Environment, technology, and the social articulation of risk in West African Agriculture. Economic Dvelopment and Cultural Change 45(3): 557-591.

Chambers, R. (1981). Rapid rural Appraisal. Public Administration and Development 1: 95-106.

Chambers, R. (1992). Rural appraisal: rapid, relaxed and participatory. 311, Institute of Development Studies, Discussion Paper, Brigthon, 85.

Collins, W. and Petit, M. (1998), 'Strategic Issues for National Policy Decisions in Managing Genetic Resources.' Environmentally Sustainable Development Agricultural Research and Extension Group *Special Report* No. 4. World Bank, Washington, DC.

Collinson, M.P. (1981). The exploratory survey: content method and detailed guidelines with farmers. Farm System Newsletter 5:.

Commercial aquaculture in Southeast Asia: Some policy lessons, Food Policy, Vol. 34, Issue 1, February 2009, pp. 102-107, Nathanael Hishamunda, Neil B. Ridler, Pedro Bueno and Wilfredo G. Yap.

Conway, G. (1985). Agro-ecosystem analysis. Agricultural Administration 20: 31-55.

Conway, G. (1987). The properties of agroecosystems. Agricultural systems 24: 95-117.

Conway, G. (1997), *The Doubly Green Revolution: Food for all in the Twenty-First Century*. Penguin Books, London.

Crole-Rees (1992): A. *Rural Household Strategies in Southern Mali Determinants and Contribution of Income Diversification to income level and Distribution*; Thesis No. 14,586; Swiss Federal Institute of Technology (ETHZ): Zurich, Switzerland,

Cutler, P. (1986). The response to drought of Beja famine refugees in Sudan. Disaster 10(3).

Dahlberg, K. (1979), *Beyond the Green Revolution: the Ecology and Politics of Global Agriculture*. Plenum Press, New York.

Daley E. and M. Hobley (2005), Land: Changing Contexts and, Changing Relationships, Changing rights. Paper commissioned by the Rural-Urban Change Team, Policy Division, Department for International Development, UK. September 2005.

Dantwala M.L. (1996), Employment Guarantee Scheme, Economic and Political Weekly, Vol. 31, No. 9.

Davies, S. (1996). Adaptable livelihoods: coping with food insecurity in the Malian Sahel. Sciences, Technology and Development 14(1): 144-156.

Deininger K., F. Lara, M. Maertens, and A. Quisumbing (1999), Global Development Network (GDN).

Deininger, K. (2003), Land Policies for Growth and Poverty Reduction. Washington D.C: World Bank.

Deininger, K. (2004), Land Rights and Administration in Africa. Keynote Presentation in Quan *et al.* 2004. pp. 53-59.

Dev S. Mahendra *et al.* (2003), Towards a Food Secure India Institute for Human Development New Delhi.

Dev S. Mahendra *et al.* (eds.) (2000), Social and Economic Security in India Institute of Human Development, New Delhi.

DFID (2001): *Sustainable Livelihoods Guidance Sheets*; UK Department for International Development, London, UK; Available online: www.livelihoods.org/info/info_guidanceSheets.html#6

DFID (2004), Land Reform, agriculture and poverty reduction. Working paper for the Renewable Natural Resources and Agriculture Team, Policy Division, Department for International Development, UK. RNRA team incollaboration with Martin Adams.

Dias, C.J. and Joseph, C. (eds.) (1993), "The fisherfolk of Asia: justice denied. Report and statement of the Fifth Asian Fisherfolk Consultation, January 26-31, 1992, Songkla, Thailand", Asian Cultural Forum on Development (ACFOD), Bangkok (Thailand).

Dreze, J. and A. Sen (1989), Hunger and Public Action, Clarendon Press, Oxford.

_____ (1995), India: Economic Development and Social Opportunity Oxford University Press Delhi and Oxford, GOI (2000) Mid–Term Appraisal of Ninth Five Year Plan.

Fisheries and water productivity in tropical river basins: Enhancing food security and livelihoods by managing water for fish, *Agricultural Water Management, Volume 80, Issues 1-3, 24 February 2006, Pages 262-275*, Patrick Dugan, Madan M. Dey, V.V. Sugunan.

Frank Ellis, Milton Kutengule, Alfred Nyasulu (2003). Livelihoods and Rural Poverty Reduction in Malawi, *World Development, Volume 31, Issue 9, September 2003, Pages 1495-1510.*

Grimble, R. and Laidlaw. M. (1998), *Biodiversity conservation in rural development: lessons for better addressing biodiversity concerns in planning rural and agricultural development projects*. Report prepared by the Natural Resources Institute for the Environment Department of the World Bank (mimeo).

Hiremath, B.N., Raju and Patel (2004), Tecnology adption and Farm Management in Rural Livelihood Systems in Gujrat in *In search of sustainable development* by Ruedi Baumgartner and Hogger Sage Publications, New Delhi, pp. 124-29.

Integrated Agriculture-Aquaculture Systems in the Mekong Delta, Vietnam: An Analysis of Recent Trends, *Le Thanh Phong, Henk M.J. Udo, Martinus E.F. van Mensvoort, Roel H. Bosma, Le QuangTri, Dang Kieu Nhan* and *Akke J. van der Zijpp, Asian Journal of Agriculture and Development*, 2007, vol. 4, Issue 2, pp. 51-66.

Kadigi, R.M.J., Mdoe, N.S.Y., Senkondo E. and Mpenda Z. (2007), Effects of food safety standards on the livelihoods of actors in the Nile Perch value chain in Tanzania', *DIIS Working Paper* 2007/24. Copenhagen, Denmark: Danish Institute for International Studies.

Kanbur, R. (2002), 'Economics, social science and development', *World Development* 30 (3): 477-486.

Kaplinsky, R. (2000), 'Spreading the gains from globalization: What can be learned from value chain analysis?' *IDS Working Paper* 100. Brighton, UK: Institute for Development Studies.

Klooster, D. (2005), 'Environmental certification of forests: The evolution of environmental governance in a commodity network', *Journal of Rural Studies* 21: 403-417.

Kritzinger, A., Barrientos, S. and Rossouw H. (2004), 'Global production and flexible employment in the South African horticulture: Experiences of contract workers in fruit exports', *Sociologia Ruralis* 44(1): 17-39.

Kruger, S., du Toit A. and Ponte S. (2006), 'De-racialising exploitation: "Black Economic Empowerment" in the South African wine sector', *DIIS Working Paper* 2006/34. Copenhagen, Denmark: Danish Institute for International Studies.

Livelihood diversification in Uganda: patterns and determinants of change across two rural districts, *Food Policy*, Volume 26, Issue 4, August 2001, Pages 421-435, Davd Rider Smith, Ann Gordon, Kate Meadows, Karen Zwick.

Loha Choudhury Biplab (2010), Indian Paradigms of Development Man Standard and Communication, Sampark Publishing company, Calcutta.

Macdonald, K. (2007), 'Globalising justice within coffee supply chains? Fair Trade, Starbucks and the transformation of supply chain governance', *Third World Quarterly* 28(4): 793-812.

Majumdar, B. (2009), Political Economy of Public Distribution System Concept Publishing Company New Delhi.

Meenakshi, J.V. (1996), How important are Changes in Taste? A State Level Analysis of Food Demand, Economic and Political Weekly, Vol. 31, No. 50, December 14, pp. 3265-69.

Misra Sib Ranjan (2006), Inland Fisheries in India; Issues and concern Concept Publishing House Delhi.

____ 2011 Individual economics for Sustainable development—key note address delivered in the International Seminar organized in honour of Birth anniversary of Sri Sri Anukul Thakur at Guwahati on 19th February.

____ (2010), Climate Change and Food Security: Issues and Policies in Climate Change and Development (Proceedings of the International Seminar organized by Department of Environment, Visva–Bharati.

Mooney, P. (1998), 'The parts of life: agricultural biodiversity, indigenous knowledge and the role of the Third System' *Development Dialogue*.

Morgan, M.G.; Fischhoff, B.; Bostrom, A. and Atman, C.J. (2002). *Risk Communication: A Mental Models Approach*; Cambridge University Press: Cambridge, UK.

Murray, C. (2001), 'Livelihoods research: Some conceptual and methodological issues'. *CPRC Background Paper* 5. Manchester, UK: Chronic Poverty Research Centre, www.chronicpoverty.org

Murray, C. (2002), 'Livelihoods research: Transcending boundaries of time and space', *Journal of Southern African Studies* 28(3): 489-509.

Mutersbaugh, T. (2005), 'Fighting standards with standards: Harmonization, rents, and social accountability in certified agrofood networks', *Environment and Planning A* 37: 2033-2051.

Norr, J.L. and Norr, K.F. (1992), "Women's status in peasant-level fishing", Society and Natural Resources, 5 (2): 149-163.

Osmani, S.R. (2007), 'When endowments and opportunities do not match: Understanding chronic poverty', *CPRC Working Paper* 78. Manchester, UK Chronic Poverty Research Centre, www.chronicpoverty.org

Pacey, A. and Payne P. (eds) (1985), Agricultural Development and Nutrition, FAO /UNICEF Hutchinson /West view Press Colorado.

Palpacuer, F., P. Gibbon and L. Thomsen (2005), 'New challenges for developing country suppliers in global clothing chains', *World Development* 33(3).

Pattberg, P. (2006), 'Private governance and the South: Lessons from global forest politics', *Third World Quarterly* 27(4): 579-593.

Peters, P.E. (1994). Dividing the Commons: politics, policy, and culture in Botswana. The University Press of Virginia, Charlottesville.

Pido, M., Pomeroy, R.S., Carlos, M.B., and Garces, L.R. (1996). A Handbook for appraisal of fisheries management systems. ICLARM, Manilla, Philippines.

Pido, M., Pomeroy, R.S., Garces, L.R., and Carlos, M.B. (1997). A rapid appraisal approach to evaluation of community-level fisheries management systems: framework and field application at selected coastal fishing villages in the Philippines and Indonesia. Coastal Management 25: 183-204.

Platteau, J.P. (1989). The dynamics of fisheries development in developping countries: a general overview. Development and Change 20(4).

Ponte, S. (2007a), 'Governance in the value chain for South African wine', *TRALAC Working Paper* 9/2007. Stellenbosch: Trade Law Centre for Southern Africa.

Ponte, S. (2007b), 'Bans, tests and alchemy: Food safety standards and the Uganda fish export industry', *Agriculture and Human Values* 27(2):179-193.

Ponte, S. and P. Gibbon (2005), 'Quality standards, conventions and the governance of global value chains', *Economy and Society* 34(1): 1-31.

Posey, D.A. (1995), *Indigenous peoples and traditional resource rights: a basis for equitable relationship?* Green College, Oxford University, Oxford.

Prowse, S. (2003), 'Towards a clearer understanding of "vulnerability" in relation to chronic poverty', *CPRC Working Paper* 24. Manchester, UK: Chronic Poverty Research Centre, www.chronicpoverty.org

Radhakrishna, S. (200), Food Security: Emerging Concerns in Social and Economic security in India by S. Mahendra Dev (ed.) Institute of Human Development New Delhi pp. 103-118.

Raju S.S., P. Shinij and P.K. Joshi (2008), Sustainable Development of Bio-fuels: Prospects and Challenges, Economic and Political Weekly October 25, pp. 265-69.

Rao Chandrasekhar and S. Mahendra Dev (2009), Biotechnology and pro-poor; Agricultural Development Economic and Political weekly November 28, pp. 56-65.

Ravi, C. (2000), Complete Demand Systems, Welfare and Nutrition: An Analysis of Index Consumption Data, Centre for Economic and Social Studies, Hyderabad.

Rhoades, R.E. (1982). The art of informal agricultural survey. Training document 1982-2, Social Science Department, International Potato Center, Lima, Peru.

Sarch, M.T. (1997). Fishing and farming in Lake Chad: implications for fisheries development. Development Policy Review 15: 141-157.

Sekan, J. (1992). Seasonal coping strategies in Central Mali: five village during the "soudure". Disaster 16(1,): 66-73 cited in Hussein and Nelson 1998.

Skaptadóttir, U.D. (2000), "Women coping with change in Icelandic fishing community", Women's Studies International Forum, 23 (3): 311-321.

Smith, I. (1979). A research framework for traditional fisheries. 2, ICLARM, ICLARM Studies and Reviews, Manilla, 45.

Smith, I. (1981). Improving fishing incomes when resource are overfished. Marine Policy 5(1): 17-22.

Sultan, S. (1991), "Role of women in fisheries", FISH. CHIMES., 11 (4): 43.

Suryanarayana, M.H. (1995), Growth, poverty and Levels of Living: Hypotheses, Methods and Policies, Journal of Indian School of Political Economy, Vol. 7, pp. 203-55.

Sustainable rural livelihoods? Evaluating the potential of small-scale aquaculture in the Western Cape, Najma Mohamed; Belinda Dodson, Development Southern Africa, 1470-3637, Volume 15, Issue 1, 1998, pp. 103 – 121.

Touray, I. (1997), "Gender issues in the fisheries sector and effective participation", in Report workshop on gender roles and issues in artisanal fisheries in West Africa, Lomé, Togo, 11-13 December 1996. Horemans, B.W., and Jallow, A., M. (eds.), Cotonou, Benin, Programme for the Integrated Development of Artisanal Fisheries in West Africa, IDAF/WP/97: 42-47.

United Nations (2000), Fourth Report on World Nutrition Situation, Geneva.

Vosti, S.A., and Reardon, T. (1997). "Sustainability, growth, and poverty alleviation: a policy and agroecological perspective.", I.F.P.R. Institute, ed., John Hopkins University Press, 388.

Index